Coaching and Mentoring

Coaching and Mentoring
Theory and Practice

Bob Garvey, Paul Stokes and David Megginson

Los Angeles | London | New Delhi
Singapore | Washington DC

First published 2009

Reprinted 2009, 2010

SAGE Publications Ltd
1 Oliver's Yard
55 City Road
London EC1Y 1SP

SAGE Publications Inc.
2455 Teller Road
Thousand Oaks, California 91320

SAGE Publications India Pvt Ltd
B 1/I 1 Mohan Cooperative Industrial Area
Mathura Road
New Delhi 110 044

SAGE Publications Asia-Pacific Pte Ltd
33 Pekin Street #02-01
Far East Square
Singapore 048763

Library of Congress Control Number: 2008928183

British Library Cataloguing in Publication data

A catalogue record for this book is available from
the British Library

ISBN 978-1-4129-1216-7
ISBN 978-1-4129-1217-4 (pbk)

Typeset by C&M Digitals (P) Ltd, Chennai, India
Printed and bound in Great Britain by TJ International Ltd, Padstow, Cornwall
Printed on paper from sustainable resources

Mixed Sources
Product group from well-managed
forests and other controlled sources
www.fsc.org Cert no. SGS-COC-2482
FSC   © 1996 Forest Stewardship Council

DEDICATIONS AND ACKNOWLEDGEMENTS

Bob Garvey dedicates this book to his father, Arthur Garvey, and his uncle, the late Alan Garvey (1927–2006). Thank you both for introducing me to and developing in me the capacity for argument.

Paul Stokes dedicates this book to the memory of his father, Bob Stokes (1933–2005). Thanks also to Liz and Louri for their support and encouragement as always.

David Megginson thanks Vivien for constant support and a string of great ideas, and to all the groups who have contributed to our understanding of coaching and mentoring processes, practices and principles, especially the MSc Coaching and Mentoring cohorts at Sheffield Hallam and in Switzerland, the SHU Research Days, the Bristol University Critical Coaching Conferences and numerous EMCC events. I am particularly grateful for the gracious hospitality of Prabhu Guptara and UBS, Wolfsberg, in hosting me as Scholar in Residence at Wolfsberg during the summer of 2006, when one of 'my' chapters was drafted.

CONTENTS

LIST OF FIGURES

ABOUT THE AUTHORS

Bob Garvey is Professor of Mentoring and Coaching at Sheffield Hallam University. He works with a range of people, either one-to-one or in groups. He is an EMCC (European Mentoring and Coaching Council) member and formerly the editor of the *International Journal of Mentoring and Coaching*. Bob is obsessed with coaching and mentoring!

Paul Stokes is a Senior Lecturer at Sheffield Hallam University. He is course leader for the MSc in Coaching and Mentoring and an experienced coach-mentor. He has worked in a range of different types of organization and has a particular interest in the idea of a skilled coachee or mentee.

David Megginson is Visiting Professor of HRD at Sheffield Hallam University. He is co-founder of the former EMC (European Mentoring Centre), a Director of the EMCC (European Mentoring and Coaching Council) and the founder of the Coaching and Mentoring Research Unit. David is a dedicated listener, an experienced coachmentor and obsessive runner.

Dawn Chandler studied with Kathy Kram and earned her doctorate at Boston University. She is Assistant Professor of Management at California Polytechnic University, San Luis Obispo. Her research interests include mentoring, career development and adult development.

INTRODUCTION

In recent years, the activities of coaching and mentoring have developed, evolved and expanded at a phenomenal rate (see CIPD Surveys, 2005/6/7/8). There is interest in the different forms of coaching and mentoring right across all sectors of society around the globe. Coaching and mentoring, as developmental activities, are truly global in their application.

Mentoring and coaching are used for a variety of purposes, including to:

- Develop managers and leaders
- Support induction and role changes
- 'Fast-track' people into senior positions
- Reduce stress
- Support change
- Gain employment for the long-term unemployed
- Reduce crime and drug taking
- Develop and foster independence
- Increase school attendance and support anti-bullying policies in schools
- Improve performance in whatever context employed
- Support talent management
- Improve skills and transfer knowledge
- Support equal opportunities policies and diversity
- Aid social integration
- Develop SMEs
- Support retention strategies.

The items on this list, although incomplete, have one thing in common – change. This may mean changes of thinking, behaviour, attitude or performance. Whatever the case or the context, all these applications of seemingly the same processes raise many issues and questions about how mentoring and coaching are understood and perceived by those who engage in practice.

There is still much debate about the similarities and differences between coaching and mentoring practice and we address these in Chapter 1 with some new research.

We wanted to call this book 'The Inner Odyssey' to combine a core coaching book, Gallwey's (1997) *The Inner Game of Tennis*, with the foundation of mentoring, Homer's *Odyssey*. This hints at our views on the similarities and differences between the two! Whatever they are called, this book is all about coaching and mentoring in a wide range of settings for a wide range of purposes.

We, the authors, are *for* coaching and mentoring but that does not mean that we are partial or partisan. This book, which draws on the literature, extensive research, our own experience as coaches, mentors, coachees, mentees, practice supervisors, scheme designers and evaluators, and academics, is accessible, academic, critical and practical. It offers both challenge and support to all who are interested in mentoring and coaching. The challenge is found in our critical perspective on coaching and mentoring in theory and practice, and the support is in the theoretical underpinning and positive practical experiences we present. We have sought to write it in the spirit of coaching and mentoring by writing it in what we call the 'coaching and mentoring way'. This is our philosophical position and includes qualities of:

- Mutual respect and valuing differences of viewpoint
- Acknowledgement of our influences
- Listening and sharing.

We hope that when we are critical, it is respectful.

We work together within the Coaching and Mentoring Research Unit at Sheffield Hallam University and think it fair to say that we are obsessed with coaching and mentoring! We engage with the processes and skills in our daily work and we help others from different sectors of society to do the same. We work with individuals, large and small businesses, the public sector and the voluntary sector, so we have experienced first hand the power of coaching and mentoring to transform lives and working practices. We also read and write about coaching and mentoring; we believe that there is much still to learn about mentoring and coaching and, in some ways, we set an agenda here for learning about this fascinating and developing world.

ORGANIZATION OF THE BOOK

The book has four parts; the chapters within the parts have a different emphasis on theory and practice. As academic practitioners, we believe that this blending is important and reflects the title of the book which links the theoretical with the practical. We agree with the old adage that there is nothing as practical as a good theory. All chapters have a critical element.

Part 1: An Introduction to Coaching and Mentoring

Part 1 offers an introduction to coaching and mentoring. It starts with the historical development of coaching and mentoring, moves through current issues in coaching and mentoring research, and goes on to look at the broad issue of organizational cultures which support coaching and mentoring. In Part 1, we look at the issues of scheme design and evaluation, and consider the widely different models of coaching and mentoring found in today's society. Finally, we look at the power of conversational learning.

Chapter 1 is about the development of the meaning of the terms 'mentoring' and coaching' and is drawn from substantial historical research. It shows how, in practice, coaching and mentoring have been applied and demonstrates how the meaning of the terms has changed over history through practice. It helps to explain the wide discrepancies in meaning found in current practice and concludes with a way forward. Many of the themes identified in the historical research and in the sections on current practice are developed in later chapters in the book.

Chapter 2 takes a critical look at research practice in coaching and mentoring. It presents some opposing but fundamental philosophical positions and links these to research practice. The chapter suggests that there are various 'archetypes' of research practice in coaching and mentoring research. These archetypes are aimed at different audiences and have different purposes in mind. There is a cautionary note here for researchers, practitioners and scheme designers that research findings need to be understood from the 'gaze' of the writer. No one method is better than the other but the chapter suggests that a blended approach offers the most potential to inform all users of research material.

Chapter 3 looks at creating or developing coaching and mentoring cultures. This chapter offers both theoretical and practical insights into the development of environments supportive of coaching and mentoring. The chapter introduces models of mentoring and coaching culture while outlining strategies and practices for leaders, managers and specialist coaches and mentors to widen the impact of what they do. The chapter raises some challenging questions and issues for organizations wishing to develop coaching and mentoring. There is not 'one best way' but, rather, many choices in specific contexts.

Chapter 4 offers insights into scheme design and evaluation. There are many resonances in this chapter with earlier chapters in the book. The chapter focuses towards practitioners and places more emphasis on the pragmatic issues of scheme design and evaluation that confront those who organize formal coaching and mentoring schemes in an organizational context. The chapter draws on the authors' work and experience as well as reports the work of others.

Chapter 5 looks at the wide variety and range of models and perspectives in coaching and mentoring. The chapter aims to reflect the breadth and depth of the field, and to explore some of the assumptions that underpin these various approaches and models. The chapter captures the essence of each approach, using selected references. It raises many challenging questions about the theory and practice of mentoring and coaching.

Chapter 6 is about the power of one-to-one developmental dialogue. It explores the influence of the social context on learning; it discusses and compares the 'linear' view of learning with the 'non-linear' view. There are links in this chapter to the opposing views taken in research philosophy and mind-set presented in Chapters 1, 2 and 4. We show that these viewpoints influence thinking and behaviour in practice. The chapter looks at the non-linear nature of coaching and mentoring conversations, presenting and analysing an example of a live conversation.

Part 2: Influences on Coaching and Mentoring

In Part 2, we discuss the various influences on the form one-to-one develop-ment takes, in particular the influence of power, the development of 'learning networks', the use of technology and, finally, organizational issues such as pur-pose and goal orientation in coaching and mentoring. Part 2 covers a range of organizational and practice issues found in coaching mentoring. The chapters take a critical look at the various influences on the forms coaching and men-toring take within an organizational setting.

Chapter 7 discusses the concept of power in coaching and mentoring. This is a key concept that permeates through all units of analysis in coaching and mentoring. Given that coaching and mentoring relationships are often located within organizational schemes or wider community through various mentor-ing engagement schemes, it is necessary to subject them to an analysis of power. Coaching and mentoring are generally intended to enable some sort of exchange of knowledge, wisdom, understanding between their participants, so, inevitably, power will be involved. Also, coaching and mentoring are often closely associated with transition, development and growth, so, again, it is inevitable that, as people grow and develop (often at different rates and times), this will alter the power dynamics between them. It is therefore impor-tant to try to understand power and extent of its impact.

Chapter 8 considers the notion of coaching and mentoring networks. Coaching and mentoring conversations are social interactions facilitated in specific contexts and with a variety of purposes. This chapter explores the idea of multiple coaching and mentoring relationships in the context of the knowledge economy and the consequential implications for on organizational structures and practices.

Chapter 9 investigates the growing use of electronic media used to make social connections between people. This may include the use of email as well as dedicated coaching or mentoring software designed to facilitate developmental relationships. We examine the impact of these innovations on coaching and mentoring.

Chapter 10 is a chapter which blends research, theory and practice. It exam-ines some of the issues raised when introducing coaching or mentoring into organizations. It builds on the pragmatic findings of Chapter 3 on creating a coaching culture and on the theoretical considerations of Chapter 7 on power in organizations. We address some of these through the lens of 'goals'.

Part 3: Contemporary Issues in Coaching and Mentoring

Part 3 explores some of the contemporary debates in coaching and mentoring. This includes the concept of practice supervision, diversity issues and standards.

Although, as has been shown in Chapter 1, mentoring and coaching have a long history, as a professional and fully developed activity they are very nascent. This section explores some contemporary debates that are influencing the development of coaching and mentoring. These debates could be viewed as tensions within the worlds of coaching and mentoring. They involve debates that are influenced by mindset, territory, power and control. There are no straightforward 'solutions' to these issues but we suggest that the discussion and debate should be kept alive because this will eventually lead to the main themes of Chapter 12 – tolerance, acceptance and a recognition that diversity is healthy in the context of coaching and mentoring.

Chapter 11 discusses the issue of 'supervision' in coaching and mentoring. Supervision is a relatively new term in coaching and mentoring. We explore the reasons for the explosion of interest in supervision as well as examining the different approaches, functions and roles that supervision can play. Some argue that contemporary demands towards the professionalization of coaching and mentoring have created this need. Others, for example paying clients, are considering issues of quality control and competence. A further driver for supervision is the training or development of coaches and mentors. The chapter takes a critical look at the arguments.

Chapter 12 is about diversity. The chapter takes a critical perspective on the issue of diversity and its relationship to coaching and mentoring. It discusses the meaning of diversity and examines current philosophies and practices found in organizations. We present a new case example and the chapter ends with a challenge.

Chapter 13 looks at the debates around competencies, standards and professionalization. The chapter raises many questions and presents a comprehensive list of arguments for and against competencies in coaching and mentoring, standards of practice and professionalization.

Part 4: Towards a Theory of Coaching and Mentoring

Part 4 draws together the themes discussed in the book and moves towards a theory of coaching and mentoring. It looks at emerging issues for coaching and mentoring and presents a view of developments in the US. We conclude with extrapolated views for the future development of coaching and mentoring drawn from the current emerging trends and patterns.

Chapter 14 is a view from the US. It is the only guest chapter in the book and we are very grateful to Dawn Chandler for her contribution and insight. The chapter discusses the current developments in coaching and mentoring practices and research in the United States. The discussion begins with an overview of coaching and mentoring as practices, starting with a brief review of their historical roots in the United States. The chapter then delves into the topics as subjects of research with a particular emphasis on their distinctiveness from each other. Because of the mentoring literature's maturity as a field, the discussion highlights key conceptual features and trends. Next, the chapter turns to the American culture bias that permeates much of the mentoring literature. Finally, Dawn offers areas for future research.

Chapter 15 develops a diverse typographic heuristic to describe coaching and mentoring. We place this into the public domain, not as a finished and tested theory but as a framework for debate and discussion. This heuristic is both a challenge and a basis for support. We value critical thinking and as such offer our thoughts up to criticism in the spirit of learning and the generation of new thinking. The chapter highlights some key themes in the book and concludes with our view of future developments drawn from current practices.

PART I

AN INTRODUCTION TO COACHING AND MENTORING

THE MEANING OF COACHING AND MENTORING

CHAPTER OVERVIEW

This chapter traces the historical discourses related to mentoring and coaching and relates them to modern writings. It shows that the meanings associated with the use of the words 'coaching' and 'mentoring' have subtly altered over time to become more or less inter-changeable in the modern world. The research is drawn from a substantial number of historical and modern sources. The chapter helps to explain the wide discrepancies in meaning found in current practice and concludes with a way forward through the application of the dimensions framework previously presented by Garvey (1994a). We develop the themes identified in the historical research and in the sections on current practice in later chapters in the book.

INTRODUCTION

There is lively debate among academics and practitioners alike as to the meaning of the terms 'mentoring' and 'coaching'. This debate is fuelled and further confused by:

- Variations in the application of mentoring and coaching
- The wide range of contexts in which coaching and mentoring activities take place
- The perceptions of various stakeholders as to the purpose of these conversations
- Commercial, ethical and practical considerations.

In the mentoring and coaching literature there are many descriptions and definitions. These differences raise a key question for those interested in definition: *are mentoring and coaching distinctive and separate activities or are they essentially similar in nature?*

In the coaching and mentoring worlds, there are examples of distinct 'camps' and in some cases these 'camps' are almost tribal (see Gibb and Hill, 2006) in their disdain for one another. In the book *Making Coaching Work* (2005: 15–17) Clutterbuck and Megginson present a range of quotes listed as 'coaches on coaching', 'mentors on mentoring', 'mentors on coaching' and 'coaches on mentoring'. It seems as though each writer positions their own particular understanding of either coaching or mentoring as distinctive and different, often by making a disparaging and inaccurate remark about the other.

There is an explanation for the discrepancies and the crude positioning of different viewpoints and this chapter seeks to develop this explanation through an analysis of the 'folk wisdoms' (Bruner, 1990) of the past.

METHODOLOGY

We base this chapter on extensive and rigorous literature searches. In the various catalogues and on-line databases we used to search, we only paid attention to the direct use of the words 'coach', 'coaching', 'mentor' or 'mentoring'. Any description from the past, either in the original text or translations, that did not directly use these words were discounted and at times we suggest that the link to coaching or mentoring is associative and not direct.

We investigated the meanings of these words by examining the descriptions and comments made by the various authors. We also compared and related these historical meanings to modern uses of words 'coach', 'coaching', 'mentor' or 'mentoring'.

We do not seek a justified or 'proved' position here but present a descriptive account based on literature, research and practice.

FOLK WISDOMS AND MEANING

This research is unique and extensive. It is not exhaustive because we believe that there is yet more to be explored in the hundreds of years of literature on the subject but the significance of these historical links is demonstrated by Bruner's (1990) notion of 'folk wisdoms'. He argues that folk wisdoms or stories play a vital role in shaping understanding of any social phenomenon. Bruner (1990: 32–3) suggests that this is central to the notion of human psychology: 'The central concept of human psychology is meaning and the process and transactions involved with the construction of meaning.'

Bruner states that it is the surrounding culture and external environment, not biological factors, that shape human lives and minds. People do this by imposing the patterns inherent in their culture's symbolic systems, 'its language and discourse modes, the forms of logical and narrative explication, and the patterns of mutually dependent communal life' (p. 33). Therefore, with social phenomena such as mentoring and coaching it is necessary to interpret language, symbols and myths in the environment in which they are displayed in order to explicate meaning: 'we shall be able to interpret meanings and meaning-making in a principled manner only in the degree to which we are able to specify the structure and coherence of the larger contexts in which specific meanings are created and transmitted' (p. 64).

Bruner believes that 'folk wisdom' is communicated through narrative and that 'we take meaning from our historical pasts which gave shape to our culture and we distribute meaning through interpersonal dialogue' (p. 77). Bruner's views, we believe, relate very strongly to coaching and mentoring but Bruner does not use either word in his writings – we have therefore made an associative link.

INDIRECT EARLY LINKS TO MENTORING

Plato and Socrates

There are resonating links but no direct references in translation to mentoring in Plato's (427–347 BC) writings (1997). In his earlier work Plato employs Socratic (469–399 BC) philosophy and some translators and introduction writers (Nehamas and Woodruff, 1989; Taffel, 2004) refer to Socrates as Plato's mentor. In brief, according to Plato, the main thrust of Socrates' teaching is that true knowledge emerges through dialogue, systematic questioning and participation in critical debate. Further, Socrates calls learners to 'know yourself'. Mentoring activity today is associated with dialogue, questioning and developing self-knowledge but we could find no evidence in translation of Plato (1997) using the word 'mentor' despite his references to Homer. We therefore conclude that links between Socratic dialogue and mentoring in the modern world are associative and not direct.

Aristotle

Some (e.g. Cottingham, 2007) state that Plato was Aristotle's mentor. Aristotle was among the first of the ancients to develop a philosophy of learning. This involved three aspects: the *practical* (as associated with political and ethical life); the *theoretical* (the seeking of truth through thought, observation, consideration and the achievement of knowledge for its own sake); and the *productive* (making something). A learner may separate or combine these different elements to achieve varied understandings of different types of knowledge through the application of different techniques (Carr and Kemmis, 1986). We believe that the modern concept of mentoring draws on this ancient tradition of the triangle of knowing. But, in the translations of Aristotle we explored there is no direct use of the word 'mentor'.

DIRECT EARLY LINKS TO MENTORING

Homer

The first mention of mentoring in literature was about three thousand years ago. The original mentor was a friend and adviser of Telemachus, Odysseus' son, in Homer's epic poem *The Odyssey*. The Indo-European root 'men' means 'to think' and in ancient Greek the word 'mentor' means adviser. So, mentor is an adviser of thought.

Within Homer, there are many confusing and contradictory events. Some writers have drawn selectively on them in order to make a point; for example, the violence of the original story is often glossed over (see Garvey and Megginson, 2004), the social norms and context of the day are inadequately explored and some (Harquail and Blake, 1993) raise confusing gender issues found in the original story. Others (see, for example, Whitmore, 2002) suggest that the Odyssey implies a directive approach to mentoring but our reading of the Odyssey leads us to believe that the mentoring is more based on experiential learning with support and challenge. There can be little doubt that some of the ideas presented in Homer's version of mentoring remain relevant today and we discuss these later in this chapter.

EIGHTEENTH CENTURY WRITINGS ON MENTORING

Fénélon (1651–1715), Archbishop of Cambrai and later tutor to Louis XIV's heir, in his seminal work *Les Aventures de Télémaque*, developed the mentoring theme of *The Odyssey*. It is a case history of human development and demonstrates that life's events are potential learning experiences. Fénélon shows us that the activity of observing others provides both positive and negative learning opportunities. He suggests that pre-arranged or chance happenings, if fully explored with the support and guidance of a mentor, provide opportunities for the learner to acquire a high level understanding of 'the ways of the world' very quickly.

Eighteenth century France viewed Fénélon's work as a political manifesto presenting an ideal political system based on the concept of the paradox of a monarchy-led republic. There was a clear focus on the development and education of leaders – something with which both mentoring and coaching are associated today. Fénélon implied that leadership could be developed through guided experience. Louis XIV saw this as a challenge to the divine right of kings and he banished Fénélon to Cambrai and cancelled his pension.

Les Aventures de Télémaque appears again in France in Rousseau's educational treatise *Emile* (1762). Rousseau, probably the founder of the notion of 'experiential learning', was profoundly influenced by Fénélon's ideas on development.

He focussed on dialogue as an important element in learning and gave clear guidance on the ideal class size for effective education – one-to-one! In his book *Emile*, Telemachus becomes a model, perhaps a metaphor for learning, growth and social development. The central character, Emile, is given a copy of *Les Aventures de Télémaque* as a guide to his developmental journey.

Further early writings on mentoring can be found in the work of Louis Antonine de Caraccioli (1723–1803). As Engstrom (2006) noted, Caraccioli wrote *Veritable le Mentor ou l'education de la noblesse* in 1759 and it was translated into English in 1760 to become *The True Mentor, or, an Essay on the Education of Young People in Fashion*. This work describes mentoring mainly from the perspective of the mentor. Caraccioli acknowledges the influence of Fénélon's work on his own. Caraccioli writes: 'we stand in need of academics to form the heart at the same time that they enrich the mind' (1760: vii). Caraccioli was also interested in the therapeutic effects of mentoring conversations when he says 'Melancholy, so common a complaint with the most voluptuous' has no effect on the man who possesses reflection' (vs 35, 88).

In 1750, the term 'Mentor' (according to the *Oxford English Dictionary*) was used in the English language by Lord Chesterfield in a letter to his son (8 March 1750, letter number CVII) to describe a developmental process:

> These are resolutions which you must form, and steadily execute for yourself, whenever you
> lose the friendly care and assistance of your Mentor. In the meantime, make a greedy use
> of him; exhaust him, if you can, of all his knowledge; and get the prophet's mantle from
> him, before he is taken away himself.

Later, Lord Byron (1788–1824) used the term 'Mentor' in his poems *The Curse of Minerva* and *Childe Harold's Pilgrimage* ('Stern Mentor urg'd from high to yonder tide'), and in *The Island* Byron refers to the sea as 'the only mentor of his youth'. Given the classical educational background of these writers (ancient Greek literature was a part of their curriculum), it is likely that they derived the concept from Homer. It is also interesting to note the dual description of 'mentor' as either 'friendly and caring' or 'stern'.

Two volumes of the publication *The Female Mentor* appears in the English language in 1793 with a third volume in 1796. These works are recordings of conversations about topics of interest among a group of women referred to as '*the society*'. The author, Honoria, identifies and describes the characteristics of the female mentor, not as the substance of the book but rather as a commentary and series of asides made throughout the volumes. The introduction to Volume 1 gives the reader the purpose of the books and states: 'If the following conversations should afford you some amusement, and if you should think them calculated to lead the youthful and unbiased mind in the ways of virtue, I shall feel highly gratified' (Vol. 1: i). The mentor, Amanda, was aware of Fénélon, and his approach to education and life seemed to have been a model for '*the society*'.

The philosophical underpinnings of the discussions in the books are broad and draw on, for example, the philosophy of ancient Egypt, Christianity, Greek civilization and ideas on nature. There are also a number of discussions about famous women as positive role models, for example 'Anne Boleyn, Queen Consort of Henry Eighth' and 'On Learned Ladies'.

DETAILED HISTORICAL DESCRIPTIONS OF MENTORING PRACTICE AND THE LINKS TO MODERN DISCOURSES

Homer

The original Mentor has two personas. One is Mentor, the Ithacan and friend to Odysseus. Odysseus asked Mentor to be the guardian of his son, Telemachus. The other is Athena, 'the goddess of civil administration, war and, most notably, wisdom' (Harquail and Blake, 1993: 3). Athena takes on the guise of Mentor to protect the stability and wealth of Ithaca during Odysseus' absence. Athena sees Telemachus as key to the achievement of this aim. She establishes Telemachus' potential, first in the guise of Mentees, with a series of tests and sets about taking him on a voyage of discovery and learning. This story is therefore about Athena as mentor rather than Mentor himself.

The following characteristics of mentoring displayed by Homer's Athena are drawn from Garvey's (1998) narrative research. We suggest that modern discourses in both coaching and mentoring draw on these early descriptions of mentoring. To support this claim, we have put two references from modern literature after each bullet point. The first reference comes from mentoring literature and the second from coaching. We use this approach in all the following historical descriptions:

- Athena assessed and helped develop potential (Cox, 2000; Wilson, 2004).
- The relationship had a clear sense of purpose and direction (Bush and Coleman, 1995; Cramm and May, 1998).
- Athena was aware of the balance and split of attention between the learner (Telemachus) and the organization (Ithaca). Athena was supportive and loyal to both (Garvey and Williamson, 2002; Downey, 2003).
- Telemachus had a range of developers and some of these developers had specific skills and motives in mind to help him progress (Bowerman and Collins, 1999; Higgins and Kram, 2001).
- Trust was present in all the learning relationships (Connor, 1994; Bluckert, 2005).
- There was both challenge and support in the relationships (Gladstone, 1988; McCauley et al., 1998).
- Athena enabled Telemachus to make his own decisions by fostering and encouraging independence (Clutterbuck, 1992; Krazmien and Berger, 1997).

The Fénélon Development

In Fénélon, we discover, through the narrative, descriptions of the benefits, characteristics and skills of mentoring. These include:

- Mentors use reflective questions (Hallett, 1997; Garvey and Alred, 2000).
- Mentors support and help to remove 'fear of failure' by building confidence (Ellinger et al., 2005; Megginson et al., 2005).
- A mentor is assertive and calm in the face of adversity (http://www.prospects.ac.uk/downloads/occprofiles/profile_pdfs/A6_Learning_mentor.pdf; Atkinson, 2005).
- A mentor is confident and self aware (Nelson and Quick, 1985; Byrne, 2005).
- A mentor has charismatic leadership abilities (Hjermstad, 2002; Goldsmith, 2006).
- Role modelling goes on in mentoring (Robertson, 2005; Fracaro, 2006).
- Mentoring involves experiential learning (Kellar et al., 1995; Salimbene et al., 2005).
- A mentor is inspirational (Nankivell and Shoolbred, 1997; Vermaak and Weggeman, 1999).
- Trust is essential (Connor, 1994; Bluckert, 2005).

Caraccioli's contribution

In Caraccioli a mentor:

- Expresses wisdom (Garvey et al., 1996; Bluckert, 2005)
- Has self-knowledge leading to the enhanced knowledge of others (Nelson and Quick, 1985; Byrne, 2005)
- Builds rapport and establishes trust (Tabbron et al., 1997; Giglio et al., 1998)
- Is empathetic and inspirational (Giglio et al., 1998; Hansford and Ehrich, 2006)
- Is sought out rather than seeks pupils (mentees/coachees) (Garvey and Galloway, 2002; Jones et al., 2006)
- Has a sense of goodness based on deep religious values (Lantos, 1999; no reference found to this in modern coaching literature)
- Understands the cultural climate of the pupil (coachee/mentee) (Johnson et al., 1999; Lloyd and Rosinski, 2005)
- Prefers the positive and distinguishing truth from falsehood (Garvey et al., 1996; Murray, 2004)
- Acts from the principle of conscience and not self-interest (Appelbaum et al., 1994; no direct reference could be found in modern coaching literature to this quality of the coach – the closest is 'person centredness' found in Bluckert, 2005)
- Does not deal with trifles (Garvey et al., 1996; Giglio et al., 1998)
- Draws on experiences (Kellar et al., 1995; Salimbene et al., 2005)
- Helps to direct attention and assists in making decisions (Brunner, 1998; Pegg, 1999)
- Encourages varied reading and discussing literature (not mentioned in either discourse)
- Develops and encourages reflection (Barnett, 1995; Ellinger and Bostrom, 1999).

Caraccioli provides a staged and progressive mentoring process model:

Observation leading to...
Toleration leading to...

Reprimands leading to...
Correction leading to...
Friendship leading to...
Awareness.

Caraccioli's model aims to develop 'awareness' as the main outcome of mentoring and it offers two versions of mentoring within the same model. One is the 'stern mentor' alluded to by Byron who 'reprimands' and 'corrects', while the other is the 'friendly mentor' in Lord Chesterfield's letter to his son who 'observes', 'tolerates' and offers 'friendship'.

Making allowances for historical changes in the meanings of words, this model also resonates with modern discourses on mentoring and coaching. For example, 'observation' can be an aspect of performance coaching and 'toleration' could be linked to listening and acceptance, 'reprimand' with challenge, 'correction' with skills coaching, 'friendship' is often discussed in mentoring literature and 'awareness' is discussed within both mentoring and coaching.

Caraccioli contributes two further concepts. The first is what we now call 'supervision'. Caraccioli's view is that a mentor needs an experienced and successful mentor as a guide. The second is a description of the phases of life:

1. The torrid, which is our youth.
2. The temperate (the state of manhood).
3. The frigid or old age where our imagination falters and our passions and desires subside.

Modern discourses on mentoring also refer to 'life cycles' and stages or phases of the relationship (see, for example, Kram, 1983 and Alred et al., 1997).

Honoria

In *The Female Mentor or Select Conversations* by Honoria (1793/6) we find further and similar descriptions of a female mentor, Amanda. Honoria was Amanda's daughter and she writes: 'she [Amanda] endeavoured to instil instruction into our tender minds by relating either moral or religious tales, and by entering into a course of reading, which while it inculcated a lesson, was calculated to engage our attention' (p. 6). *The Female Mentor* is an account of group mentoring. The group, started by Amanda, was originally for her own children but word soon spread and *the society* developed to include other people's children, and later, adults. Deep religious values underpin Amanda's work.

These works show that the female mentor has many of the qualities of those described by Homer, Fénélon and Caraccioli, and that the main approach for acquiring these qualities is through role modelling.

THE BEGINNINGS OF COACHING

In the modern coaching literature, Hughes (2003) suggests that the term coaching also has its origins in ancient Greece and links to Socratic dialogue. De Haan (2008: 1) also suggests that coaching originates from ancient Greece: 'It is important to realize here that inspiring coaching conversations have been passed down from classical times…'. His book has many classical images within it as if to reinforce the link. However, as this section demonstrates, the link to classical times is speculative and associative. Brunner (1998: 516) takes this link further with a more direct association when he asks the question, 'Would coaching thus be the modern version of the Socratic dialogue?' This is an important question and, according to Krohn (1998), there are four indispensable components within Socratic dialogue.

The Concrete

By keeping with concrete experience it becomes possible to gain insight by linking any statement with personal experience. In this way the dialogue concerns the whole person.

Full Understanding Between Participants

This involves more than simple verbal agreement. All parties to the dialogue need to be clear about the meaning of what has just been said by testing it against her or his own concrete experience. Limiting beliefs need to be made conscious in order for them to be transcended.

Adherence to a Subsidiary Question Until it is Answered

For a dialogue to achieve adherence, each participant in the dialogue needs to be committed to their work and develop self-confidence in the power of reason. This means: to be persistent in the face of challenge, calm and humble enough to accept a different course in the dialogue in order to return to the subsidiary question. It is about honouring digressions while being persistent.

Striving for Consensus

This requires honesty, trust and faith in the examination of the thoughts of both self and others. These are the conditions of consensus and it is the striving that is important and not necessarily the consensus itself.

Clearly, there are many resonances in this explanation of Socratic dialogue with modern writings on both coaching and mentoring. There are no translations of Plato that we looked at that used the term 'coaching' and therefore modern writers like Brunner (1998), Hughes (2003) and de Haan (2008) have made associative and not direct links to classical times and, in particular, Socrates. Additionally, Socratic dialogue was about groups of people and not pairs as in coaching.

Brunner (1998: 516), however, does offer an insightful comment on the meaning of coaching when he states: 'coaching takes many forms, from technical counselling to the psychological domination that flirts with suggestion, for this is a domain devoid of any fixed deontology.' According to Brunner, then, coaching has multiple meanings and is subject to contextual variation. History supports this view.

The *Oxford English Dictionary* Online, states that the earliest uses of the term 'coaching' in the English language can be traced to 1849 in Thackeray's novel *Pendennis*. This probable first use of the term is in fact a pun. Some university students are travelling back to university in a horse-drawn coach:

> 'I'm coaching there,' said the other, with a nod. 'What?' asked Pen, and in a tone of such wonder, that Foke burst out laughing, and said, 'He was blowed if he didn't think Pen was such a flat as not to know what coaching meant.' 'I' m come down with a coach from Oxford. A tutor, don't you see, old boy? He's coaching me, and some other men, for the little go...'

Following this publication, the term 'coaching' seems to have been associated with supporting university students and academic attainment, for example, F. Smedley writes in 1850: 'Besides the regular college tutor, I secured the assistance of what, in the slang of the day, we irreverently termed "a coach".' It is not clear why the term was regarded as 'irreverent'.

During the nineteenth century the term coaching was used extensively in association with the development of boating and rowing skills as well as to enhance performance in these activities. For example, in 1867 the *Evening Standard*, on 14 February, reported: 'The crew being coached by Mr. F. Willan and Mr. G. Morrison, from the former gentleman's steamboat.' And in 1885 the *Manchester Guardian*, on 28 March, reported: 'A thoroughly clever coach was able to advise them from first to last. Under his careful tuition the crew have improved steadily.' Also associated with boating in 1889 the *Daily News*, on 29 January, commented on the Oxford and Cambridge Boat Race: 'The President superintended the coaching from horseback.'

Additionally, another nineteenth century link to sport (cricket) can be found in Harrison's (1888) *The Choice of Books and Other Literary Pieces*: 'To call in professional "coaches" to teach the defence of the wicket.'

Presumably referring to life skills, in 1887 Sir R.H. Roberts, in *In the Shires* (viii, 128), wrote: 'These young ladies, although ably coached by their mother...'

There is comment in the 1866 edition of the *London Review*, on 18 August (180/1), which says: 'The coach and the coachee can soothe their consciences by the reflection.' This is a very interesting reference for two reasons. First, it is probably the first recorded use of the term 'coachee' to describe the focus of the coach's activity. Second, the emphasis on *reflection* contrasts with the rather more didactic stance of the previous citations associated with coaching.

As far as we can discover, there are no works predating the nineteenth century devoted to exploring or describing the meaning and practice of coaching. We therefore conclude that coaching, relative to mentoring, is a newer term.

THE DYADIC RELATIONSHIP

Both mentoring and coaching are dyadic partnerships and to further explore the discourses surrounding them, we draw on Simmel's (1950) seminal theoretical sociological work on the nature of the dyad.

Simmel's Dyads

Simmel observed that one element of the dyadic relationship is that *two* is the maximum number of people needed for the security of a 'secret'. In modern parlance 'secrecy' could be replaced by the word 'confidentiality'. Confidentiality is fundamental to the success of both coaching and mentoring relationships as described in many recent texts; see, for example, MacLennan (1995), Clutterbuck and Megginson (1999), Grodzki and Allen (2005) and Megginson et al. (2005).

According to Simmel, the element of 'secrecy' also places a mutual dependency on the relationship. This is because, if another person is added to the pair, the social structure fundamentally alters, for example, if one person 'drops out' of the relationship of three, the group can still exist in the remaining two. Clearly, in a dyad if one drops out, the group is at an end. Modern writings on both mentoring and coaching regard dependency as a problem and something to be avoided. However, the modern discourses on coaching and mentoring do stress the allied notions of 'trust', 'commitment' and 'active involvement' as important elements of the relationship.

The certainty that any dyadic relationship may end can be a powerful influence on the partnership. According to Simmel, the sense of the inevitable end has the potential to lead to either greater dependency or a lack of trust due to the inherent risk of closing down within the relationship. However, the risk of the end can also have the effect of bringing the pair closer together in a sense of uniqueness.

Within the discourse of coaching and mentoring, the issue of 'the ending' is important and both discourses raise the issue of proper closures and endings of the relationship (see Garvey, 1994b; Clutterbuck and Lane, 2004; Grodzki and Allen, 2005).

Simmel also mentions the concept of 'triviality' in relation to the dyad. Simmel suggests that this is created by the initial expectations in the relationship failing to materialize in practice. Additionally, the regularity and frequency of experiences within the relationship may create a sense of 'triviality' and this can result in the dyad closing down. In short, the pair or one of the pair may run out of things to say and get bored! The 'content' of a relationship can be measured by its rarity and in partnerships that 'do not result in higher units, the tone of triviality frequently becomes desperate and fatal' (Simmel, 1950: 126). So, there is a need for continued renewal and stimulation within the dyad for it to survive. Neilson and Eisenbach (2003) found in mentoring that renewal through regular feedback about the relationship within the relationship was a significant contributor to successful outcomes.

Simmel also states that within the dyad there is potential for great intimacy. He suggests that the dyadic form provides the ingredients for deep friendship and has an in-built tendency for intimacy and mutual dependence. Simmel makes it clear that this is not due to the 'content' (the things the individuals discuss) within the relationship but the unique shared quality of the relationship. Intimacy exists 'if the 'internal' side of the relation is felt to be essential; if its whole affective structure is based on what each of the two participants give or show only to the one other person and to nobody else' (Simmel, 1950: 126).

Many modern writers raise the issue of intimacy in mentoring, for example: Levinson et al. (1978); Torrance (1984); Bennetts (1995, 1996); Hurley and Fagenson-Eland (1996); Scandura et al. (1996); Hale (2000); Samier (2000); Friday et al. (2004). In these writings 'intimacy' is discussed as both an important and positive element of the relationship and a potential source of difficulties and abuse. Levinson et al. (1978: 100) state that 'mentoring is best understood as a form of love relationship' and as such 'it is a difficult one to terminate'.

Within coaching, the element of 'intimacy' in dyad is not widely discussed in the literature. To illustrate, using The Emerald Online Library, we completed a literature search by searching the word 'coaching' and 'mentoring'. We then randomly selected 25 articles from the search list and searched for the word 'intimacy' in these 25 articles. The 'mentoring + intimacy' search resulted in 25 hits and 'coaching + intimacy' resulted in no hits.

It seems then that there is some resonance between Simmel's writings of the early twentieth century and the modern discourses of coaching and mentoring. There are also differences. Simmel describes some of the qualitative elements such as friendship, intimacy and mutuality and it seems that the modern discourses of mentoring also tackle these elements whereas these elements are not so commonly approached within the coaching literature. We suspect that this difference may be explained with reference to the different social contexts in which mentoring and coaching sometimes take place. We will elaborate on this comment later in the chapter.

PULLING THE THREADS TOGETHER

The history of mentoring is very long. The core mentoring model, as described in the past, is one of the more mature and experienced engaging in a relationship with a younger and less experienced person. In these early accounts, the central purpose of mentoring is to assist the learner to integrate as a fully functioning person within the society they inhabit. This still remains as one of the purposes (but not the only) of modern coaching and mentoring. However, the mentor or coach, in current times, may be a peer.

In the historical writings on both coaching and mentoring, specific knowledge and skills are transferred from one to the other but with the intention of fostering independence. There is some confusion here in some of the modern literature. A typical example is in Rosinski (2004: 5), where he states:

> Although leaders can act as coaches, I have found that this role is often confused with mentoring. Coaches act as facilitators. Mentors give advice and expert recommendations. Coaches listen, ask questions, and enable coachees to discover for themselves what is right for them. Mentors talk about their own personal experience, assuming this is relevant for the mentees.

Later, he presents the issue of knowledge transfer in coaching and says: 'In my view coaches are also responsible for transferring knowledge. Coaches don't simply help resolve coachees' issues. They actually share their knowledge so that coachees can become better coaches. For example, the coach will briefly explain his frame of reference' (2004: 245).

In the first comment, 'mentor' is perhaps characterized as the 'stern mentor' giving advice or perhaps the 'reprimand' and 'corrective' model put forward by Caraccioli, with the coach represented as the 'friendly facilitator'. In the later comment, Rosinski presents the coach as a 'giver of advice' or, in his words, the 'knowledge transferer' but Rosinski reduces its significance by using the word 'briefly' almost as if 'briefly' makes the advice-giving less important. Further, it is difficult in our minds to distinguish between 'personal experience' and 'frame of reference'.

This example shows how modern writers on mentoring and coaching draw selectively on certain, albeit subliminal, dominant narratives and present them as versions of the truth. Bruner's (1990) point made earlier in this chapter about the importance of the social context to illuminate meaning seems to hold true. A coaching writer has a particular story to tell as does a mentoring writer. Sadly, this is often at the expense of one over the other.

Homer, Fénélon, Caraccioli and Honoria offer similar, comprehensive and complementary descriptions of mentoring qualities, processes and skills and these attributes feature in modern writings on both mentoring and coaching. Many of the characteristics of 'mentor' outlined in these texts are desirable in modern coaching practice.

The term coaching, when compared with the term mentoring, seems to have a more recent history in the English language. The nineteenth century writings on coaching focus on performance and attainment, originally in an educational setting but also in sport and life. There is some historical evidence that coaching was also about reflection and the development of 'life skills'. Similar to the mentor, the coach is the skilled, more experienced or more knowledgeable person.

Crucial to the success of mentoring, as outlined in the historical texts, is the development of the *relationship* between mentor and mentee. Historical writers describe this as forms of friendship. In modern writings (Clutterbuck and Megginson, 1999) 'friendship' is still strongly linked to mentoring but the link between 'friendship' and coaching is not so strong.

To illustrate, we completed the same search exercise explained above for 'intimacy' using the word 'friend'. In articles about coaching, 'friend' is mentioned in five of them, with the writers referring to the coach as 'friendly', positing this as a key characteristic of the coach. The 'mentoring + friend' search yielded 14 hits. In these articles 'friendship' is posited as an outcome of mentoring or as an element of relationship building.

All 50 articles discussed either mentoring or coaching in a range of settings but, in the main, they were work-related contexts.

Coaching is still a dominant practice in sport and the term is used extensively in business environments. This is either in the form of internal line manager coaches or with the use of external and paid coaches. These are often positioned as 'executive coaches'. Life coaching is almost exclusively linked to paid practice. Coaching is still associated with performance improvement of a specific kind related to a job role but it is also increasingly linked to leadership development, transition and change and generally developing a focus for the future (see Chapter 5). We believe that coaching is adopting the historical descriptions of mentoring.

Mentoring activity is found in all sectors of society and includes both paid and voluntary activities. It is also associated with 'off line' partnerships. The relationship elements are important and terms like 'friendship' in the modern literature generally views this as acceptable and natural. Mentoring is more associated with 'voluntarism' than coaching, although we do accept that it would not be possible to compel anyone to be coached (see Chapter 5).

Coaching is not as strongly associated with mutuality as mentoring is (see Chapter 5), although we suspect, as Simmel (1950) suggests, that mutuality is inevitable. If both benefit, this raises a question around the issue of payment which we discuss in Chapter 15.

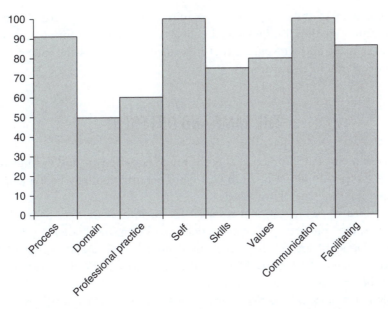

Figure 1.1   Percentage of agreement among practitioners about mentoring and coaching competencies

Modern concepts of coaching and mentoring also include explorations of the emotional self which resonate with Caraccioli's call, when writing about mentoring, to educate the 'mind' and the 'heart'.

CURRENT RESEARCH

Recent research (Willis, 2005) into mentoring and coaching standards undertaken by the European Mentoring and Coaching Council (EMCC) suggests that in practice there is much common ground between mentoring and coaching (see Figure 1.1). The research identified eight main categories in which competencies might be identified as follows:

- Process.
- Domain specific knowledge, expertise and focus.
- Professionalism and building a practice.
- Self.
- Skills.
- Values and approach.
- Communication.
- Facilitating.

Within the categories of 'Domain specific knowledge, expertise and focus' and 'Professionalism and building a practice' the respondents give a lack of agreement as to the competencies required of a mentor or coach. Both of these represent the different social contexts in which mentoring and coaching takes place and we suggest that it is this that explains the lower level of agreement among practitioners.

THE SAME AND DIFFERENT

It would seem that in practice, there is much common ground despite claims to the contrary found in modern writings. This situation may be explained by considering the issue of 'mindset'.

The idea of 'organizational mindset' is an important one. Senge (1992) describes the concept as 'mental models' and Bettis and Prahalad (1995) call it 'the dominant logic'. They argue that mental models and dominant logic greatly influence both behaviour and thinking process and have the potential to inhibit or enhance learning capabilities.

'Mental modes are deeply ingrained assumptions, generalizations or even pictures or images that influence how we understand the world and how we take action' (Senge, 1992: 8).

According to Burrell and Morgan (1979) there are two opposing 'mindsets' in social science – the 'objectivist' and the 'subjectivist'. The 'objectivist' tradition favours cause and effect and positivistic methodologies, whereas the 'subjectivist' tradition views social research from an antipositivist perspective and favours a descriptive framework (see Chapter 2).

Arguably, many decision makers, managers and funders who employ mentoring and coaching tend towards the objectivist perspective, consequently seeking cause and effect justifications to support expenditure on mentoring and coaching. This, we believe, has led to the general widespread 'commodification' of coaching in particular as those who engage in its practice seek to demonstrate its impact in 'objectivist' terms. Our experience shows that managers of some publicly funded schemes are also moving towards this belief (see Colley, 2003). The consequence of this shift is reflected in a change in the discourse as we have seen earlier in this chapter in a movement away from using the language of 'the heart' towards a cleaner language of rationality or the 'brain'. Coaching and mentoring may suffer from what Habermas (1974) refers to as 'misplaced concreteness'. Here, the social phenomenon is attributed with a hard, solid, rational reality as though it were a product of a factory and, in the case of mentoring and coaching, they are placed in the discourse as 'tools' of production. We also believe that, either consciously or unconsciously, modern writers on coaching make the links to classical times to add credibility and substance to the coaching phenomenon.

Mentoring and coaching draw on different traditions of research. Coaching research, currently at least, tends to focus on outcomes and return

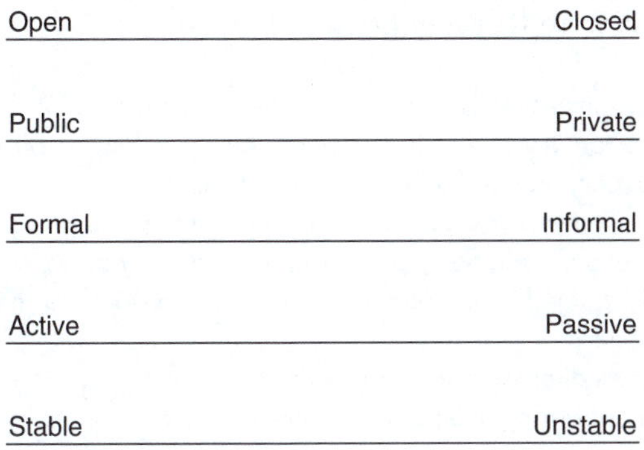

Open	Closed
Public	Private
Formal	Informal
Active	Passive
Stable	Unstable

Figure 1.2   Dimensions framework

First published in Garvey, B. (1994) 'A dose of mentoring', *Education and Training*, 36(4): 18–26.

on investment calculations. Mentoring research tends to look at the functional issues (see Chapter 2).

Schön offers insight into this as follows: 'On the high ground, management problems lend themselves to solution through the application of research-based theory and technique. In the swampy lowland, messy confusing problems defy technical solution' (1987: 3).

Mentoring and coaching, in our view, despite the 'commodification' are quite firmly in the 'swampy lowlands' and, if there is to be enhanced understanding, we must continue to 'thickly describe' (Geertz, 1971) coaching and mentoring in as many different contexts as possible.

DIMENSIONS

The 'objectivist' tradition favours definition over description but by their very nature definitions seek to simplify and condense. In this age of increasing complexity, simplification may have appeal. The range of contexts or domains in which mentoring and coaching is found suggests that definition alone cannot adequately reflect the complexity of meaning and we argue that the meaning of coaching and mentoring is fundamentally determined by the social context.

A way forward is to view mentoring and coaching from a 'subjectivist' tradition and view mentoring and coaching descriptively. The notion of 'dimensions' in mentoring was first put forward by Garvey in 1994 (see Figure 1.2). By looking at the dimensions of dyadic relationships in context it is possible to consider their characteristics not as fixed positions but in relation to a moving and changing dynamic over time.

The dimensions were first identified as follows:

The *open/closed* dimension is about the content. What kind of things will be talked about? This is up for discussion. If it is open, then anything is on the agenda. If it is closed, the discussion may be focussed on specific issues.

The *public/private* dimension is about who knows mentoring is going on. If the mentoring is in an organization, keeping it private may lead to speculation about its purpose and nature. Making it public is good for mentoring and good for the relationship in the organizational context.

The *formal/informal* dimension is about the administration and management of the relationship. In a formal arrangement, the mentoring pair may agree meetings in advance, take notes, time limit the discussion, agree to meet in a regular venue at regular intervals. If it is informal they will meet on an 'as required basis' and generally work on a 'go with the flow' basis.

The *active/passive* dimension is about activity. Who does what in the relationship? The mentee is the more active in the relationship as he or she is the one undergoing change and carrying out action plans. The mentor may also agree to take some actions, such as gathering information for the mentee, and may indeed, at times, ask the mentee for a meeting. If both feel the mentoring is passive, if not much is happening, it is probably time to review the mentoring relationship.

The *stable/unstable* dimension is about trust and consistency. It is about sticking to the groundrules while being prepared to jointly review them. It is about sticking to the meeting schedule and not changing it (particularly at the last minute). It is about developing momentum to the mentoring process and maintaining it.

The 'dimensions' framework describes the type of coaching or mentoring within a particular setting without needing to resort to definitional positioning.

CONCLUSIONS

In conclusion, there can be no 'one best way' in mentoring and coaching and therefore no one definition. Practitioners draw on similar traditions of one-to-one developmental dialogue and position their particular brand according to the environment in which they operate. Both traditions draw on a similar range of skill sets and adapt them according to the nature and form of the dialogue in use within the environmental setting.

The question 'Whose agenda is it?' helps to highlight the similarities and the differences between the terms mentoring and coaching and we discuss this further in Chapter 7.

Another issue is the dynamic quality of the relationship between the two participants over time. The dimensions framework offers a way of agreeing the nature and form of the relationship at the start, reviewing it over time or noticing the changes as they happen. In this way both the similarities and the differences can be understood descriptively rather than by a positioning or tribal definition.

The meaning of coaching and mentoring is a changing dynamic with certain elements remaining constant but with others changing, and it is this that explains the confusing array of definitions found in modern discourses.

To return, then, to the original question: *are mentoring and coaching distinctive and separate activities or are they essentially similar in nature?*

The above evidence suggests that, although the original roots are different, both mentoring and coaching in the modern context selectively draw on a range of the same narratives or, in Bruner's (1990) term, 'folk wisdoms' to describe the activity. However, it seems that coaching and mentoring are essentially similar in nature.

The Future

We acknowledge and accept that it is very unlikely that there will ever be widespread consensus as to the meaning of coaching and mentoring in any particular context. As Garvey suggests: 'in whatever the setting the terminology is used, there needs to be a common understanding of meaning within that setting' (2004a: 8). This suggests that localized understanding is important and perhaps that is the best that can be done in a social practice that has such variation of purpose, scope and application. However, the term coachmentor seems to be in use fairly commonly in the UK at least and we wonder if this may be another way forward.

QUESTIONS

What is in a name? Does a name make any difference to practice?
How do you meet the challenge of definition in your organization?
Do you agree that coaching and mentoring are becoming commodified? Does this matter?

RESEARCHING COACHING AND MENTORING

CHAPTER OVERVIEW

This chapter takes a critical look at research practice in coaching and mentoring. It presents some opposing but fundamental philosophical positions and links these to research practice. We suggest that there are various 'archetypes' of research practice in coaching and mentoring research and that these are aimed at different audiences and have different purposes in mind.

This chapter is a multi-perspective, descriptive account, which characterizes research traditions and discourses in both mentoring and coaching and we create a framework of research approaches grounded in an analysis of a range of research articles in the field.

We aim to illustrate the characteristic strengths and weaknesses of each discourse thus illustrating the preoccupations that researchers have about mentoring and coaching. We also highlight the historical differences between the two traditions in a way that throws light on current preoccupations of those who focus on either coaching or mentoring.

Additionally, we examine the context of the studies we review and highlight how this impacts on research choices.

Finally, we offer implications and prescriptions derived from our arguments presented in this chapter that may be useful for researchers and practitioners alike.

INTRODUCTION

As raised in Chapter 1, there are many different perspectives on the meaning of coaching and mentoring, and the research traditions similarly fall into various camps or tribes. In Chapter 1, we also raised the issue of social context and its impact on coaching and mentoring in practice. Within research, the social context also shapes the researcher's purpose and often influences the practitioner's activities as they act on a researcher's findings.

Within our framework of analysis, we examine the gaze, strengths and weaknesses of each. 'Gaze' refers to the issues that various research strands privilege (by giving predominant attention to them), and an example is taken from our recent collaborative research study to illustrate how gaze operates in shaping the perceptions of researchers and determining the findings that they uncover. This is akin to the concept of 'mindset' raised in Chapter 1 but the difference between gaze and mindset is that gaze refers to what the researcher looks at, whereas mindset refers to what they are likely to see. We therefore see gaze as a particularly relevant intellectual tool in discussing research paradigms.

Nonetheless, there is a cautionary note here for researchers, practitioners and scheme designers that research findings need to be understood from the 'gaze' of the writer. As raised in Chapter 1, Burrell and Morgan (1979) offer some helpful insight into the 'gaze' in the task of classifying research approaches. Morgan (1993: 276–7) comments:

> One of the main insights emerging from this work was that social scientists, like people in everyday life, tend to get trapped by their perspectives and assumptions. As a result, they construct, understand, and interpret the social world in partial ways, creating interesting stets of insights but obliterating others as ways of seeing become ways of not seeing.

Burrell and Morgan used a two-by-two matrix to describe four of these partial ways of seeing: the subjectivist versus the objectivist paradigms and the concept of radical change versus regulatory change. A widely used simplification of this model is to contrast the two approaches of positivism and phenomenology (or interpretive). Others (e.g. Ruona and Lynham, 2004: 157) add to these two core methodologies a third – critical science. Critical science is aligned to Burrell and Morgan's concept of radical change.

To illustrate one such approach in a recent lecture on mentoring research David Clutterbuck suggested that there are a dozen things wrong with most mentoring research:

1. Failures of definition. What is mentoring? Do respondents self-select?
2. Context of relationship not specified. Internal/external; formal/informal; in-line/off-line/external.
3. Outcomes not explored. For mentee/for mentor; sponsorship/career (some of Kram's (1985) functions are processes, not outcomes – e.g. friendship).
4. Individual demographic variables not taken into account. For example, age, education, gender, race.
5. Quality of relationship. Nature of conversation; training of parties; effects of power on disclosure; effects of coercion to participate.
6. Stage of relationship. How many meetings? Duration of meetings; elapsed time since end of relationship.
7. Lack of triangulation. Just mentee; just mentor; a line manager view; no 360° view; no scheme organizer view.
8. Over-reliance on retrospective accounts.
9. Single point samples. No attempt to track movement of the relationship by longitudinal study.
10. Direction of gaze. If you can't measure it, it doesn't exist.

11. Researcher bias not addressed. Who sees the relationship? Who asks the questions?
12. Sample size. Number of respondents; representativeness is not considered.

We could critique mentoring and coaching research publications against such a list; however, Clutterbuck's perspective is largely a positivist one. While this is not a problem in itself and we maintain the position that no one method is better than the other, we do suggest that a blended approach offers the most potential to inform all users of research material. In this chapter we seek our own grounded methodology to analyse our selection of current research articles in mentoring and coaching.

METHODOLOGY

To introduce the different research traditions in mentoring and coaching we have picked two archetypal accounts of research that typify their respective traditions. We give a review of each.

We set out to build a typology of discourses found in the research literature of mentoring and coaching by drawing on a relatively random set of research accounts to give a picture of the field as it is currently developing. Our criteria for selecting the accounts were as follows:

- Published in or after 2003.
- Published in peer-reviewed journals.
- Selected from a range of journals – no more than three in either coaching or mentoring from the same journal.
- The same number of articles about coaching and mentoring. This resulted in 18 mentoring and 18 coaching articles.

In this way, we sought to build a picture of research practice that was current, high quality, eclectic and offering comparison between traditions in coaching and mentoring. The criterion of eclecticism was especially important because we could easily (for example) have concluded that all research in mentoring and coaching was in the tradition of a particular journal or its editors if we had over-relied on one source.

Using SWETSWISE and Business Source Premier Search engines, we identified the articles for mentoring as listed on p. 25 and analysed them using Table 2.1 on p. 38. The numbers in front of each source referring to the column where they are listed.

We also examined practically the research 'gaze' of a group of experienced researchers. At a meeting of the European Mentoring and Coaching Council's (EMCC) Collaborative Research Group, we examined the first few minutes of a DVD of the fifth coaching session between one of the group and a client. The group member, who was the coach on the DVD, took notes of the comments made and these are noted below in the section Research 'Gaze'. The research question was 'What is the reviewer's "gaze" in their analysis of the interaction?'

ARCHETYPES OF MENTORING AND COACHING RESEARCH

The Mentoring Archetype

For mentoring, the example is Phyllis Tharenou's article in the *Australian Journal of Management* (30(1): 77–109) entitled 'Does mentor support increase women's career advancement more than men's? The differential effects of career and psychosocial support' (Tharenou, 2005). From reading this title, we already know a great deal about this work. For instance:

- It addresses a group who may be disadvantaged in employment – in this case, women.
- It is grounded in an established theory – there is reference in the title to 'career' and 'psychosocial' functions of mentoring, a framework first established by Kram (1985) and continuously used by mentoring researchers ever since.
- It seeks to study the relationship between variables – in this case 'career advancement' and 'career and psychosocial support'. This may imply a 'positivist paradigm' to the research – a point that we will explore more in what follows.
- The question about comparison of effects on women and on men implies a large sample – and indeed, in this case, 3,220 respondents.
- The size of the sample implies that the researchers would be more interested in statistical relations than in stories or accounts of experience, and this is indeed so.
- The author's affiliation is described as University of South Australia – so embedded in the research community.
- This article is from the 30th volume of the *Australian Journal of Management*, so it is published in a prestigious and longstanding journal.

A perusal of the abstract of the article will yield further information about the nature of this work:

- The study examines the differential effects of men and women mentors upon the male and female subjects – thus introducing intervening variables and implying a sophisticated statistical treatment of the data.
- The abstract specifies that respondents came from Australians in the public sector and finance and business service industry – characteristically acknowledging the possible limitations to relevance of the findings.
- The study is described as being 'based on past research' so its findings seek to be cumulative building on (or contradicting) other contributions.
- This particular study is, although limited in terms of time, longitudinal – the subjects being surveyed twice, a year apart. This feature is not found widely in mentoring research accounts, but still represents an ideal. Cross-sectional research accounts (a snapshot taken at one time only) frequently refer to this feature as a weakness of their study and recommend longitudinal research designs.

Moving to the body of the article, in addition to confirmation of the points listed above, we also find that:

- A structure of hypotheses is set out and then tested in the remainder of the study.
- The limitations of the study are acknowledged.
- The sophisticated statistical treatment is borne out by a reading of the complete article, which has six pages of tables and reference (*inter alia*) to chi-squared tests, alpha coefficients, *t*-tests, intercorrelations, control variables, moderated hierarchical regression analysis and multivariate multicollinearity.
- Some variables that might affect the results are presented and where possible the statistical procedures to discount the effects of these variables are described.
- A large number of other mentoring research studies are cited and their findings and methodology are compared with the author's own study, placing it in an evolving body of knowledge.

In our view, in spite of the great strengths of this article, there are also some potential weaknesses that moderate the powerful impact of its story.

The subjects are described as 'protégés', a term that implies to an English speaker a passive 'done to' approach to mentoring. In fact, the approach or approaches to mentoring used in this study are not discussed. We suggest that with such a large sample, the approaches are likely to have been widely variable, but the use of this term illustrates a disembodied and simplifying approach to the research.

The researcher does not seem to be interested in what went on in the mentoring relationships she is examining. What happened in these relationships is in a 'black box', and not investigated.

There is no discussion of the 'treatment' that the protégés received or how they perceived it.

There is a sense here that the author examines reality principally through the statistics. What there is in the relationship is selected by examining statistical significance rather than personal meaning. As a result of this orientation the author can get into quite a tangle as illustrated by the following sentence: 'It should also be noted that, although mentor support is not related to men's career advancement for this sample, having a male mentor does increase men's managerial levels' (Tharenou, 2005: 102). The statement 'increasing managerial level' sounds to us like an important part of 'career advancement', but because they are two different technical measures in this aspect of the research, the rather striking conflict of data embedded in this sentence is not taken up by the author. This example illustrates a main theme in this book of the strong desire of many writers, researchers and organizations to seek simplicity in complexity.

There is an implication that the reader will be deeply knowledgeable about statistics and therefore able to make sense of such sentences as, 'Formal tests were made of multivariate multicollinearity, resulting in high tolerances (generally > 0.07), except for training and managerial level, and low variation inflation factors (all < 2)' (Tharenou, 2005: 91). We can see that this level of statistical sophistication is a useful means of gaining publication in a prestigious journal and in examining relationships between variables. However, we are not so sure that, presented in this way, it is effective in communicating with those interested in outcomes of mentoring research from a point of view of practice. As pointed out in Chapters 3 and 8, this approach to communication both includes and excludes different social groups.

The implications for practice are brief – less than a page in a 32-page article. They also seem contradictory. The author says, on the one hand, 'mentor career support explains women's career advancement more than it does men's…The effects are strongest for women with female mentors' (p. 105). This sentence seems to us to imply that we would have more positive career effect on women protégés by matching them with women mentors. But in the very next sentence the author says, 'Male mentors also help their protégés (male or female) advance more than female mentors do' (p. 105).

We do not make these criticisms to traduce the author of this interesting and painstaking study. Rather we raise them to highlight weaknesses of the type of research represented here and of which this article is an archetype.

THE COACHING ARCHETYPE

Moving on to the archetypal coaching article, we explore the features of Vernita Parker-Wilkins' 2006 article 'Business impact of executive coaching: demonstrating monetary value' from the journal *Industrial and Commercial Training* (28(3): 122–7). Again this information begins to tell us about the nature of the article:

- Business relevance is a concern – the 'business impact' is privileged. This writer is addressing practitioners of coaching or buyers of coaching services, rather than the community of researchers.
- The criterion of relevance is 'Return on Investment' (RoI) – the sub-heading speaks of 'demonstrating monetary value'.
- The author's affiliation is described as Executive Development Manager with a consultancy', Booz Allen Hamilton, so a practitioner rather than an academic.
- This article is from a well-established practitioner journal, where some articles are accepted without blind peer review.

The abstract adds the following aspects, all of which emphasize the practical, business related focus of the author:

- Being clear that the purpose is to 'enhance the utilization of coaching throughout the firm'.
- The RoI study is an evaluation of the scheme from the perspective of the business-significant stakeholders.
- This evaluation research focuses on practical effects rather than social science understanding.

- The abstract account showed how all the figures had been reduced to demonstrate that the results were conservative, and did not include remarkably massive individual cases, which were excluded from the study, thus giving the impression of 'reasonableness' in the study.
- The practical policy implications are spelled out in detail.

Reading the article itself indicates that the research was a mixture of quantitative and qualitative, and that there is more interest in what went on, but less attention to describing the research processes than in the mentoring archetype:

- The data are presented in summary form or with examples rather than spelling out in detail the processes and protocols for the research.
- The research was a case study of one company – and in fact this company was the author's own organization.
- Applicability and generalizability was not considered.
- The author delegated the design of the protocols to a survey company.
- The data were gathered by interview, giving a great deal of business-relevant circumstantial detail, which was described.
- The basis for the RoI calculation was given.
- Only 26 respondents were interviewed, though all those who might have responded were asked.

The weaknesses we identify in this account of coaching include the fact that the interests of the author in working for the firm studied and having a role in the delivery of the programme were not discussed.

The detail of the calculation of benefits or costs were not discussed in detail, although examples were given. This means that any reader is unable to assess the legitimacy of the calculations and is also unable to employ the techniques for themselves.

There is no attempt to explore or explain any alternative possible explanations for the positive results. Given the number of variables involved, it is likely that there would be more than one explanation for either positive or negative results.

No other studies are cited to confirm or contrast with the findings so there is no attempt to link this study to the broader body of literature on the subject.

Rather like the communication difficulties we raised about the previous paper, this article is written to appeal to a particular social group with a particular set of discourses. It is not our intention to damn this particular work by highlighting these deficiencies, as such weaknesses are characteristic of the generality of coaching research accounts.

Both pieces of work can be understood in terms of the gaze of the researcher, the imagined audience and his or her intentions in writing the paper.

IN SUMMARY

Mentoring research archetypally:

- Addresses interventions that counteract disadvantage in employment
- Is grounded in established theory and a research tradition
- Is positivist: examining relationships between variables and using analytical/inferential statistics to test hypotheses
- Uses questionnaires to survey a large sample
- Comes from a university research community and addresses other researchers and is peer reviewed
- Explores and seeks to control intervening variables
- Spells out limitations
- Is incurious about the nature of the relationships described
- Privileges statistical significance over subjective meaning
- Only touches on implications for practice and with caveats.

The archetype for coaching research, by contrast, involves:

- Focus on business relevance
- Pragmatic enhancement of practice is the declared aim
- Carrying out an evaluation study of a particular scheme
- Insider account by a sponsor of the scheme
- All other measures are subordinate to RoI
- Summaries and examples are provided rather than detailed research protocols
- Small number of respondents
- Data gathered by interview
- Sources of bias not addressed
- No other studies cited.

List of Mentoring Articles Selected

1. Tharenou, P. (2005) Does mentor support increase women's career advancement more than men's? The differential effects of career and psychosocial support. *Australian Journal of Management*, 30(1), June: 77–109.
2. Allen, T.D. and O'Brien, K.E. (2006) Formal mentoring programs and organizational attraction. *Human Resource Development Quarterly*, 17(1), Spring: 43–58.
3. O'Neill, R.M. (2005) An examination of organizational predictors of mentoring functions. *Journal of Managerial Issues*, XVII(4), Winter: 439–60.
4. Rhodes, J.E., Reddy, R. and Grossman, J.B. (2005) The protective influence of mentoring on adolescents' substance use: direct and indirect pathways. *Applied Developmental Science*, 9(1): 31–47.
5. Eby, L., Butts, M., Lockwood, A. and Simon, S.S. (2004) Protégés' negative mentoring experiences: construct development and nomological validation. *Personnel Psychology*, 57: 411–47.

Table 2.1 Mentoring article features by frequency of occurrence

Feature	1	2	3	4	5	6	7	8	9	10	11	12	13	14	15	16	17	18	Total
A Many citations (>15)	66	58	71	69	60	51	59	53	38	58	45	37	65	16	35	28	54	68	18
B Independent academic author	x	x	x	x	x	x	x	x	x	x	x		x	x	x	x	x	x	16
C Data from mentees	x	x	x	x	x	x	x	x					x	x	x	x	x	x	15
D Large N (>30)	3220	190	479	928	239	323	262	88	192	249	217					34		94	13
E Protégés term used	x	x	x		x	x	x	x	x	x	x		x				x		12
F Data by questionnaire	x	x	x	x	x	x	x	x	x	x	x	x							12
G Intervening variables examined	x	x	x	x	x	x	x	x		x	x				x		x		12
H Use others' measures	x	x	x	x	x	x	x	x	x	x	x	x							12
I Builds on established theory	x	x	x	x	x	x	x	x	x	x	x								11
J Hypotheses set/tested	x	x	x	x	x	x	x	x	x	x	x								11
K Inferential statistics	x	x	x	x	x	x	x	x	x	x	x								11
L Limitations discussed	x	x	x	x	x	x	x	x	x	x	x								11
M Informal mentoring					x		x	x	x	x	x		x	x	x	x	x		10
N Contingent variables controlled	x				x	x	x	x	x	x	x	x							9
O Formal mentoring		x	x	x	x	x	x	x	x	x		x							9
P Benefits to mentees	x				x								x	x	x	x	x	x	9
Q Practice relevance		x				x	x						x		x		x	x	8
R Data from mentors						x	x		x	x				x			x	x	8
S Data by interview					87								15	15	10		10		7
T Data from students		x	x		x	x						x						x	7

Table 2.1

Feature	1	2	3	4	5	6	7	8	9	10	11	12	13	14	15	16	17	18	Total
Article																			
U Kram functions used	X		X	X	X	X		X			X								7
V Qualitative data method specified													X	X	X	X	X	X	6
W Verbatim quotes								X				X	X	X		X		X	6
X Single case organization							X	X				X		X				X	5
Y Disadvantaged group	X			X											X		X		4
Z Longitudinal study	X			X										X				X	4
AA Treatment discussed													X	X	X			X	4
BB Benefits to mentors							X				X		X	X					4
CC Focus on negatives					X		X					X					X		4
DD Basis for sample spelt out								X	X						X				3
EE Benefits to organization		X												X					2
FF Qualitative data from e-sources												X						X	2
GG e-mentoring												X						X	2
HH Data from observation															X	X			2
II Data by focus group															X		X		2
JJ Control group				X															1
KK Descriptive stats only																		X	1
LL Mentoring by line boss															X				1
MM Data from mentee's staff																			0

6. Young, A.M. and Perrewé, P.L. (2004) The role of expectations in the Mentoring Exchange: an analysis of mentor and protégé expectations in relation to perceived support. *Journal of Managerial Issues*, XVI(1), Spring: 103–26.

7. Van Emmerik, H., Baugh, S.G. and Euwema, M.C. (2005) Who wants to be a mentor? An examination of attitudinal, instrumental, and social motivational components. *Career Development International*, 10(4): 310–24.

8. Boyer, N.R. (2003) Leaders mentoring leaders: unveiling role identity in an international online environment. *Mentoring and Tutoring*, 11(1): 25–41.

9. De Janasz, S.C., Sullivan, S.E. and Whiting, V. (2003) Mentor networks and career success: lessons for turbulent times. *Academy of Management Executive*, 17(4): 78–91.

10. Borredon, L. and Ingham, M. (2005) Mentoring and organisational learning in research and development. *Research and Development Management*, 35(5): 493–500.

11. Barrett, I.C., Cervero, R.M. and Johnson–Bailey, J. (2004) The career development of black human resource developers in the United States. *Human Resource Development International*, 7(1): 85–100.

12. Lines, D. and Robinson, G. (2006) Tough at the top. *International Journal of Mentoring and Coaching*, IV(1).

13. Crossland, C. and O'Brien, M. (2004) Informal mentoring: a source of indirect entry into informal male networks? *International Journal of Mentoring and Coaching*, III(1).

14. Friedman, A.A., Zibit, M. and Coote, M. (2004) Telementoring as a collaborative agent for change. *The Journal of Technology, Learning and Assessment*, 3(1): 2–41.

15. Finklestein, L.M., Allen, T.D. and Rhoton, L.A. (2003) An examination of the role of age in mentoring relationships. *Group and Organization Management*, 28(2): 249–81.

16. Niehoff, B.P. (2006) Personality predictors of participation as a mentor. *Career Development International*, 11(4): 321–33.

17. Allen, T.D. and Eby, L.T. (2003) Relationship effectiveness for mentors: factors associated with learning and quality. *Journal of Management*, 29(4): 469–86.

18. Godshalk, V.M. and Sosik, J.J. (2003) Aiming for career success: the role of learning goal orientation in mentoring relationships. *Journal of Vocational Behavior*, 63(3): 417–37.

THE SURVEY OF MENTORING RESEARCH

The picture painted in the previously presented mentoring archetype is partly confirmed in our wider survey of the 18 mentoring articles listed above. The studies numbered 1–7 and 15–18 conform to the archetype. The group numbered 8–14, however, are embedded in a different tradition, as will be discussed below.

Findings

Our collection of mentoring research articles split into two parts having very different characteristics. On the one hand, we found mainstream, social science studies in a positivistic tradition, very like the archetype of Tharenou (2005). On the other hand, there were also articles that resembled the practitioner coaching literature – they were concerned to report what respondents said in long open interviews, and to examine the implications for practice. The two types – positivist and practitioner are described below. The pattern of characteristics in Table 2.1 indicates graphically the differences.

Positivist Studies of Mentoring

The hard social-science studies were very uniform in their type and all had the following characteristics:

1. *Relation to established theory.* These articles described mentoring theory, making reference to a strongly overlapping cannon of texts. Kram's (1985) analysis of career and psychosocial functions is used as a base, and scholars such as Allen, Ragins and Scandura are everywhere cited. A large number of references (52–69) to the work of other authors positioned these studies in a research tradition. Authors of these papers seek to build upon what their predecessors have found, and they frequently make use of concepts operationalized in other fields of social science to examine the effects of features of mentoring. So, the studies in our collection looked, for example, at dimensions in organizational theory such as attraction, context, position and type, social exchange and so on. A feature of these studies related to this last point is that they made wide use of established measures of social phenomena – citing other sources to justify the operationalizations they adopted for the concepts that they wished to examine.
2. *Positivist methodology.* These studies sought to make their contribution to established theory by a hypothesis testing methodology. In the light of earlier mentoring studies and well-founded research in other areas, a set of hypotheses was posited, and then examined. The hypotheses were examined by collecting a large number of responses from mentees (numbers varied between 190 and 3,220), and subjecting them to relatively complex statistical analysis. This analysis used tools that went beyond the descriptive statistics of percentages, standard deviations and correlations, and used *t*-tests, regression analysis and (as suggested earlier in this chapter) tests of multivariate multicollinearity.
3. *Intervening variables examined.* Part of the statistical sophistication of the studies lies in their attention to intervening variables that may explain some of the variance described. By using multiple regression analysis and other tools these studies seek to illustrate the presence of relatively complex pathways of cause and effect between a variety of phenomena.
4. *Passive language for mentee.* Following Levinson et al. (1978) and Kram (1985) the studies used the term 'protégé' to describe the person mentored. We have long argued against this term (Gibb and Megginson, 1993) on the grounds that it implies a dependency on the part of the actor, and it also emphasizes the sponsorship form of mentoring, which is countercultural in some contexts, notably the public service and in northern European cultures.
5. *Distance from the participants of the study.* The authors of these articles are academics who are studying experiences in organizations of which they are not a part – they are outsiders rather than insiders. They also distance themselves from the people that they study by the methods that they use to collect data – postal, email or web-based survey. Similarly, the data that they gather by these means is standardized, quantifiable, tick box responses to pre-determined questions. These authors do not seem interested in the meaning making of the participants in their survey. This distance has its virtues in that the accounts are dispassionate, balanced and avoid partisanship from the authors. The authors acknowledge the limitations of the study and suggest what further research is needed. On the other hand, they do not enquire into the experience of the participants, and thus do not give a taste or

feel of that experience. They also run the risk of not measuring the same 'thing' as other studies, because they do not specify the kind of experience that the subjects have had.

Practitioner Studies of Mentoring

The practitioner studies resemble the studies of coaching described below and differ markedly from the positivist studies of mentoring that we have just considered. There is also more variation among them than in the positivist studies. It is clear that here, as with coaching, we are examining a field of practice where the research protocols have not yet coalesced into a widely accepted form. Insofar as patterns can be discerned, we describe them below:

1. *Insider accounts.* The reports are often from one organization, and the accounts are given by people involved in the scheme rather than dispassionate outsiders.
2. *Data from mentees.* Typically, the studies are based on a relatively small number of interviews of mentees (10–15). The accounts show interest in the experience of the respondents and often include verbatim quotes of their own words. So the treatment these mentees received is not seen as a black box that cannot be examined; rather it is open to investigation and often is at the centre of the study, which therefore has considerable implications for practitioners. These accounts are often about the benefits experienced by the mentees, who are often referred to neither as mentees nor protégés.
3. *Informal mentoring.* Accounts suggest that the kind of mentoring under study is usually informal rather than being part of a formal scheme.
4. *Qualitative studies.* The research processes seem less deeply considered than the previous group, but there is evidence of justification of qualitative data gathering or analysis (notably in de Janasz et al. (2003: 88–9), where the authors make a case for target sampling, reflexive interviews and narrative analysis.
5. *Outside an established tradition.* The articles often include a great many references, though on average less than the positivist group (range 16–68). The references are used differently, they often relate to areas other than mentoring and are not used as thoroughly as in the first group to formulate questions from which the research will build.

THE SURVEY OF COACHING RESEARCH

When we came to study the range and quality of coaching research we knew that, as a new field of practice, the theory had lagged and the research was rudimentary. We were still surprised at how marked this situation was. The quality of research was fragmented, partisan and impressionistic.

Our own search for peer-reviewed, research-based articles (that have been published after 2003) highlighted the weaknesses in the field. Articles that looked promising when we found their titles often were recommending research rather than describing it or had accounts that were so flimsy that they did not contribute to the genre which they purported to represent. We did not seek, for example, to criticize case studies by the lights of the positivist tradition. However, many of the cases we read did not match up to the criteria for good case study research (Stake, 1998; Kilburg, 2004).

We concluded by focussing on peer-reviewed articles that were either cited widely by others, or, if new, came from reputable peer-reviewed journals. To these we added a small number of professional journal articles that addressed current issues and gave a taste of the range of writing in the field. We added two rich case studies from recently published books to produce 18 texts to match the 18 texts we had selected from the huge mass of mentoring research articles available.

We struggled hard to find our target of 18 articles and the ones we selected in the end did not meet all our criteria – two being chapters from recent books and several being from journal articles that were not peer referenced.

We then read these 18 accounts and identified characteristics as we worked through them and then listed the characteristics or issues. The full list is shown in Table 2.2, where the items are ordered by frequency of mention.

List of Coaching Articles Selected

C1 Parker-Wilkins, V. (2006) Business impact of executive coaching: demonstrating monetary value. *Industrial and Commercial Training*, 38(3): 122–7.

C2 Natale, S.M. and Diamante, T. (2005) The five stages of executive coaching: better process makes better practice. *Journal of Business Ethics*, 59: 361–74.

C3 Longenecker, C.O. and Neubert, M.J. (2005) The practices of effective managerial coaches. *Business Horizons*, 48: 493–500.

C4 Bennett, A. (2006) What can be done when the coaching goes 'off-track'? *International Journal of Mentoring and Coaching*, IV(1).

C5 Robinson, J. (2005) GROWing service improvement within the NHS. *International Journal of Mentoring and Coaching*, III(1).

C6 Abraham, A., Collins, D. and Martindale, R. (2006) The coaching schematic: validation through expert coach consensus. *Journal of Sports Sciences*, 24(6): 549–64.

C7 Hardingham, A. (2006) The British eclectic model in practice. *International Journal of Mentoring and Coaching*, IV(1).

C8 McElrath, M., Godat, L., Musson, J., Libow, J. and Graves, J. (2005) Improving supervisors' effectiveness: Mayo clinic finds answers through research. *Journal of Organizational Excellence*, Winter: 47–56.

C9 Pearson, M. and Kayrooz, C. (2004) Enabling critical reflection on research supervisory practice. *International Journal for Academic Development*, 9(1): 99–116.

C10 Mulec, K. and Roth, J. (2005) Action, reflection, and learning – coaching in order to enhance the performance of drug development project management teams. *R&D Management*, 35(5): 483–91.

C11 Hoddinott, P., Lee, A.J. and Pill, R. (2006) Effectiveness of a breastfeeding peer coaching intervention in rural Scotland. *Birth*, 33(1): 27–36.

C12 Schwartz, J.P., Thigpen, S.E. and Montgomery, J.K. (2006) Examination of parenting styles of processing emotions and differentiation of self. *The Family Journal: Counselling and Therapy for Couples and Families*, 14(1): 41–8.

Table 2.2 Coaching article features by frequency of occurrence

Article / Feature	1	2	3	4	5	6	7	8	9	10	11	12	13	14	15	16	17	18	Total
A Insider account	×	×	×	×	×		×	×		×			×	×	×	×	×	×	13
B Business relevance	×	×	×	×	×		×	×						×	×	×	×	×	12
C Aim enhance coaching	×			×	×		×			×			×	×	×		×	×	10
D Scheme evaluation of outputs	×				×			×		×	×		×	×	×		×	×	10
E Small N (<30)	26	2	10	2	3	16	1			16			2		1	4			10
F Few citations (<16)	0		10	0	0		1	2						2	1	15		8	10
G Many citations (>15)		45				49			39	37	23	44	50				35		8
H Data from coachees									×	×	×	×	×	×			×	×	8
I Benefits specified	×	×	×	×										×	×	×		×	8
J Limitations discussed							×	×		×	×	×	×			×	×	×	8
K Company or organizational scheme								×	×	×	×		×	×		×	×		8
L Large N (>30)			225				179	314		1155	254		101				1361	87	8
M Academic author		×	×						×		×	×	×				×		7
N Case study individuals				×	×		×												7
O Data by interview						×				×	33			30	25	×			6
P Bias addressed		×				×		×	×			×							6
Q Key inputs researched			×	×		×							×				×	×	6
R Data by questionnaire									×	×	×	×		×			×	×	6
S Builds on established theory										×	×	×	×				×	×	6
T Research protocols detail						×			×	×	×						×		5

Table 2.2

Article / Feature	1	2	3	4	5	6	7	8	9	10	11	12	13	14	15	16	17	18	Total
U Coaching model used	x	x			x	x	x												5
V Inferential statistics									x	x	x	x					x		5
W Not business						x			x		x	x	x						5
X Verbatim quotes						x		x		x			x		x				5
Y Prescribes unresearched practice		x		x	x										x	x			5
Z Hypotheses set/tested						x			x			x					x		4
AA Consider transferability						x			x								x	x	4
BB Set coaching agenda								x			x		x			x			4
CC Deficiency focus		x			x											x			3
DD Coach plans outcomes		x														x		x	3
EE Data by focus group			45							2	226								3
FF Data from coaches						x				x	x								3
GG Focus on coach acts							x				x	x							3
HH Compare with other HRD interventions														x			x	x	3
II Data from 360°								x						x			x		3
JJ Descriptive statistics								x						x				x	3
KK Collaborative/action research										x	x		x						3
LL Control group used								x			x						x		3

(Cont'd)

Table 2.2

Article	1	2	3	4	5	6	7	8	9	10	11	12	13	14	15	16	17	18	Total
Feature																			
MM Rol a key measure	x							x						x					3
NN Protocol for coach selection						x											x		2
OO Qualitative data analysis method specified						x				x									2
PP Data from coachees' staff															x		x		2
QQ Team coaching										x	x								2
RR Research as intervention											x		x						2
SS Theory development													x				x		2
TT Data by observation										x									1
UU Line manager as coach								x											1

C13 Trevitt, C. (2005) Universities learning to learn? Inventing flexible (e)learning through first- and second-order action research. *Educational Action Research*, 13(1): 57–83.

C14 Colone, C. (2005) Calculating RoI in executive coaching, in Jarvis et al. (2006) *The Case for Coaching – Making evidence-based decisions on coaching*. CIPD: London. pp. 219–26.

C15 Goldsmith, M. (2005) Chapter 9 in Morgan, H., Hawkins, P. and Goldsmith, M. (eds), *The Art and Practice of Leadership Coaching*. Hoboken, NJ: Wiley.

C16 McMahan, G. (2006) Doors of perception. *Coaching at Work*, 1(6): 36–43.

C17 Smither, J.W., London, M., Flautt, R., Vargas, Y. and Kucrie, I. (2003) Can working with an executive coach improve multisource feedback ratings over time? A quasi-experimental field study. *Personnel Psychology*, 56(1): 23–44.

C18 Wasylyshyn, K.M. (2003) Executive coaching: an outcome study. *Consulting Psychology Journal: Practice and Research*, 55(2): 94–106.

One interesting observation is that there are almost more surveys of the field bemoaning its quality than there are quality studies doing something to improve the situation! However, these reviews are useful to build an agenda for developing research in the field. We have found six reviews particularly helpful: Kilburg, 2004; Feldman and Lankau, 2005; Joo, 2005; the Lowman case and the Tucker case, in Morgan et al., 2005; Jarvis et al., 2006.

These reviews all point to a tiny number of studies that meet our criteria of good research outlined above. It is interesting to us that the positivist criteria that drive mentoring research are not present in these gatekeepers for coaching research. Rather their passion is for Return on Investment (RoI) research. The recent paper most widely referred to is Smither et al., 2003, which is praised by Feldman and Lankau, 2005, Joo, 2005, Tucker, 2005 and Jarvis et al., 2006. Another study by Wasylyshyn (2003) is valued by Feldman and Lankau, 2005, Joo, 2005 and Jarvis et al., 2006.

So, what are the characteristics of these and other papers?

In the main, they are evaluation studies that seek to measure bottom line or other business-critical variables; second, they also sometimes compare coaching with other HRD interventions.

Some of the most frequently identified issues – all of which apply to at least eight of the 18 items – are discussed below:

1. *Insider account.* 13 of the articles were written by someone who is involved in the project or relationships studied. This has the advantage of giving an insight into the processes that are being examined – so that it can be contextualized for the reader and a view from the inside can be seen. However, this approach runs the risk of being partisan, omitting the possibility of alternative explanations for phenomena, or being simply self-aggrandizing. Wasylyshyn's (2003) study is a role model of how to do an insider account and to avoid these pitfalls. She studies responses from 87 of her own clients, but in a clear-sighted and careful way that yields insights for the reader and at the same time is humble and thoughtful about the limitations of the study (see 8 below).

2. *Business relevance.* Coaching research by and large addresses a business audience. Five of the 18 articles were not about business, being concerned with sport, research

supervision, breast feeding, parenting and curriculum development, respectively. So, of the 13 remaining, 12 were written for business users or practitioners of coaching. This contrasts with the style of the mentoring articles where the intended audience seems to be the academic community. The one article from our 18 that is about business but not primarily written for a business audience is Mulec and Roth's (2005) study of drug development project teams. This offers a direction forward to coaching research balancing theoretical and practical considerations emerging from the study.

3. *Aiming to enhance the practice of coaching* – 10 articles met this criterion. The findings were expressed in normative terms – describing what coaches might do to improve practice. In some of these articles, it seemed to us that these prescriptions emerged from the prior commitments of the authors, rather than as findings from the research. In others, prescription comes from investigation, notably Longenecker and Neubart, (2005) who identify the ten practices most desired by coachees.

4. *Scheme evaluation citing outputs/outcomes of coaching*. 10 of the 18 studies focus on one particular scheme, company or organization. This contrasted with the mentoring research articles that tended to cover a range of schemes and informal relationships, brought together in large, wide-ranging surveys. Three of the schemes sought to give an account of the return on investment (RoI) from the scheme (Parker-Wilkins, 2006; McElrath et al., 2005 and Colone, 2005), a feature often demanded by those seeking improvement in the quality of coaching and mentoring research.

5. *Small samples.* Seven of the studies gave between one and four individual case studies and three others had only a small number (16, 16 and 26). This contrasted with the norm for mentoring studies, but the other eight coaching papers had large numbers of respondents, ranging from 87 in Wasylyshyn's (2003) study mentioned above to 1,361 in Smither et al., 2003. Smither and colleagues seek to bring to coaching research the positivist methodology associated with mentoring research, with the apparatus of control samples, interpretive statistics, controlling for other causes and building and testing hypotheses in a theory-rich context that embeds the work in a stream of existing scholarship. Another manifestation of the rarity of Smither's approach in the field of coaching research is the observation that 10 of the 18 cases only cited a few references to others' work – seven of them to two or less sources. On the other hand, this is beginning to change, with the other eight sources citing between 23 and 50 sources. Not all these studies, however, embed their enquiry explicitly into a research tradition or theme. Interestingly, six of these eight cite literature having no connection with coaching – three concern education and learning, while the others explore the literature of sport, health, parenting. Of the remaining two articles one is the Smither et al. (2003) study focussing on feedback and on coaching, and the other is by Natale and Diamante (2005), which is embedded in the psychology of emotion.

6. *Data from coachees.* The most frequently investigated sources of information in coaching research are the coachees (eight studies). This compares with the data from coaches (three cases) and data from coachees' staff (two cases). The remaining studies did not describe a specific process for gathering data from anyone, usually presenting data on individual cases *ex cathedra* without building a case for the care with which it might have been gathered. The richest studies of the coachee's perspective are Smither et al., 2003 and Wasylyshyn, 2003.

7. *Benefits of coaching identified and specified.* The eight papers identifying benefits were often based on a small number of individual cases and outlined the putative benefits from a particular approach to coaching. Goldsmith (2005) is interesting in that he shows how the benefits can ramify throughout the organization following coaching of a senior executive.

He also displays commendable modesty in recognizing that much of the credit for this is owed to the coachee, not to himself as coach.

8. *Limitations discussed*. Good practice in a wide range of research traditions is to discuss the limitations of the study and the constraints on its generalizability. This can usefully lead to suggestions about future research as well as begin to set up a debate on the direction of research in the field. The clearest accounts we have identified in our sample of coaching research are (again) Smither et al., 2003 and Wasylyshyn, 2003.

RESEARCH 'GAZE'

As suggested earlier, the gaze of the researcher cannot be over-emphasized. Schostak (2002: 2) has identified how the existential quality of our own experience always 'meets the other in dialogue' and describes how a process of 'self-election' in relation to our worlds has many consequences in the choice of what and how to research. This was apparent in attempts by the Collaborative Research Group (a group of scholars coming together through the European Mentoring and Coaching Council (EMCC) to review research and practice from multiple perspectives). From subsequent discussions around our joint and separate attempts to analyse the raw data of a number of coaching interventions (mainly video) it was evident that the events that shape us as people, our educational, political, ethical, cultural 'make-up', plus our current affinities and interests, impacted on the way we each viewed the data.

At one of the meetings of the Collaborative Research Group, we examined, with permission, the first few minutes of a DVD of the fifth coaching session between one of the group and a client. The group member who was the coach on the DVD (and is also an author of this chapter) took notes of the comments made and these are noted below. He then went on to review these review comments by asking the question, 'What are reviewers privileging in their analysis of the interaction?' From a learning point of view, these data raise the important question of where issues arise in a dialogue between two people. Is it from the prior commitments made by individuals, or is it from the direction that the dialogue happens to take? Process awareness offers a means of making choices among these and other causal factors.

The number in brackets after each comment refers to the 'gaze' category. These categories are discussed after this presentation of this raw data. The letters refer to different members of the group so that the reader can piece together the preoccupations of these different members.

The Review Comments

B. The process sets the agenda. Focus is instrumental, not development. Where's the coachee? What's in it for coachee? He seemed anxious about his meeting with his boss. (1).

A. He held it at a safe distance from himself – focussed on the organization not himself. (1).

C. He showed anxiety (his leg 'going') when he spoke. He talked about we/us, not me; about over there, not in here. It felt very busy. (2).

B. His boss is going to watch this; he needs to look at how he's developing into his new role. (3).

E. Coach stuck with what the coachee wanted. The phrase 'hurtling towards the end' reset his focus. 'Big win' was also a big statement. They agreed what was and wasn't an outcome. (4).

D. Neither did much work – both stayed in a frame. What is the coaching culture? I would ask about self-grounding questions. I feel he would be thankful to follow if the coach led. (5).

B. Agenda for coachee is projects. (1).

E. He may be talking about IIP, but it may help him address his issues. (4).

A. The coach worked hard at summarizing. (6).

B. Coachee descriptive – coach probes him. (6).

E. Exercising influence rather than working. (3).

D. He needs a strong style – intervention: more help on focus. He looks at his life from the stage; he needs to look at how the play is constructed. (5).

E. It may be the first time he ever reflected. (4).

D. He may need more comments on process. (5).

A. 'Who's influencing?' is an interesting question; then we can ask 'What is the nature of that influence?' (3).

D. Look at coach's style and coachee's learning style – do they match or form an alliance? If you got better at this, how would your life be better for you? Where are you in this? How might your boss notice? (5).

C. There is a multiplicity of interpretations/lenses. (7).

A. Is three minutes from the relationship enough? (7).

C. It depends on your research question. (7).

D. The coach has a specific style; with soft and small interventions he won't shift his approach. Is an educational approach within the coach's range or should the coachee find out for himself? Give him homework and check with him. (5).

E. List 20 things that have worked for you since last time. He was working – giving information, being very prepared, staying with it, turning up, answering questions, giving lots of information. (4).

The 'Gaze' Categories

1. *The individual and his or her development over the organization agenda.* Both B (twice) and A see the interactions as lacking a valuable personal focus and the emergence of the striving, feeling, inquiring individual.
2. *Interpretation – what do ticks and tropes mean?* C in her first comment focusses on two features. First, the body language – the apparently involuntary leg movements and, second, the use of language – the failure to use 'I', allegedly blurring personal responsibility by talking about 'we' and 'us'.
3. *Context and power relations.* B switches focus from privileging individuality to explaining why the coachee does not do this, by examining the context and power – the coachee's boss will be viewing the DVDs as a member of the collaborative research group.
4. *Autonomy of the coachee.* E mostly stays focussed on what the coachee wants in this interaction and whether and how the coach respects this. These observations by E greatly heartened the coach, as they seemed close to his impulse in behaving as he did, and left him feeling recognized, appreciated and not judged in the way he felt he had been by previous observations (however cogent and salient these judgements might have been).
5. *Education of coachee by coach-examining process.* D makes a series of internally coherent observations about the strength and nature of interventions necessary from the coach in order to shift the coachee into a learning/development stance from being on *the stage* of his life, to directing this from *the stalls or the wings*.
6. *Coach behaviours.* A and B make comments about the coach's individual behaviours – summarizing, describing, probing.
7. *Meta-commentary.* C starts a cluster of meta-comments by recognizing the multiplicity of lenses through which we have examined this short excerpt of a coaching interaction. A wonders how much of an interaction is needed to capture the 'gaze'.

Another theme in these comments, which overlays many of the above was

8. Who does the work? Some commentaries (D particularly) observe that not much work is being done; others see the coach as doing it (A, B); yet others see the coachee (E) doing the work.

Patterns of 'gaze' emerge in phases of the conversation – A's comment, which privileged the 'gaze' of process, for example, elicits a comment from B which also privileges process; C's meta-comment presages further meta-comments by A and again by C. However, there are also strong preferences – all five of D's comments have an education 'gaze', three of E's four comments have the 'gaze' of the autonomy of the coachee. From a learning point of view, these data raise the question as to where issues arise in a conversation. Is it from the prior commitments made by individuals, or is it from the direction that a conversation happens to take? An awareness of a coaching process offers a means of making choices among these and other causal factors.

Commentary on the Commentaries

The coach writes:

> I am conscious as I write these re-descriptions of my colleagues' descriptions of me – that I am exercising the ultimate freedom described by Richard Rorty (1989), and taking back some personal power, which I experienced having been taken away from me by my friends' comments, and, to an extent, by the intractable nature of the interaction with the coachee, who will not bend to my preferences, but remains, obdurately and magnificently, himself. I reflect, not for the first time, that it is a good job that humans have this inertia. If they didn't, then all the good work that I did, changing people for the better, might be immediately undone by the next person they met, who would change them again to suit the new helper's preferences.

We give this account to remind the reader that choices about research articles that we have made in the other sections of this chapter are just as arbitrary and partial as the views of our co-researchers in the description above. Knowing and naming is an exercise of power. In doing it we claim the right to organize the field to suit our purposes and also recognize the right of the reader to re-organize our organizing.

CONCLUSIONS

There is an established, widely referenced positivist tradition of mentoring research based on mentoring functions (Kram, 1985) and using hypothesis testing, large samples of mentees, controlling or testing the effect of intervening variables, and inferential statistics. This tradition can be described as normal science (Kuhn, 1970). The tone and direction of this strand of mentoring research seems to indicate that it is written by academics for academics. No equivalent tradition has yet been established for coaching research, though this may be emerging with scholars such as Smither et al. (2003) carrying out quasi-experiments on the longitudinal effects of coaching interventions.

The majority of coaching articles, however, describe case studies focussing on the meaning of the experience for the participants (principally the coachee, though sometimes they are spoken for by the coach, without the basis for the views being ascribed to them being expressed). Coaching articles are often insider accounts, written by people who have a stake in the scheme or the relationship – usually as the coach. This has an advantage of giving insights into the dynamics of the coaching intervention, though it can mean that they do not pay attention to alternative explanations for the phenomena that they observe, and that they tend to emphasize the positive and effective while ignoring data that could be seen as negative. Many of these studies are in the tradition of evaluation research, and they are written to catch the eye of practitioners and purchasers of coaching.

There is a tradition in mentoring research that parallels this approach to coaching research.

The Future of Mentoring and Coaching Research

In this section, we offer our view on the routes forward that mentoring and coaching research might usefully take. There is a need for conference debate to build critical mass in this meta-discussion about the direction for research. The positivist tradition in mentoring research could develop usefully by:

- Including more longitudinal studies and quasi-experiments
- Examining the effects on other stakeholders (mentors and sponsors)
- Break out of the productive but increasingly restricted ghetto of Kram's functions and pay systematic attention to other formulations of goals and purposes for mentoring
- Looking inside the 'black box' and exploring the nature of the mentoring interaction
- Paying attention to the development of good practice as well as elegant theory.

The professional strand in mentoring research could be developed by:

- Paying attention to good practice in case study research (Stake, 2004)
- Develop more powerful evaluation models as in some coaching research (Tucker, 2005; Parker-Wilkins, 2006).

Coaching research, which has been described as evaluative and professional, could be developed by:

- Following the dictates of good case study research (Stake, 2004)
- Making more studies across coaching approaches rather than within a preferred approach, to test Kilburg's (2004) contention that we are all running towards Alice in Wonderland's 'Dodoville' (where all approaches have equal effect and all must have prizes).

There is a question as to whether coaching research needs to develop a strand of positivist research as mentoring has done. There is evidence that this can be done, notably in the study by Smither et al., 2003. If other researchers see this as desirable, it would require them to:

- Build a typology of coaching inputs and outcomes
- Conduct studies built on the edifice of positivist research outlined in this chapter
- Conduct longitudinal studies and quasi-experiments
- Continue to pay attention to the 'black box' of what goes on in the coaching relationship
- Explore systematically the experience of coaches and others impacted or involved in the experience.

A final alternative would be to seek an integration of positivist and professional traditions to pay attention to the best in both and develop mixed methodological approaches to research. This direction could also include comparing and contrasting coaching and mentoring interventions across a range of contexts.

QUESTIONS

Which traditions of research do you value? Does this lead you to ignore and down-play research in other traditions?

Do you focus on the findings from mentoring research or coaching research? Could you broaden your enquiry to embrace both?

When conducting your own research what research tradition will you embed your work within? How might you ensure that you follow best practice for research in that tradition?

CREATING A COACHING AND MENTORING CULTURE

CHAPTER OVERVIEW

In this chapter, we look at creating or developing coaching and mentoring cultures and offer both theoretical and practical insights into the development of environments supportive of coaching and mentoring. This chapter explores the literature on the subject of coaching and mentoring cultures. We present various models of mentoring and coaching culture while outlining strategies and practices for leaders, managers and specialist coaches and mentors to widen the impact of what they do. The chapter raises some challenging questions and issues for organizations wishing to develop coaching and mentoring.

INTRODUCTION

One of the frontiers in the field of coaching and mentoring is how to harness organizational impact. We have seen the variations of meaning of coaching and mentoring in Chapter 1 and the approaches to gathering evidence to justify and understand coaching and mentoring in Chapter 2. Here, we continue with the same themes of variation and move away from the tired and well-worn track of 'one best way'. Coaching and mentoring are social phenomena and are therefore influenced by social processes. One size does not fit all. There are many choices that relate to specific contexts. However, in the business world dominated by the rational, pragmatic manager (Garvey and Williamson, 2002), coaching and mentoring advocates risk losing much of their potential to influence how people manage and work in organizations unless the organizational implications of a coaching and mentoring way of working are considered and acted upon.

Coaching and mentoring are essentially one-to-one practices and so those studying, researching and working in the area tend to ignore the wider, social and organizational implications of their work. However, research (McGovern et al., 2001; Garvey and Garrett-Harris, 2005) suggests that the impact on the organization is considerable. This chapter seeks to address this issue.

METHODOLOGY

We approach the concept of coaching and mentoring cultures in this chapter from a practical and applied position by drawing on some of the literature on coaching, mentoring and culture as well as practical experience. Consistent with the themes already established in Chapters 1 and 2, we recognize that the form coaching and mentoring take is related to the social context and its perceived purpose. Consequently, we try to avoid prescription and, instead, raise what we see as important questions about the idea of developing a cultural environment that will support and sustain coaching and mentoring activity.

THE MENTORING ORGANIZATION

Megginson et al. (2005) build on case study research in Clutterbuck and Megginson (2005: 7) to identify characteristics of a mentoring culture. Eight features of mentoring schemes that pay attention to the organizational dimension are:

1. Clear link to a business issue, with outcome measured
2. Part of a culture change process
3. Senior management involvement as mentees and mentors
4. Established link to long-term talent management
5. Mentees in the driving seat
6. Light-touch development of individuals and scheme
7. Clear framework, publicized, with stories
8. Scheme designed to focus on business issues and change agenda.

Reading the case examples on which this list is based highlights the perspective noted elsewhere in this book (Chapter 12) that mentoring is often actuated by a social impulse to support those disadvantaged in employment and elsewhere (schools, for example) – women, ethnic minorities, people experiencing bullying, and so on. Nonetheless, in all the cases cited, there was also an emphasis on supporting the development of talent, working with people at the top of the organization and with future potential leadership.

Carden (1990: 276), when suggesting that mentoring works with the dominant culture of the organization, states that mentoring could 'exclude(s) the socially different, clone managers and administrators, and maintain a status quo based on "accumulation of advantage" and replication of hierarchical systems'. And Garvey (1994c, 1995b) indicates that mentoring cannot be a 'cure-all' for organizational ills and is least effective when viewed as a 'new initiative' rather than a natural process and part of normal behaviour at work. Such findings would suggest that mentoring, on its own, is neutral with regard to fundamental organizational cultural change. However, the challenge of mentoring, as argued by, for example, Caruso (1996) and Turban and Dougherty (1994), is to recognize the need to synthesize individual and organizational aspirations as a central condition of organizational success. This coincides with Nonaka's (1996) recognition of the importance of personal commitment in a knowledge-creating organization.

Caruso (1996) also introduces the concept of power (see Chapter 7) in the organization when he says that often the mentee's agenda is replaced by the mentor's or the organization's objectives (see Chapter 10 for a full exploration of the problem of goals). Given the point made so far in this book that learning happens in a social context, an organization can make it more or less possible for people to learn by its values, processes, policies and actions. Caruuso (1996) argues for a theory of mentoring, in which the qualities of learning, as conceptualized, for instance, in the theory of situated learning (Lave and Wenger, 1991), and the potential benefits of mentoring move away from the traditional one-to-one mentoring relationship to characterize relational activities in the organization as a whole. In practice, this means that a mentor can be a 'variety of individuals and/or institutions who provide help to a protégé' (Caruso, 1996). It then becomes appropriate to talk about a 'mentoring organization'. We characterize this as:

- The compatibility of individual and organizational aspirations
- High employee commitment
- A focus on collaboration and team development
- A complex web of practices and relationships that are supportive and developmental of the individual and the organization.

Above all, people who have a developed and enthusiastic sense of themselves as learners inhabit a 'mentoring organization'. This concept resonates well with Higgins and Kram's (2001) notion of 'multiple mentoring relationships' (discussed in Chapter 8) where any one individual may have a range of developers including coaches and mentors. Therefore, the links between mentoring, coaching and organizational development are strong and this is perhaps why so many different types of organization engage with it.

THE COACHING ORGANIZATION

The literature on the coaching organization is more robust and fuller than that on a mentoring organization. It is nonetheless very thin compared with the huge amount of writing (both academic and professional) on the one-to-one coaching relationship. We speculate that one reason for coaching organization literature being more developed than mentoring organization literature is that coaching is widely seen as a mainstream way of managing (Zeus and Skiffington, 2000; Whitmore, 2002; McLeod, 2003; Pemberton, 2006). An early example of this strand in the literature is Megginson and Boydell (1979: 5), where they describe coaching as 'a process in which a manager, through direct discussion and guided activity, helps a colleague to learn to solve a problem, or to do a task, better than would otherwise have been the case'. This definition sees coaching as being the responsibility of the line manager, and sees it as being centrally 'concerned with improved task performance' (p. 5). With this focus on performance, it is easier to justify coaching as being a fundamental way of managing work relationships rather than mentoring, which is seen as a special intervention to be called upon for certain particular and unusual purposes (making major transitions, challenging inequalities, increasing opportunity, and so on).

Clutterbuck and Megginson (2005) have developed one framework, grounded in the practices of major organizations, for creating a coaching culture. This study produced a model of four levels of depth against six main areas that are divided into four sub-areas to produce a 4 by 24 matrix for assessing a coaching culture (pp. 99–100). They describe the four levels as:

- Nascent.
- Tactical.
- Strategic.
- Embedded.

This framework marks a multi-strand journey from:

- Having the idea of making an organizational impact
- Through to doing disjointed things to bring it about
- To doing integrated things
- To establishing these things in the DNA of the organization.

The 24 areas identified from the case studies are listed below with the items in italics being those that were found in a high proportion of the cases studied (Clutterbuck and Megginson, 2005: 28–9):

1 Coaching linked to business drivers

    1.1   *Integrate coaching into strategy, measures and processes*
    1.2   Integrate coaching and high performance
    1.3   Coaching has a core business driver to justify it
    1.4   *Coaching becomes the way of doing business*

2 Being a coachee is encouraged and supported

    2.1   *Encourage and trigger being a coachee*
    2.2   You can challenge your boss to coach

2.3 Extensive training for both coach and coachee

2.4 External coaches used to give coaches experience of being coached

3 Provide coach training

3.1 Integrate coach training for all
3.2 Coaches receive feedback on their use of coaching
3.3 After their training coaches are followed up
3.4 *Coaches are accredited, certificated or licensed*

4 Reward and recognize coaching

4.1 People are rewarded for knowledge sharing
4.2 *Coaching is promoted as an investment in excellence*
4.3 Top team are coaching role models (who seek and use feedback)
4.4 Dedicated coaching leader

5 Systemic perspective

5.1 Assume people are competent
5.2 Organic, not process driven
5.3 Initiatives decentralized
5.4 Constructive confrontation

6 The move to coaching is managed

6.1 Senior group manages move to coaching
6.2 Line takes responsibility for coaching culture
6.3 *Integrate coaching and culture change*
6.4 Coaching supports delegation and empowerment

This study clearly points out that developing culture change in an organization is not a quick-fix process and that there are many approaches and options.

Other authors who have written about coaching culture include Whitmore (2002), Caplan (2003), and Hardingham et al. (2004) while more recent contributions to the coaching culture literature include Pemberton (2006) and Hunt and Weintraub (2007).

Hunt and Weintraub (2007) offer an American perspective on the topic. Hunt and Weintraub (2007) adopt a similar case study methodology to Clutterbuck and Megginson (2005), so comparison is possible. They focus on what they call 'developmental coaching', which they define as 'relationship-facilitated, on-the-job learning, with the most basic goal of promoting an individual's ability to do the work associated with that individual's current or future work roles' (p. 27). Within this definition, however, they include 'whole life' issues such as 'career direction and work-life balance' (p. 34). Their approach focusses heavily on organization readiness. They also develop an assessment framework that helps individuals or organization representatives to assess readiness to create a coaching organization, and to identify areas for further work within the organization. As such, their list seeks to serve the same function as the one from Clutterbuck and Megginson (2005) outlined above. However, Hunt and Weintraub (2007) focus more on the cultural context and social qualities; for example, they emphasize trust, employees and relationships as ends in themselves, valuing learning, truth telling, diversity, continuous improvement, and place a high bar to entry into the process of developing a coaching culture.

The Pemberton (2006) study is from the UK rather than the US, and examines how to spread coaching practice widely in an organization. Her book focusses on the manager as coach and she argues (p. 3) that a tipping point (see Gladwell, 2002) has been reached with coaching so that it is now a pervasive phenomenon in the life of staff in organizations. Pemberton (2006) argues that staff expect to get it and the only people who can deliver it in the amount required are line managers. In summary, Pemberton (2006) suggests that all managers need to work in a coaching way because:

- There is now a growing expectation from the organization that managers should coach
- Employees have experienced coaching outside work and expect it at work too
- It responds to what is sought by demanding and egocentric staff
- It delivers the 'deal' that employees expect
- It harnesses the motivation that employees have to contribute to the organization.

Some sources, particularly those that focus upon externally provided, psychologically grounded coaching, seek to emphasize the weaknesses or dangers of coaching. Berglas's (2002) much cited article is an example of this literature. Another is the chapter in de Haan and Burger (2005) entitled 'Limitations of coaching with colleagues' (pp. 151–9). At the centre of their concerns are the points that 'the internal coach is less free with respect to the coachee's organization' (p. 153) and 'the internal coach has a less well-defined relationship to the coachee' (p. 154). They make the challenging but reasonable point that coaching managers 'sometimes find it hard to put the coachee and his/her issues truly at the centre and to intervene in a way that respects the autonomy of the coachee' (p. 155). This difficulty is related to points made in Chapters 6, 7 and 8 of this book about the power, control and obedience expectations of managers. It may also be another example of either 'mindset' or 'gaze' raised in Chapters 1 and 2. While these points have legitimacy, it is also important to remember that these authors also have an agenda and a position to defend.

To extend this argument, we are grateful to Bruno Rihs, a Swiss colleague, for drawing to our attention Platt (2001), who highlights the weaknesses of a particular and specific approach to coaching:

I have generally found that people who practice NLP are not receptive or even prepared to countenance critical reviews of this field of study. Indeed, I have come to recognize that 'Hell hath no fury like an NLP practitioner scorned' as a result of daring to question some of the practices framed by NLP...When I published the negative findings of a large number of clinical trials focusing on NLP techniques and also the research of Dr Heap, Principal Clinical Psychologist for Sheffield Health Authority...the response almost universally condemned the findings stating that they were 'unscientific' or that the particular aspects of NLP could not be clinically trialled, or that the areas studied were minor and insignificant when viewed against the entire gamut of the NLP approach. A mass of anecdotal evidence was also cited to challenge the clinical research findings.

In our view, there are two points here. Coaches adopting a strong frame for their interaction need to also have a robust approach to critiquing that frame if they are to avoid the defensive, cult-like reactions noted by Platt. Additionally, we argue for a celebration of difference rather than viewing it as a problem or a challenge to one's very being. In a world of increasing polarization and extreme positioning, we suggest that an accepting and tolerating position is a more constructive way forward. Creating a coaching culture, even more than individual coaching, requires an ability to liaise and co-operate with others who have differing views of the organization and of the purposes of coaching. In other words a diversity perspective as discussed in Chapter 12.

COACHING AND MENTORING CULTURE – THE NEW FRONTIER

The above literature review has helped to both define the field and identify the parameters to address in taking coaching and mentoring organization-wide.

What is needed next to develop this frontier is a series of organizational quasi-experiments, where scholars and practitioners can co-operate to build a long-term development alliance to make an impact on an organization. To start this process of developing a range of models for creating a coaching and mentoring culture fit for a variety of contexts, we believe it is necessary to examine a number of cultural features. This section introduces these features and offers a rationale for making the choices about each. The features, similar to the dimensions framework presented in Chapter 1, are set as opposite points on a continuum as follows:

Change	or	Stability
Deficit	or	Appreciative inquiry
Problem	or	Solution
Internal	or	External coaches
All managers	or	Master-coaches/mentors
Performance	or	Whole life
Roll-out	or	Creep in

Figure 3.1   Dimensions of coaching and mentoring culture

Change or Stability

This variable is key to the development of a mentoring or coaching culture. Megginson and Clutterbuck (1995) noticed that in some companies such as the Swedish part of Nestlé, Svenska Nestlé, retired executives were invited to mentor up-and-coming high potential managers. This seems to be an example of a strong culture, confident in itself and wanting to perpetuate the 'shared meaning, shared understanding, and shared sensemaking' (Morgan, 1986: 128). In another organization in Megginson and Clutterbuck (1995), each of the 20 members of the top team had an external coach because the chief executive was convinced that no-one in the firm (with the possible exception of himself) had the characteristics necessary to drive the organization forward. In our view, this is a weak culture because there is little within the organization to sustain the desired culture. Balancing the amount of help offered to individuals in a culture change process therefore represents a major challenge and leads to the question, 'How can just enough help be provided from outside to develop coaching so as not to swamp internal efforts and thus to avoid the possibility of dependency being created?'

In one bank we studied some years ago, we found evidence of dependency being deliberately created by a coaching firm that was widely used throughout the bank, in order – it seemed to us – to maximize revenues for the coaching provider. However, strong cultures also present challenges. If people in an organization are good at replicating what they already do well, then what happens when the environment changes and what is needed begins to change? Many strong cultures, for example in the UK retail sector Marks and Spencer, suffer when market circumstances change. For some organizations, a pattern of using internal or quasi-internal coaches (such as ex-staff who have gone 'independent') needs to change to engaging genuinely external resources to prepare experienced staff to deal with the new situation in new ways.

Being clear whether the culture that is desired is a changed one or a stable one is the first question to ask and will influence the form of the answer to many of the questions that follow.

Deficit or Appreciative Inquiry

Implicit in much writing about coaching is a very traditional HRD model based on identifying needs, planning, implementing and evaluation. This sometimes glories in the name 'gap analysis', which implies that there is a gap between what the job requires and what the employee can provide (for a thorough-going critique of this position see Roy Jacques' 1996 book *Manufacturing the Employee*).

Models of individual and organizational functioning based on standards and competencies (see Chapter 13 for a fuller account of this issue) are grounded in a similar understanding to the HRD gap analysis model.

Some psychologists also adopt a 'needs' model. This bases coaching on what the learner may need to develop into a fully functioning person. For example, Hardingham et al. (2004: 71–7) suggest that coaching must address such topics as belonging, control and closeness needs.

Standing in contrast to these, deficit perspectives, is positive psychology. This cluster of interrelated theories and practices suggests that creating a coaching culture will involve building on strengths. Strands of this movement are interested in 'flow' (Csikszentmihalyi, 2002), 'appreciative inquiry' (Cooperrider, 1995) and, particularly in the world of coaching, the 'solutions focused approach' (Berg and Szabó, 2005).

Many HR systems in organizations are posited upon the gap model, for example appraisal, performance management and, in many instances, coaching and mentoring. The psychological effect of such a perspective, where people get training, education, development, coaching or mentoring because there is something missing or wrong with them is considerable. As Garvey and Williamson (2002) suggest, those entering a developmental session of any form may not engage in a positive state of mind if they think they have been sent to be mended.

If one is to develop a coaching or mentoring culture based on strengths, a major piece of work will be to address the challenge that these embedded systems place in the way of a culture that celebrates, extends and develops strengths. In one such attempt we made some years ago in an insurance company, the biggest challenge the strength-oriented developers faced was the opposition from the HR department. The systems we were advocating would have required a rewriting of every policy HR had. After working with HR, the challenges of engaging line management seemed relatively straightforward!

We leave this dimension with a question: do you think that you are better off going with the grain of existing policies or seeking to develop an alternative set of assumptions about how best to engage people in their own evolution?

Problem or Solution

Related to the dimension about deficit or appreciation is this simple dichotomy in coaching and mentoring thinking. Many well-established models of coaching and mentoring suggest starting by identifying a problem that the client wants to work on. Flaherty (1999) and McLeod (2003) are examples of the needs orientation. Flaherty being a psychologist, emphasizes assessment as a process for determining needs; McLeod, with his performance coaching perspective, focusses upon organizational issues such as communication, 'Who's the boss?' and interpersonal conflict.

Grant and Greene (2001); Jackson and McKergow (2002); Berg and Szabó (2005) and Pemberton (2006) offer an alternative perspective based on attention to solutions rather than problems. So, where do the efforts to create a coaching and mentoring culture need to focus? Should they focus on fitting in with the problem-focussed orientation so prevalent in our wider culture, or seeking to create a new orientation to building on strengths, which may set people against powerful organizational interests and societal taken-for-granted assumptions?

Internal or External Coaches/Mentors

This dimension relates to the change and stability dimension. In particular, to the question of whether the power-holders believe that there are managers in the organization who display the characteristics sought by change leaders. However, other considerations also shape where the emphasis is placed. One such factor is the extent of the proposed spread of coaching or mentoring. If it is for a relatively narrow group, top management or high potentials, for example, then the costs of using external, professional coaches may not be prohibitive. On the other hand, if the intent is to coach everyone in the organization, then clearly the costs of external help become too huge to bear. For some organizations, budgets for development are so modest that external coaching for anyone is out of the question.

Many authors (see Caplan, 2003; Hardingham, 2004; Clutterbuck and Megginson, 2005) argue that there is a great advantage in engaging managers in the coaching enterprise. There is also considerable evidence that mentoring is beneficial to the organization, the mentor and the mentee (see Wilson and Elman, 1990; Garvey, 1995a; Devins and Gold, 2000). In fact, many authors on culture in relation to coaching and mentoring suggest that this is a crucial plank in its creation. So does necessity (or capacity) push the organization in the direction of using internal coaches? Do the benefits of engaging people widely in coaching others justify the expenditure of money and effort in enabling everyone to perform in this way?

All Managers or Master-coaches/Mentors

Some companies seeking to create a coaching or mentoring culture have relied upon a cadre of skilled leaders to develop high-level coaching and mentoring skills. In Clutterbuck and Megginson (2005), a case study example of such a company would be Kellogg's. In the mentoring literature, Garvey and Galloway (2002), for example, illustrate the skills approach to developing a mentoring culture. A number of banks in the UK, for example HBOS, have developed internal mentors while others, such as Lloyds TSB, have created a job role of internal coaches, giving this aspect of the manager's role to specialists. Other cases from Clutterbuck and Megginson (2005) focus on giving all managers the same training, for example in Vodafone.

An argument for specializing is that the master-coaches/mentors can then use their enhanced skills to coach/mentor other managers in coaching/mentoring skills. An argument for the 'train everybody' orientation is that it sends a signal that coaching and mentoring is a central part of the manager's job and not something that can be delegated to anyone else. Sometimes the choice is a function of the size of the business. Sometimes it is a cultural choice based on perceptions of power (see Chapter 7), democracy, individualism or collectivism within the organization, and sometimes it is a function of cost. So, which strategy should be emphasized – a specialist cadre or the widest possible engagement?

Performance or Whole Life

Some developers of coaching and mentoring culture will want to narrow the coaching or mentoring manager's attention with laser focus onto performance. Authors who support this view include McLeod (2003). Paradoxically, Whitmore's book *Coaching for Performance* (2002) has a much wider remit than the title suggests. Other sources, such as Brockbank and McGill's 2006 book *Facilitating Reflective Learning through Mentoring and Coaching*, direct their attention more widely, while Alred and Garvey (2000) advocate a wider application of mentoring for a more holistic development of people. And the same can be said for the radically participative, content-free coaches such as Downey (2003). So, how focussed on performance should coaching and mentoring be in any particular organization?

Roll-out or Creep In

The picture in the heads of the leading coalition about how to introduce change will dictate to which end of this spectrum organization leaders are drawn. The choice is between 'driving the change through the organization', which leads to a tendency to roll out training to all in a high-cost, high-profile campaign on the one hand, and on the other to a systemic perspective based on 'creep in'.

The creep-in approach was characterized by the engineering company cited in Clutterbuck and Megginson (2005: 68–9), which focussed on key decision makers, took time to explore options, thought through the integration of coaching with other initiatives the company was exploring, and did not go for extensive training of large numbers as a separate initiative. So, should an organization favour roll-out or creep in? Is the greatest chance of success achieved by following the organization's norms or by trying something different?

Summary

By examining these variables – change or stability; deficit or appreciative inquiry; problem or solution; internal or external coaches/mentors; all managers or master-coaches/mentors; performance or whole life; roll-out or creep in – it becomes possible to set out the broad direction and strategy for a favoured approach within a specific organization to creating a coaching/mentoring culture.

SITUATIONS TO FOCUS ON TO CREATE A COACHING AND MENTORING CULTURE

We have found from working with organizations in recent years that the strategy of focussing on creating a culture can seem abstract to some decision makers. In such cases, an approach that can be followed is to attend to opportunities to build coaching and mentoring into the fabric of the organization. Some impactful examples of these opportunities are:

- C&M as preparation for new roles
- C&M as delegation
- C&M as management style
- C&M as problem solving.

We discuss each of these below.

Coaching and Mentoring Preparation for New Roles

Ever since Levinson et al. (1978) first suggested that mentoring was associated with transition, mentoring and, latterly, coaching has been linked to supporting people in new job roles. The first 90 days in new roles is a period of intense learning (Porter, Lorsch and Nohria, 2004; Neff and Citrin, 2005; Watkins, 2005). For example, Porter et al. (2004) and colleagues say that a new CEO is faced with seven surprises:

- You can't run the company.
- Giving orders is very costly.
- It's hard to know what's really going on.
- You are always sending a message.
- You are not the boss.
- Pleasing shareholders is not the goal.
- You're still only human.

This represents a strong agenda for coaching and mentoring, and similar issues face new jobholders at every level in the organization.

Thinking about the strategic options addressed in the previous section, decisions will need to be made about the extent to which external and internal coaches or mentors will be used. If they are internal, will this be line managers or especially appointed and trained people?

Coaching and Mentoring as Delegation

Building the expectation of delegation in encounters with managers is the fundamental basis for creating a developmentally aware culture. Companies starting from here do not even have to use the word 'coaching' or 'mentoring'. If it is known that asking a boss what to do will lead to the following sequence of questions, then a delegation culture, and thus a coaching/mentoring culture will have been established:

- What are the options?
- Which of these would you prefer or recommend?
- Why don't you try that and let me know how it goes?

Coaching and Mentoring as Management Style

Building a coaching and mentoring approach into all leadership training is a starting point for this opportunity. There are implicit views about how to manage in all leadership training programmes. Advocates for a coaching and mentoring culture need to spend time exploring with development and training colleagues what these messages are and how they integrate with what is being done and said to propagate coaching and mentoring. They are not two processes, but one.

Coaching and Mentoring as Problem Solving

Coaching and mentoring are not soft forms of managing staff; in fact, they are not even a form of managing staff hard or soft. They are a means of addressing issues and problems (or, as solutions-focussed coaches would say, achieving solutions) that can be used in a wide range of contexts. We have frequently remarked upon the enthusiasm with which managers have grasped a coaching framework, like GROW, and found that they can use it in a team setting to deal with a big issue. So, how does an organization's project-management approach fit with its coaching and mentoring approach?

CONCLUSIONS

In this chapter, we have sought to introduce some dimensions of coaching and mentoring that are directed towards impacting the organization as a whole, rather than the usual focus upon an individual or a tranche of individuals. We have explored what the literature says about the process and have outlined our sense of the strategic decisions that have to be made and the tactical opportunities that exist to progress this agenda.

In the next chapter, we focus upon questions of the design and evaluation of coaching and mentoring schemes.

Future Directions

We discern a widespread interest in creating coaching culture, less so in creating a mentoring culture. This seems appropriate in so far as mentoring is seen as an off-line process and coaching as something that can be done by a line manager. An emphasis on paid external one-to-one coaching takes the eye of the coaching leaders in organizations off the question of creating a coaching culture – indeed it could be seen as threatening the market for external coaching. Similarly, external coaches can leave the topic alone as they are the ones who may feel supplanted. The drive to link the outcomes of coaching to some organizational purpose persists and may be considered as a force shaping the approaches to coaching and mentoring as an organizational intervention.

QUESTIONS

How far do/does the organization/s you work with want to push the development of a coaching/mentoring culture? Are they ready to begin, or (if already on the journey) how far have they progressed with this project already?

What is the business case for developing this culture? If that is unclear, how might clarity be developed? What components of such a culture need to be developed? Who needs to take what responsibility for this project?

To what extent should a coaching style be seen as the default style of leading and managing in the organization?

DESIGN AND EVALUATION

CHAPTER OVERVIEW

This chapter mainly focusses on practice and practitioners. It places emphasis on the pragmatic issues of scheme design and evaluation that confront those who organize formal coaching and mentoring schemes in an organizational context. We start by exploring some literature on evaluation and then draw this through into a discussion on scheme design. We also attempt to bridge theory and practice and argue that positivistic thinking tends to dominate organizational life and this is a further example of 'misplaced concreteness' as discussed in Chapter 1. To address this, we suggest that an action-oriented approach offers a way forward.

INTRODUCTION

In an organizational context, there are many competing demands on managers. Organizations, however conceived, are complex places and in such complexity, there can be a tendency to simplify and reduce the complexity to a set of principles or rules. When an organization is attempting to develop coaching and mentoring there is no less a demand to simplify and attempt to position, control, ignore or smooth over social factors. The inherent risk of this approach is that those practising coaching or mentoring within a scheme may encounter difficulties. As we argued in Chapter 2, researchers whose work we categorize as falling within the mentoring research archetype are likely to have quite different answers from those whose research is more coaching orientated. Furthermore, it is also likely that the answers will differ depending on whether the person answering them is a coaching or mentoring practitioner or whether they are an academic researcher.

METHODOLOGY

Keeping in mind the points raised in Chapters 2 and 3 about gaze, the perceived purpose of mentoring or coaching and the social context, we explore the challenges of scheme design and evaluation. Additionally, we, the authors, are practising coaches and mentors, consultants and academic researchers. As a result, we intend to put forward an approach to the scheme design and the evaluation of coaching and mentoring which draws on the strengths of these different approaches. In doing so, we acknowledge the possibility, as Gill and Johnson (1997) argue, that multi-methodological processes can be difficult and time consuming. Nevertheless, our intent is to suggest a process that can encompass a range of approaches. In doing this, we draw on some selected literature, previously presented themes and we celebrate, as a virtue, a blend of theory and practice.

APPROACHES TO EVALUATION

Beginning a discussion on scheme design with a discussion on evaluation may seem strange. Evaluation is often only considered in depth once a scheme is under way or when a pilot programme has ended. This is because it seems to be axiomatic to argue that it is only possible to evaluate something once there is something to evaluate! Furthermore, it seems to make sense to think about how to evaluate something once it is known what there is to examine. For example, if a scheme co-ordinator exceeded his or her recruitment targets for a mentoring programme and has a far greater number of participants than anticipated, it seems sensible to adjust the evaluation methodology accordingly. Additionally, and perhaps the most persuasive of all these arguments, is it only possible to evaluate something once it is known what the outcomes are?

All too often schemes are evaluated later in their development and the success factors are identified post hoc. According to Megginson et al. (2006: 9), it is important to be clear about the success criteria before the scheme starts. For us, this seems to depend on the answers to three key questions:

1. How will I know whether the scheme has been successful or not?
2. What criteria will I use to make these judgements?
3. What measures will I use to assess the scheme against these criteria?

Models of Evaluation

Kirkpatrick

Perhaps the best-known goal-based model of evaluating training interventions is Kirkpatrick's model (Kirkpatrick, 1959). Kirkpatrick bases the model on four different levels as follows:

1. Reaction – participants' responses and reactions to the training, whether they themselves found it useful.
2. Learning – whether participants have increased their capability or knowledge as a result of the training.

3. Behaviour – what impact the training has had on participants' behaviour.
4. Results – what impact the training has ultimately had on business results or the wider environment.

Although this model was developed to evaluate training, it is useful in the context of coaching and mentoring evaluation because it draws our attention to a number of issues.

First, it recognizes that the success of a scheme is multi-layered and it is not just about whether participants thought it was useful or enjoyable. Often, training event evaluation is limited to the reaction level because this is easy and quick to measure. This has led to the evaluation forms handed out at the end of training events being somewhat derisively known as 'happy sheets'. However, the Kirkpatrick model recognizes that this is only one measure.

Second, it also acknowledges that participants are not the only source of data for judging the success of a training intervention, even if the focus is on them and their capability. The model offers other stakeholders the opportunity to identify the positive impact of an intervention on an individual's learning or behaviour even when that individual's reaction to it is a negative one or vice versa. It also recognizes that, as with the case with formal mentoring and coaching schemes, the ultimate aim of a development intervention is to improve organizational results in some way, for example increased profits, improved performance, greater employee retention or reduced costs.

Finally, it also recognizes the importance of time as another key element in the process. In Chapter 2, we identified the relative paucity of longitudinal studies. The difficulty with this is that we are less likely, in studies that take a 'snapshot' approach, to be able to identify the distal outcomes.

However, what the framework does not do is completely resolve the issue of different research paradigms and 'gaze' that we identified in Chapter 2.

A positivist approach to evaluation is likely to seek to prove a causal link, for example between coaching and improved business performance, with the researcher attempting to discount alternative and competing explanations for such an improvement.

With a phenomenological approach, the researcher is attempting to evaluate the scheme in terms of the subjective understandings of the impact of the intervention. Further, it is not clear what happens if multiple levels of evaluation conclude that there are competing conclusions about the effectiveness of the intervention. Similarly, different stakeholders may have different reactions, learning, behavioural responses and impacts upon business results, the net effect of which makes outcomes difficult to measure.

Finally, perhaps the most important drawback with the Kirkpatrick's model is, whilst allowing the possibility of different stages of evaluation, it does not lend itself to ongoing evaluation and feedback, throughout the life of a coaching or mentoring scheme. As will be seen in Chapter 6, this form of evaluation has also led to the pre-specification of learning outcomes that are independent of and detached from the learner.

CIRO

The CIRO model is another approach to evaluation. Developed by Warr et al. (1978), it again has four levels:

1. Context – involves gathering data about the context in which the development intervention is located, including the identification of needs.
2. Input – involves evaluation of the inputs used in the intervention.
3. Reaction – using participants' reactions to improve the process.
4. Outcome – obtaining information about the outcome or results.

Similarly, although this model does pay more attention to the context in which the learning takes place, it still does not seem to suggest ways in which ongoing feedback can be incorporated into the intervention. Eseryl (2002) comes to similar conclusions about the current practice in training evaluation. She provides a useful taxonomy of evaluation in her article on approaches to the evaluation of training where she identifies six general approaches:

- goal-based evaluation
- goal-free evaluation
- responsive evaluation
- systems evaluation
- professional review
- quasi legal.

She suggests that the majority of evaluations are either goal based or systems evaluations. Similar to the key question often raised in coaching and mentoring – 'Whose agenda is it?' – the question 'Whose goals are we evaluating?' becomes a key question. This question does not necessarily have a simple answer and, as we discuss in Chapter 7, the question of power is rarely far away and, in Chapter 10, goals aren't always what they seem.

In the case of a systems evaluation, we may gain an understanding of processes and specific interventions but we may not develop an understanding of individual impact. With these dominant preferences in mind (Eseryl, 2002: 96) calls for a unifying model for evaluation theory:

> There is a need for a unifying model for evaluation theory, research and practice that will account for the collaborative nature of, and complexities involved in, the evaluation of training. None of the available models for training evaluation seem to account for these two aspects of evaluation. Existing models fall short in comprehensiveness and they fail to provide tools that guide organisations in their evaluation systems and procedures.

Mentoring and coaching are social processes that depend on active engagement and positive participation of individuals and the social context is important. Consequently, the personal commitment and personal involvement inherent in a coaching or mentoring scheme mean that it is important to treat evaluation as an ongoing developmental process. The consequences of an evaluation that discovers a problem 12 months after it occurs could be serious for the future of coaching and mentoring in that organization.

Additionally, there are tensions in scheme design and evaluation. One is acknowledging that not all possible outcomes will be or can be recognized, and therefore measured, before the coaching or mentoring intervention begins. Therefore, this lends weight to the argument that an ongoing, development-focussed evaluation is the best strategy for capturing this learning throughout the life of a scheme. Nevertheless, it is possible to anticipate some of the challenges and issues that need to be resolved in terms of designing an effective scheme. The following section explores these.

SCHEME DESIGN

Purpose

First, as we have already argued in previous chapters, it is important to be as clear *as possible* about the intended purpose of a coaching or mentoring scheme. Different stakeholders within a scheme – senior managers, coaches, mentors, other managers, customers – may have different and competing views about the purpose of the scheme. Again, this can be linked back to our earlier discussion about different ways of dealing with evaluation research. A phenomenological approach to evaluation will tend to emphasize the exploration of different subjective views of the purpose within a scheme in a relative way. However, a positivistic approach will tend to emphasize the need for clarity around purpose. This is because the positivist research agenda is focussed on 'testing' or 'proving' a causal relationship between coaching and/or mentoring and the dependent variable, for example organizational performance. In doing this, the evaluator must be able to isolate the effect of the coaching and mentoring on organizational performance. In other words, if organizational performance improves after coaching and/or mentoring has been used as an intervention, the evaluator must be able to discount other competing explanations for this variance in performance – for example, the arrival of a new managing director, a general economic upturn, other developmental interventions (see Gill and Johnson, 1997: 40 for a summary of other research design problems using this approach).

Our preferred approach is to adopt a phenomenological approach to understanding purpose. This approach acknowledges, rather than attempting to downplay, differences in understanding. Inevitably, however, *initial* responses to the questions reproduced below tend to be decided on by the most powerful stakeholders, for example the senior managers or sponsors of the scheme.

1. How will I know whether the scheme has been successful or not?
2. What criteria will I use to make these judgements?
3. What measures will I use to assess the scheme against these criteria?

In Colley's (2003) work, the 'agency' of the mentors and mentees within engagement mentoring schemes meant that the purpose of the mentoring, as defined by government and other powerful stakeholders, was fundamentally altered and undermined by these seemingly less powerful stakeholders. In a different way, in Beech and Brockbank's (1999) work, we can see how different understandings of what mentoring was about and what people's roles were in it led to 'psycho-social dysfunction' (p. 24) within the mentoring scheme.

Recruitment and Selection

Another question that could be added to our evaluation questions is, 'Who is the scheme for?' Often, this question stimulates a statement around purpose and an intended target for an intervention. However, as our work on the NHS-sponsored 'Expert Patient Mentoring Programme' (Garrett, 2006) revealed, the answer to this question is not always obvious, as the following case study illustrates.

Case Study: NHS Expert Patient Mentoring Programme

This programme was intended to build on the national Expert Patient Programme. The national programme was aimed to recognize the tremendous savings that can be made in the NHS when patients successfully self-manage their own long-term health conditions such as, arthritis, ME or asthma. This programme works by successful self-managers tutoring other patients in how to do this by delivering self-management training courses. The Expert Patient Mentoring (EPM) programme was a more radical departure from this model. The EPM programme used mentoring as a vehicle for introducing some of the learning from this initiative back into the health service. This happened through a mentoring programme where successful Expert Patient tutors were developed as mentors to health care professionals. This presented some challenges both in terms of power dynamics but also in terms of recruitment and selection.

Ostensibly, the scheme was set up for the health care professionals (mainly nurses) to help them work more effectively with their own patients who had similar long-term health conditions to that of their mentors. The notion of 'expert' was therefore widened from that of a specialist health care professional to include that of someone intimately acquainted with living with a long-term health condition on a day-to-day basis. Interestingly, and in line with Brockbank and Beech's (1999) findings, this led to some asymmetry in terms of expectations and understandings of what the mentoring relationship entailed. For some of the health care professionals, access to an 'expert patient' seemed to tick the box of patient involvement and feedback and they invited their mentor along to team meetings. For others, their relationship sometimes mirrored a patient-health care professional relationship and they attempted to work with their patient on that basis.

However, for the mentors (the patients), the experience of being developed as a mentor was a radical departure from what they were used to in terms of their previous experience of the NHS. Rather than being a passive recipient of a process, for some, it reconnected them to other parts of themselves, prior to their illness, where they conceived of themselves as being helpful, resourceful and purposeful human beings. In that sense, the pilot programme was, in several ways, more successful in terms of empowering mentors than its effect on the mentees. Consequently, any attempt to evaluate the scheme based on its initial criteria would not have captured the learning that had ultimately emerged.

However, it remains important in general for the scheme organizer to try to establish some early clarity about who should be involved, even if this is likely to shift as the programme moves forward. This decision revolves around the following four key areas.

Eligibility

Organizational schemes consume resources, therefore scheme sponsors need to make decisions about who they will allow to be involved in the coaching/ mentoring process. In particular, they need to be clear about the criteria for acceptance as either a coach or coachee. For example, a FTSE 100 company based in the north of England is currently, at the time of writing, offering external one-to-one coaching for a range of aspiring senior managers as part of a 19-day development programme. However, they are talking in terms of 'targeted' coaching, using a 'push' approach, rather than offering it to all and working via a demand-led system. Additionally, these managers have an internal mentor to support application of the learning from the programme into the workplace.

Credibility

Coaching and mentoring work best when both parties are willingly involved and make active choices about who they want to work with. Therefore, each party must be credible to the other in terms of their willingness to invest the time in the process. This can lead to competition for key organizational members as coaches or mentors and does suggest that, inevitably, not everyone can have exactly who they want to work with. Some years ago, we were involved in creating a mentoring programme putting together senior executives from experienced exporting organizations together with those from less experienced exporting organizations, as part of a publicly funded project (see Megginson and Stokes, 2004). Mentees were often quite fastidious in terms of who they would work with (see matching below) and were often very clear at the outset about what their mentor should have achieved and what sort of business they would like them to be in. Conversely, the mentors were happy to work with anyone from any background. Garvey and Galloway (2002) also found examples of what they called 'mentee fastidiousness' and 'mentor indifference' in the mentoring scheme they developed within HBOS plc. In practice, if mentees were matched with someone not meeting their specification, they found that the relationship could still be very useful to them. In this sense the mentees were clear about what they wanted, but wrong about the importance of their pre-specification.

Availability

Related to the above, the scheme organizer must consider the likely availability of both coaches/mentors and mentees/coachees and the impact of any imbalances on the success of the scheme in terms of its stated purpose. At the time of writing, we are currently working with South Yorkshire Police and their Positive Action Mentoring Scheme (PAMS (see Chapter 12)). The intention of the scheme is to make progression and development within the organization accessible to those who are currently under-represented within its hierarchy. One of the challenges facing newly trained mentors is that there are relatively few formal referrals via the scheme; because of the confidential nature of the scheme, mentees either make direct contact with the mentors or mentors make offers to prospective mentees.

Motivation

It is important to be aware of possible motivations for being involved in a scheme that both coaches/coachees and mentors/mentees might have. Our experience with a range of schemes (see Megginson et al., 2006) suggests that it is often more helpful if the coach or mentor has a clear idea about what they want to get out of the relationship, in addition to being helpful to the coachee/mentee. In contrast, a desire to 'give something back' and to 'offer people the benefit of my experience' can suggest that the coach/mentor has more of an interest in being admired and having a willing and receptive audience than actually focussing on what they might do to help their partner further their agenda. There is nothing wrong with altruism as a motive for becoming a coach or mentor, but we have found that if it is the only motive, then this is a contra-indicator. It is often better that mentors/coaches are also interested in learning for themselves.

Coaching and Mentoring Training and Development

Once the decision has been made about whom the coaching is for, and methods of recruitment and selection have been established, it is important to consider the mode and methods of development. Megginson et al. (2006) suggest there are a number of ways to do this. The one that we shall focus on here is our preferred approach to development, rooted as it is in adult development theory. Garvey and Williamson (2002: 39–40) use the term 'open curriculum' to describe this approach to learning – the following quote seems to capture, for us, the essence of coaching and mentoring development work by first contrasting it with a 'closed curriculum' approach:

> The type of learning embedded by the 'formal' or 'closed' curriculum is associated with high 'teacher' control of the knowledge and it socialises a sense of order and rationality...As the formal curriculum is driven so strongly by assessment and evaluation it offers a greater opportunity for managerial control and direction.

This approach seems to us to explain, particularly with publicly funded coaching and mentoring initiatives, the strong drive towards accreditation and standards found among those interested in coaching and mentoring (see Chapter 13). This can be contrasted usefully with the open curriculum: 'In contrast, the "open curriculum" places the "learner" in control and consequently encourages challenge, questioning, high initiative, innovation and creativity. The open curriculum socializes a sense of "disorder"...' (p. 110). The latter definition of a learning agenda seems to us to be much more consistent with coaching and mentoring philosophy because it places the learner in the centre and he or she becomes responsible for and in control of the learning agenda. However, we recognize that, by referring to disorder, this does not sit well with the modernist discourse which sets great store by efficiency. McAuley et al. (2007: 54) summarize modernism well: 'The modernist approach to organizations is based on a belief that if we adopt a rational, scientific approach to organizational life, our organizations can be effective and efficient machines for the delivery of industry, business and public services.'

Our contention is that, often, having a closed curriculum-based approach to coaching and mentoring development, which has its roots in a modernist approach to organizational life, is ineffective in delivering the intent of the curriculum developers. This is because such approaches tend not to leave room for the experience and contribution of the participants. As Garvey and Williamson (2002) point out, it is important to consider the situated nature of learning (Lave and Wenger, 1991) and, in the case of coaching and mentoring, enable legitimate peripheral participation in coaching and mentoring, via experiential learning (see Beard and Wilson, 2006 for an analysis of experiential learning).

Matching

Matching coaches and coachees, and mentors and mentees is often messy and difficult. Megginson et al. (2006) argue that it is important to take account of a number of factors when matching as follows.

The Criteria for Matching

These should follow from a clearer understanding of purpose and identification of who the coaching or mentoring is for. For example, in the export scheme referred to earlier (Megginson and Stokes, 2004), the focus of the matching was around putting people with experience of export together with those who had not. As we later explore, this was not the only factor.

Rapport

The quality of the relationship and chemistry is something that we have argued (Chapter 1) is particularly underplayed in the literature on coaching. In both the export scheme and the PAMS scheme mentioned earlier, the success of the intervention seems to crucially depend on the quality of the relationship.

The Balance between Similarity and Difference

In all coaching and mentoring, it is crucial to achieve a balance between there being sufficient difference, in order to add value, and sufficient similarity, in order to enable rapport. As mentioned above, the quality of the relationship and the strength of the rapport between the two individuals is referred to much more in the mentoring literature than the coaching literature although this trend is beginning to change (see Bluckert, 2005). Colley's (2003) work on engagement mentoring also reminds us that each individual will want different things from the relationship and that this may not always be consistent with the stated aims of the scheme.

Marketing a Scheme

Coaching and mentoring can sometimes be seen as 'nice to have' options within an organization. Our view is that, as coaching and mentoring is such an intrinsic and natural part of adult development (see Chapters 1 and 3), it should be recognized and embedded as a central and legitimate work activity. For those new to coaching and mentoring, it is important to give them an opportunity to find out about what is involved before committing to it. Consequently, marketing the scheme is important but there are two key approaches that can be taken with marketing.

Formal Launch and New Initiative Approach

This is where the usual organizational mechanisms for promoting any change is done in a formal and organized way, for example, team briefings, formal papers, presentations. This has the advantage of legitimizing the activity, particularly if key players (see Chapter 8) are seen to be involved. However, it also brings pressure to bear on people to be involved. This can militate against the spirit of voluntarism which underpins coaching and mentoring. Also, it can sometimes put too much pressure on the coaching and mentoring itself to solve a whole host of organizational issues and raise expectations too highly (see Garvey's case study in Megginson et al., 2006: 124–33).

The Organic Approach

This is where coaching and mentoring is promoted in a low-key way by using other, less formal, channels of communication, for example newsletters, word of mouth, lunch-time get-togethers. To draw on Gareth Morgan's work on metaphors (Morgan, 2006), this approach tends to require scheme organizers to think of the scheme rather like an organism, a living thing, that needs to be nurtured and developed under the right environmental conditions. This has the advantage of relieving some of the pressure on a scheme that the formal launch approach brings while still giving people access to the experience in a way that might pique their interest as opposed to pressurizing them to be involved. Case studies in Clutterbuck and Megginson (2005: 137–45) of KPMG and the Scottish Executive illustrate this approach where they conclude that this approach has the potential disadvantage of not seeming to have the full weight of the system behind it and, therefore, possibly fizzling out.

Cranwell-Ward et al.'s (2004: 68–9) book on mentoring provides a useful list of support tools which a scheme organizer may use to market their coaching or mentoring scheme. These include:

- Booklets – giving details of objectives, benefits, roles and responsibilities of participants.
- Policy/process documents – giving details of eligibility, processes involved and possible content of meetings.
- Websites – giving details contained in the above two categories but also links to other resources, e.g. models, useful questions, FAQs.
- Use of champions – identifying people who have been coaches, coachees, mentors or mentees and who have benefited from the scheme.
- Information workshops – short lunch-time sessions to inform people about the scheme.
- Email and voice mail – two normal organizational communication mechanisms which might be used to promote the scheme.

CONCLUSIONS

In this chapter, we have chosen to focus the unit of analysis on the coaching and mentoring scheme itself. As mentoring and, in particular, coaching have become more popular and commonplace in organizations, it is noticeable that evaluation and return on investment have become more prominent as discussion topics, particularly within the practitioner-based literature. As we have suggested in this chapter and in Chapter 2, it is important to reflect on and be clear about the rationale for conducting such evaluations. Furthermore, the approach to evaluation that is employed has critical implications for scheme design and should be considered first of all.

Our own preferred position on evaluation is one that sees evaluation as an ongoing and collaborative process; in research methodology terms, it is more akin to action research. Gill and Johnson (1997: 76) summarize this approach well:

> Action research, then, is clearly an important approach to research in business and management, particularly given its declared aim of serving both the practical concerns of managers and simultaneously generalizing and adding to theory. Most researchers using this approach wish to do immediately useful work and at the same time to stand back from the specific so that their research may be more widely utilized.

It is unfortunate, in our view, that many publicly funded coaching and mentoring evaluation projects seem to reject this approach in favour of a more positivistic evaluation strategy. This latter approach tends to emphasize distance between the evaluator and what is being evaluated, which, in our view, can militate against a deep understanding of what is happening within the complexities of a coaching and mentoring scheme. Crucially, evaluating any pilot coaching and mentoring scheme at the end of its life means that the scheme organizer, the participants and the organization as a whole do not benefit from the evaluation until the end, when, in fact, it may have been possible to improve the experience for all concerned had a more collaborative approach been used. As a result, this can have the effect of influencing the scheme organizer's behaviour so as to make sure they appear to 'hit their targets' at the expense of identifying useful learning that may come out of the scheme.

Furthermore, we have also argued, using Kirkpatrick's (1959) model of evaluation, that, as well as adopting an ongoing approach to evaluation, there are some strong arguments in favour of extending the evaluation over a longer time period so as to capture the effects and implications for participant learning, behaviour and its impact upon the organization's results.

Drawing on our experience of conducting evaluations, we have attempted, following the traditions of action research, to identify broader challenges in terms of scheme design that have come out of our work and that of others. We offer these to scheme organizers and practitioners, as well as other researchers in the hope that they are useful in generating a deeper understanding of coaching and mentoring. We will continue to return to these issues and themes throughout the book.

Future Directions

It is our contention that those who fund and commission research into coaching and mentoring need to recognize the situated, contextual nature of such activity.

Our prediction is that, as the body of research in this area continues to grow, a more sophisticated and reflexive approach to scheme design and evaluation will emerge. Central to this approach will be some recognition of the impact of the evaluation process itself on the outcomes. We also predict that organizational coaching and mentoring schemes will become more and more aligned with and linked to existing development initiatives within the organization. This, in turn, will have implications for the way evaluation is understood, in terms of its scope and scale.

QUESTIONS

How will you know whether your coaching/mentoring scheme has been successful or not?
Who else will decide?
Who is the coaching/mentoring for?
What criteria will you use to make these judgements?
What measures will you use to assess the scheme against these criteria?

MODELS AND PERSPECTIVES ON COACHING AND MENTORING

CHAPTER OVERVIEW

This chapter looks at the wide variety and range of models and perspectives in coaching and mentoring. We aim to reflect the breadth and depth of the field and to explore some of the assumptions that underpin the various approaches and models. This is not a detailed exploration of models and perspectives but, rather, we attempt to capture the *essence* of each approach in order to raise more interesting research questions about mentoring and coaching as a domain of theory and practice.

INTRODUCTION

Megginson and Clutterbuck (2005a) suggest that raising the issue of techniques in mentoring and coaching can be reductionist and lead to a formulaic approach to practice. They also suggest that for some, having a model or framework to follow is contrary to the humanistic tradition that coaching and mentoring represents. This can inhibit empathy and a sense of giving oneself to another. However, they argue that, for others, having a conceptual framework that guides their practice is useful and does not necessarily inhibit an authentic and meaningful coaching and mentoring relationship. Taking into account these different and equally legitimate positions and by linking to other chapters in this book, we debate these issues.

METHODOLOGY

We developed this chapter using literature, general web searches and our experience in order to uncover the variety and range of coaching and mentoring models.

A simple web-based search using Google gives an illustration of the plethora of interest in coaching. Searching for 'coaching' gives 133 million hits, whilst searching more specifically for 'coaching models' still leaves over eight and a half million hits.

There do seem to be several distinct approaches to coaching which emerge within searches of both academic information databases and practitioner search engines like Google. We briefly summarize some of the main or dominant perspectives and models below and we will examine some of these in more detail as the chapter develops. We suggest that coaching is becoming more commodified into brands than mentoring and that the form mentoring takes is often related to its purpose and social context, which we refer to as 'modes'.

APPROACHES TO COACHING

Main Approaches

Sports coaching – as we claim in Chapter 1 – constitutes one of the traditional roots of many of the other approaches to coaching.

Life coaching – holistic approach to working with others. As raised in Chapter 1, we found a nineteenth century reference to life coaching but another root is in person-centred counselling.

Executive coaching – whilst this is a market-driven approach, it is emerging as a distinct field with strong links to peer and sponsorship mentoring approaches.

Team coaching – drawn from models of facilitation and action learning, this is becoming an increasingly popular field and challenges the traditional dyadic approach to coaching.

Brief coaching/solution focussed – this has its roots in therapeutic counselling and involves a goal-focussed, time-limited intervention.

Other Approaches to Coaching

There are a number of other approaches found either through Google or in books written by practising coaches. These include:

Coactive coaching – a non-directive, client-centred approach to coaching which differentiates itself on the bases of its emphasis on building a collaborative, curious approach (Whitworth et al., 1998).

Evidence-based coaching – an approach to coaching which emphasizes the importance of using only approaches and techniques that are validated by research and that are grounded in empirical data. This appears to represent a more philosophical approach to coaching research than a distinct body of work that is separate from others. Oxford Brookes University publish the *International Journal of Evidence Based Coaching and*

Mentoring and the University of Sydney run an international conference on Evidence Based Coaching. However, publications range across the coaching and mentoring spectrum.

Leadership-based coaching – similar to executive coaching, except leaders are positioned as a distinctive group of stakeholders whose goals and aspirations must incorporate those of other stakeholders in the organization (see Lee, 2003). However, it is unclear how different this approach is from executive coaching (see below).

Existential-based coaching – related to ontological coaching, this branch of coaching includes discussions aimed at positive self-actualizing, explorations of anxiety and competing motivations in order to establish better decision-making procedures.

Ontological coaching – this is a holistic approach to coaching which focusses on a way of being in relation to the world, with regard to three domains: language, emotion and domains (see Sieler, 2003).

Cognitive behavioural coaching – this approach is drawn directly from the work of Aaron Beck and Albert Ellis on cognitive behaviour therapy (see Neenan, 2006). It offers a way of dealing with limiting self-beliefs on the part of the client but, as Neenan acknowledges, research on this approach is limited.

Passmore's (2006) book – as well as some of the above – identifies other approaches such as NLP coaching (Ian McDermott), transpersonal coaching (John Whitmore), intercultural coaching (Rosinski) and his own, integral coaching.

All these above approaches and perhaps others not mentioned here represent novel and distinctive approaches to coaching on the part of their creators but they have not yet extended significantly beyond the originators to become distinctive bodies of theory and practice about coaching. This is not to say that they will not do this in time. However, it is interesting to note that the proliferation of approaches to coaching reflects the commodification thesis that we referred to earlier in Chapter 1. This is summarized well by Feldman and Lankau (2005: 845), who state: 'the domain of what coaching encompasses, the activities and responsibilities of coaches, and the kinds of recipients of coaching, are now so diverse that it is more difficult to put constructs around the construct itself and the appropriate range and scope of its associated outcomes.'

For reasons of space, we now focus our attention on approaches that have expanded beyond one or two individuals and appear to be research based.

SPORTS COACHING

As argued earlier, sports coaching has perhaps the longest history as part of the modern discourse on coaching. The academic literature on sports coaching seems to fall into three main areas:

1. Injury prevention/risk analysis (e.g. Blitvich et al., 2000).
2. Biomechanical analysis of sporting techniques (e.g. Post, 2006).
3. The performance/development of sports coaches.

This latter category is of most interest to us in terms of developing an understanding of assumptions underpinning sports coaching and contains a body of research that is focussed on coach and coachee commitment (e.g. Hollembeak and Amorose, 2005; Turner and Chelladurai, 2005). This could be characterized as the sports psychology approach to coaching. It is interesting to note that much of this research-based literature (rather like in other applications of psychology) employs statistical survey techniques, using large sample sizes (see Chapter 2 for analysis of research in coaching and mentoring). Also, there are some studies that do employ qualitative techniques. For example, Irwin et al.'s (2004) study looks at the origins of the coaching practice of elite UK gymnastics coaches. Interestingly, Irwin et al. (2004: 237) conclude that the 'most important resource identified by participants was mentor coaches'. This was the case for 91 per cent of the coaches chosen in their study. Whilst they do raise the issue of the ways in which coaches learn, they seem to stop short of critiquing sports coaching practice. However, writers such as Jones and Wallace (2005: 121) raise questions about the core assumptions of sports coaching: 'Despite its complex nature, associated literature has traditionally viewed coaching from a rationalistic perspective, a "knowable sequence" over which coaches are presumed to have command.' Jones and Wallace (2005: 121) challenge this assumption on the basis that this often equates to advice to coaches that is 'fine in theory' but that 'ignores the many tensions and social dilemmas which characterize their practice'. Whilst they recognize that the importance of sequential practice and compliance (on the part of coachees) is important in sport, they also argue that an over-reliance on this approach ignores issues such as ambiguity, the importance of reflection in action, and the diversity of goals in sport. Instead, they propose adopting the metaphor of orchestration within sports coaching. This suggests that coaches 'are unlikely to have a free hand either in selecting coaching goals or in determining how goals are to be achieved with and through their charges'. Rather, their approach emphasizes 'challenging athletes' agency (autonomy or personal power) through encouragement and incentives' more often than 'delimiting their agency through sanctions' (Jones and Wallace (2005: 129).

Potrac et al.'s (2002) study of a Nationwide league football coach suggests that the rationalistic, instructional approach to sports coaching is routed in the coaches desire to retain the respect of his coachees. In the case of Brian, the football coach, Potrac et al. (2002: 197) argue that he is consciously trying to 'create an idealized image of himself in the eyes of his players'. In doing so, Brian deliberately conflates his personal bond (based on their view of him as a person) with the professional (their view of him as a knowledgeable football professional). In other words, the need for Brian to be personally associated with the success of the football team on the pitch seems, in Jones and Wallace's (2005) terms, to mitigate against him ceding control of the coaching process to the players. Also, it seems to suggest that Brian's approach to coaching is about being directive and imposing his view of how football should be played onto his players.

Those who have taken coaching concepts from sport and attempted to apply them in other contexts resist this controlling approach. For example, Downey's (2003) book draws heavily on Tim Gallwey's (1997) concept of the inner game. Within this framework, the role of the coach is to help the 'player' to overcome their fear and negativity. Following Gallwey, Downey (2003) calls this fear 'interference' and suggests that coaching ought to enable a focus on the performance of the task rather than a focus on a fear of failure. This approach entails focussing on 'self two', a version of oneself that is character-ized by relaxed concentration, enjoyment and trust. Whilst Downey (2003: 24) does not completely reject the notion of being directive, he argues that 'the magic inhabits the non-directive end of the spectrum'. Furthermore, Downey (2003: 57) also raises the issue of the coaches intent when asking questions or making interventions:

> In coaching (and not just in coaching) understanding one's own intent at any moment is a key component in becoming more effective. When I ask novice coaches the intent question (*what is your intent with this question*), I get many kinds of answers. Mostly, they point to the coach's need to solve, to fix, to heal, to be right or to be in control. (*Emphasis not in orginial*)

We speculate that Downey's (2003: 57) view of Brian's interventions might be that they are more often about enhancing his own status rather than helping the coachee(s) 'become more aware or retain responsibility'.

These insights raise some interesting questions about coaching in general:

- What is the appropriate balance between structured coaching activity and individual coachee agency?
- To what extent should the context of the coaching relationship influence the nature of the relationship between coach and coachee?

LIFE COACHING

As Grant (2003: 253) puts it, 'the general public has a thirst for techniques and processes that enhance life experience and facilitate personal development'. This has expressed itself in coaching particularly in the area of life coaching. Using the Google search engine, the scale of this interest is shown by looking at the number of hits. Whilst a search on 'coaching' itself gives over 133 mil-lion hits, searching for 'life coaching' reveals over 45 million. This is also a sub-stantial growth in volume of self-help and personal development shows on UK television, for example Paul McKenna's *I Can Change Your Life* and *A Life Coach Less Ordinary*. In his article on work–life balance, McIntosh (2003) sug-gests that one of the drivers for life coaching is the relative imbalance that many people have in their work–life balance. He argues for life coaching as one way of redressing that balance.

However, in comparison, a search on an academic journal database Swetswise reveals only nine different hits for 'life coaching' out of a possible 21 million journal articles. This suggests that, despite the huge amount of popular interest in life coaching, there is no developed research base to support this interest.

One notable exception to this is Grant's (2003) article. This study involved 29 postgraduate students within his university. The participants completed pre-life coaching questionnaires and then identified three life goals in the areas of mental health, quality of life and goal attainment. Following this, the participants then received 10–50-minute group-coaching sessions to facilitate the achievement of these goals. The participants then answered a post-coaching questionnaire. Grant (2003: 259) concluded that there was 'preliminary empirical evidence that a life-coaching programme can facilitate goal improvement, improved mental health and enhance quality of life'. However, he qualified the results by pointing out that these were self-reported successes by potentially already well-motivated goal-focussed individuals, without the use of a control group. Nevertheless, it is still one of the few empirical studies of life coaching.

Grant's study does raise some useful distinctions between self-reflection and gaining insight. He views self-reflection as being about monitoring one's performance and understanding one's behaviour and motivations. However, gaining insight is 'a reflective process associated with goal attainment' (p. 260). In an earlier study, Grant et al. (2002) found that, when examining the impact of journal keeping, individuals who kept journals have higher levels of self-knowledge but less movement towards goal attainment. In fact, Grant (2003: 256) suggests that the journal keepers were 'stuck in a process of self reflection' or as we might call it 'analysis paralysis' rather than gaining insight and making behavioural change to reach goals. Again, this raises some interesting general questions for coaching:

- What processes best enable goal attainment?
- Is goal attainment, as opposed to self-knowledge, the primary purpose of coaching and mentoring?

EXECUTIVE COACHING

Executive coaching is perhaps the branch of coaching that has been most susceptible to the commodification of coaching services – this is particularly the case with larger organizations. Natale and Diamante (2005: 362) support this in the US context: 'Leader organizations such as Alcoa, American Red

Cross, AT & T, Ford, Northwestern Mutual Life, 3M and United Parcel Service offer executive coaching as part of their development and productivity programmes. Other organizations such as Motorola and IBM, deploy executive coaching services regularly.'

Joo's (2005) survey of the literature on executive coaching is extremely useful in identifying some distinct patterns. This work involved an analysis of 78 articles on executive coaching and a classification of these studies. Joo (2005) argues that the literature based on the sample he looked at can be placed into three different categories:

1. Definitions and designations of practice.
2. Description of specific executive coaching methodologies.
3. Case studies of executive coaching.

These categories certainly seem to resonate with what we have found in our survey of this literature. For example, Hall et al.'s (1999) article (also featured in Joo's work) is a typical example of a study that attempts to shed light on the nature and benefits of executive coaching.

Like ourselves, Joo concluded that relatively little research work (only 11 articles out of 78) underpins executive coaching although 'there are a number of case studies portraying successful instances of executive coaching' (Joo, 2005: 465). Whilst Joo makes important contributions in several areas, for example definition, distinctions between approaches to counselling and coaching, perhaps one of the most useful conceptual distinctions he offers is the difference between proximal outcomes (behavioural change on the part of participants) and distal outcomes (the ultimate purpose of coaching). This framework, drawn from Wanberg et al.'s (2003) work in mentoring, leads us to ask the following questions about the contribution that executive coaching makes:

- What behavioural changes do we hope and expect to see in coachees and coaches?
- What are the ultimate individual or organization outcomes that we hope and expect to see as a result of executive coaching?
- What is the relationship between behavioural changes (proximal outcomes) and the ultimate outcomes of executive coaching (distal outcomes)?
- How might we understand and measure all of these things?

TEAM COACHING

A search on Google on 'team coaching' reveals 25 million hits. Many of these seem to be advertisements for independent coaches moving into this area of work. Once again, however, the empirical research base to support team coaching as a distinct form of coaching is extremely thin. However, there are some academic contributions that are worth exploring. One such contribution is that of Hackman and Wageman (2005). In their conceptual article called 'A Theory of Team Coaching', they attempt to engage with the theory on group work, team dynamics, leadership and coaching to move towards a theory of team coaching. They base this on what they call four core conditions (p. 283):

1. That key group performance processes (i.e. effort, strategy, knowledge, skill) are not too constrained by task and organizations requirements.
2. That the team is well designed.
3. That coaching behaviours focus on salient group performance not on interpersonal relationships.
4. Coaching interventions are timely, i.e. the group is ready for them.

As they themselves acknowledge, 'these conditions are not commonly found in traditionally designed and managed work organizations' (p. 283).

Furthermore, they make very little reference to the existing coaching literature and much more to theories of group dynamics and team leadership. Therefore, it is by no means clear that the authors have succeeded in developing any form of team coaching that is distinct from other forms of group intervention or other forms of coaching. However, what does emerge very clearly is that there is strong support for a different approach to leading teams that moves away from traditional command and control models of management. Moreover, it is clear that leaders of teams, whether they are operational work teams or executive boards, need to pay more attention to group processes. We are doubtful, as things currently stand, if there is any evidence that can be stretched to develop a theory of team coaching.

Clutterbuck's (2007a) book on team coaching, which draws on Hackman and Wakeman's (2005) work, also tries to make a clearer distinction between a team coach and facilitator, as well as between an individual coach and a team coach, and a leader-manager and a leader-coach. His argument is that team coaches are more engaged with the team that they are working with and that the coaching role is more mutual (in terms of learning) and wider ranging than that of a facilitator. He suggests that leaders who operate as coaches to their teams are less output orientated and more process orientated than traditional team leaders. He views one-to-one coaching as similar to team coaching except that the team coach has more issues to consider. These would include, for example, group dynamics or leader credibility.

Whilst these distinctions are helpful as a starting point, it is not immediately clear as to where the evidence for these distinctions come from, in practice. Unfortunately, Clutterbuck (2007a) also points out that there is a major gap in the evidence supporting the claims for team coaching.

Mulec and Roth (2005) present one research-based study within two teams in AstraZeneca, the drug company. They describe an eight-month coaching intervention which involved two different pairs of coaches working with each team.

One of the coaches was external to the business, whilst one of them was internal. They noted that 'in between team meetings, the coaches met with the project leaders of the respective teams in a follow-up and preparation meeting where the individual leader was coaching in her leadership role' (p. 486). The results of the study seemed to be very positive, with respondents of the research pointing to better management of the agenda and greater participation in meetings on the part of team members. However, it is not clear from the study as to whether this was due to the direct interventions of the coaches in 'real time', as the authors put it, or whether this was as a result of the individual coaching, culminating in better leadership of the teams. Again, this raises some interesting questions:

- Is coaching primarily a one-to-one developmental dialogue or can coaching take place one-to-many?
- To what extent should coaching be based on direct observation of performance by the coach?

BRIEF COACHING OR SOLUTIONS-FOCUSSED COACHING

This model of coaching probably has the smallest current research base and output of the main approaches we have identified so far in this chapter. Nevertheless, it does seem to be a developing area in terms of hits on Google (2.4 million approximately) as well as published books and articles.

Brief coaching and solutions-focussed coaching are terms that often inter-linked but also referred to separately. They refer to essentially a very similar philosophy and process. Brief coaching or solutions-focussed coaching draws on solutions-focussed brief therapy (Watts and Pietrzak, 2000; Berg and Szabo, 2005). The therapeutic approach is summarized well by Watts and Pietzak (2000: 443): 'SFBT counsellors seek to help clients change clients' behaviour and attitudes from a problem/failure focus to a focus on solutions/successes and to discover and develop latent assets, resources, and strengths that may have been overlooked as clients have focussed primarily on "problems" and "limitations".' They argue, drawing on a range of therapeutic studies, that one of the key contributions that solutions-focussed brief therapy (SFBT) makes is that it 'eschews the "medical model" perspective and takes a non-pathological approach' (Watts and Pietzak, 2000). This also seems to apply to the coaching version of the approach. As Grant (2006: 74) puts it, 'the idea is that the coach primarily facilitates the construction of solutions rather than trying to understand the aetiology of the problem'. In short, this approach is rather like 'appreciative inquiry' (see Cooperrider et al., 2003) in that it focusses on what works by drawing on the resourcefulness of the client. Questions that emerge include:

- To what extent should coaching interventions be focussed on understanding the roots of client problems?
- To what extent is it legitimate to focus on solutions as opposed to issues and problems?

APPROACHES TO MENTORING

The applications of mentoring are extremely wide and range across all sectors. Megginson et al. (2006) provide an insight into the wide range of applications and features in 18 organizational case studies and nine accounts of individual relationships. The applications include:

- Mentoring young offenders and supporting victims of domestic abuse.
- Mentoring in schools and for entry into the NHS.
- Teacher development and mentoring women into science, engineering and technology roles.
- Mentoring in higher education.
- Diversity mentoring at British Telecom and for the disadvantaged in the South African mining industry.
- Mentoring with engineering firms and e-mentoring for small businesses.
- Executive mentoring within the service sector and leadership mentoring in Denmark.
- Mentoring for manufacturing managers in Australia and within financial services in UK and Switzerland.

Megginson et al. (2006) argue that mentoring has a large variety of applications in many sectors. However, this variation of application does not seem to have translated into as many distinct forms of mentoring, compared with that of coaching. As suggested in Chapter 1, mentoring, perhaps due to its holistic, educational and voluntary roots, does not have quite the same propensity for commodification as does coaching. However, we do believe that publicly funded mentoring, in particular, is moving towards commodification linked to target and measurement agenda promoted by the UK Government. As a result, approaches to mentoring tend to be differentiated by mode and by the sector in which it is applied (sectorial application is explored more in Chapter 4). However, like coaching, mentoring does seem to have some generic themes, albeit fewer.

Executive Mentoring

Rather like executive coaching, this application of mentoring has its roots in traditional mentoring and is typically focussed on developing so called 'high fliers'. However, rather than being exclusively goal focussed it enables the mentee (the executive) to identify the purpose and focus of the development. This type of mentoring is commonly linked to talent management programmes and leadership development.

Diversity Mentoring

Diversity mentoring (see Chapter 12) is a common application of mentoring, aimed not just at redressing perceived inequalities in the workplace but also at recognizing and valuing difference.

Mentoring in Education

Several foci exist here. One strand is about the educator's development. This commonly includes a more experienced teacher who mentors someone less experienced. Another strand is about developing mentoring skills in and between school/college/university learners. A further strand focusses on pastoral relationships between staff and learners and sometimes between peers in schools (see below). There is also a strand of professional mentors in secondary education called learning mentors. These people are employed in schools to work with children with special abilities, behavioural or learning problems. Managers from local businesses may also be part of a voluntary mentoring programme in schools.

Voluntary-sector Mentoring

Sometimes known as befriending or buddying, this sort of mentoring is often undertaken to help vulnerable members of society, for example ex-offenders or young drug takers.

We explore each of these further in subsequent chapters; however, it is important to examine the different modes which permeate the mentoring discourse as these have important implications for both mentoring and coaching.

MODES OF MENTORING

Traditional Dyadic Mentoring

As we have argued earlier (Chapter 1), the mentoring discourse can be traced back many hundreds of years. However, as Colley (2003: 32) argues, the work of Daniel Levinson and colleagues was one of the first to develop a 'classical model of mentoring'. Levinson's (1978) longitudinal study of 40 men as they develop through different stages of their life strongly influenced the traditional view of mentoring. The following passage from Levinson (1978: 98–9) illustrates this:

> The true mentor, in the meaning intended here, serves as an analogue in adulthood of the 'good enough' parent for the child. He fosters the young adult's development by believing in him, sharing the youthful Dream and giving it his blessing, helping to define the newly emerging self in its newly discovered world, and creating a space in which the young man can work on a reasonably satisfactory life structure that contains the Dream.

Whilst Levinson was at pains to point out that the mentoring relationship was not a parental one, it is nevertheless easy to see, based on this view, why the term protégé has been popular in the US mentoring literature (see Chapter 4). The mentoring relationship, in Levinson's view, is a close, sometimes stormy one which enables the 'protégé' to move more quickly through periods of personal transition. Sheehy's (1996) work resonates with this. Her original work 'Passages', first published in 1974, covered female development in the same way as Levinson's work on men. She updated this work in 1996 in light of the changing social patterns of women's lives and this work is now in its second edition (Sheehy, 2006). The 1996 edition, called 'New Passages', explored the development of both men and women. Like Levinson, Sheehy's research seems to indicate that the traditional notion of being mentored by someone more experienced or older is an important developmental factor for both parties. Bob Bookman, one of Sheehy's subjects, described as being 'comfortable in his own skin', drew his development from being mentored by a more successful agent in his industry and from mentoring younger people in his own organization (Sheehy, 1996: 86). As with coaching, certain questions arise about mentoring based on this view:

- To what extent is mentoring needed in order to make effective life transitions?
- How important is age/experience asymmetry in mentoring?

Peer Mentoring

Clawson (1996: 11) makes a strong case for peer mentoring as summarized in the following quote:

> In a context of rapid technological change and shifting organizational structures with confusing family and personal anchor points, there is no reason to assume that people of roughly the same age and experience could not engage in mentoring activities, especially if the natural competitiveness of the bureaucratic pyramid is replaced with an encouraging teamwork in the process oriented firm.

In other words, if we accept the rhetoric of rapid change (see Chapter 7), then peer mentoring is likely to become a more prevalent mode of learning. This echoes the earlier contributions of Kathy Kram (Kram, 1980; Kram and Isabella, 1985). In the later of the two, Kram and Isabella (1985: 118) argued that peer-mentoring relationships are distinct from traditional mentoring relationships in that they 'offer a degree of mutuality that enables both individuals to experience being the giver and receiver of these functions'. Hence, peer mentoring, in their study, seems congruent with Clawson's (1996) view of teamwork. This 'mutuality' does imply some overlap with the term 'co-mentoring' (see below). Therefore, it is important to be clear about what this mutuality/reciprocity entails.

In Kram and Isabella's (1985) study, the boundaries between who is mentor and who is mentee do not seem to be strongly drawn. Indeed, their term 'special peer' is explicitly referred to as being the equivalent of a best friend, with wide personal and professional topics being 'on the table'. However, other studies seem to see peer mentoring as being less 'mutual'. For example, Fine and Pullins (1998: 89) study of salespeople is very clear: 'Peer mentoring occurs when a more experienced salesperson (the mentor) takes responsibility for the development and guidance of a less experienced salesperson (the protégé).' Whilst they do refer to mutual support, the discussion of results makes it clear that there is one 'giver' – the mentor – and one 'receiver' – the mentee. Similarly, Fox and Stevenson's (2006) work in the UK higher-education sector makes it clear that although the final-year students (the mentors) in the study did make gains in confidence, experience and awareness, the success of the scheme was still judged in terms of the academic performance of the first-year students (the mentees).

Peer mentoring is increasingly common in UK schools. Here, the form is often an older pupil mentoring a younger pupil but Garvey and Langridge (2006: 46), in quoting users, offer a range of meanings:

> It helps young people understand the demands and expectations put on them when they start a new school, through to taking public examinations and everything in between. (Peer mentoring co-ordinator)
>
> It's about pupils supporting pupils. (Head teacher)
>
> Peer mentoring is when you work with someone in your own year group or below and build a relationship of trust and respect. (Year 10 mentor)

This raises the following questions:

- How important is it for successful mentoring that participants can relate to each other as peers?
- To what extent is mentoring a two-way process?

Co-mentoring

Co-mentoring is a way of formalizing the mutuality within a mentoring relationship. It implies that both parties in the relationship are learning and that they are equal partners. However, as Kochan and Trimble's (2000) study of their own mentoring relationship highlights, there can be different understandings of how that mutuality presents itself. For example, the following passage (p. 24) from their account demonstrates this:

> Boundaries and roles began to shift. Our relationship transcended the hierarchical mentor/mentee roles and entered into a co-mentoring relationship. Fran began to view the

relationship as one which she was also learning. Often she would ask Susan for her perceptions as a teacher and use their sessions together to talk about issues important to her and her school.

What is not completely clear from their study is how often and how much Fran (initially the mentor) was helped by Susan. As suggested above, peer mentoring and co-mentoring can often become blurred as both people in the relationship become more comfortable with disclosure. Sometimes, as with Kochan and Trimble (2000: 24), the relationship can move to one that has friendship as an important part. Indeed they talk of 'acting like friends, sharing personal hopes and frustrations, and talking about family issues'. This also appears to be similar with a case from Megginson et al. (2006: 190–5) featuring the long-term relationship – over 20 years – between two senior public-sector managers. As with Kochan and Trimble (2000), the two managers – Allen and Hinchliffe – acknowledge the mutuality of their relationship as well as the importance of friendship within it. However, what is still not completely clear (perhaps because it is not formalized and structured) is how that manifests itself within mentoring conversations.

From our own experience, one of us (Megginson) is in a more structured mentoring relationship where each person takes it in turns to be mentored by the other. The advantage of this more bounded use of co-mentoring means that time is divided equally between the two parties to ensure parity of benefit. On the other hand, the more fluid version of co-mentoring allows mutual exploration of interesting issues in which both parties are helped at the same time. Again, this raises some interesting questions about mentoring:

- To what extent should mentoring be mutually beneficial to both mentor and mentee?
- What role does friendship play in mentoring?

E-mentoring

Using information technology and other media for mentoring conversations has become increasingly popular. Megginson et al. (2006: 64–7) features three research-based case studies of e-mentoring. In his account of the east of England e-mentoring pilot, Colin Hawkes (in Megginson et al., 2006: 67) identifies several benefits of e-mentoring as a mode of mentoring:

- It is less time consuming in terms of time off work and travel for mentors.
- It is easily accessible via the internet.
- It can help to equalize the power difference between mentor and mentee.
- It removes first impression prejudice.
- It gives more time for reflection and learning.

The findings from an evaluation study of e-mentoring in Megginson et al. (2006: 134–41) supports some of these findings. However, also in Megginson et al. (2006: 216–19), e-mentoring does have its challenges in terms of its richness which is well summarized in the following extract (p. 218):

Virtual mentoring inevitably does not offer the wide range of communication and information that is available in face to face mentoring, depending as it does pretty much solely on the written word. I think this lack of opportunity to observe the mentor in action, 'read' his non-verbal messages (and he mine) and sense and hear complex intonation in the communication has affected the potential richness of the mentoring relationship.

Furthermore, studies on e-mentoring such as that of O'Neill and Harris (2004) have raised some questions about the development of mentoring skills on the part of both mentors and mentees in an e-mentoring relationship. They strongly suggest that participants need time to grow into these new conventions in order to ensure their effectiveness.

Again, this suggests some important challenges for all modes of mentoring:

- What are the advantages and disadvantages of face-to-face mentoring?
- What are the key factors which influence the effectiveness and strength of a mentoring relationship?

CONCLUSIONS

The primary purpose of this chapter was to recognize and acknowledge the variety of approaches to mentoring and coaching. In particular, the intention was to use selected literature as a way of representing approaches to coaching and mentoring, rather than exploring the structures of specific models or processes like the GROW model (Downey, 2003) or the three-stage process (Alred et al., 2006). This generates a number of questions that inform our exploration of coaching and mentoring in theory and practice (see below) and they have been refined to reflect the fact that each domain examined has something to contribute to this exploration. The questions are also phrased to recognize that it is important to ask them whether the label we are using is coaching or mentoring. In this sense, they may be seen as research questions that drive exploration.

Future Directions

Looking at the range of coaching and mentoring models is likely to raise more questions than it answers due to the breadth and diversity of applications. However, our experience of working with and analysing these models is that each new perspective adds a different angle but to a body of discourse which has more linkages and commonalties than differences. Our prediction is that there will initially be more models and perspectives to swell the existing ranks but that researchers will increasingly look for ways to integrate and build on the work of others. This is already happening with an increasing blurring between coaching and mentoring but we predict that, particularly within coaching, the multitude of approaches is likely to coalesce into a smaller number of broad approaches which will better represent the choices of approach that the coach/mentor has, including the possibility of an eclectic mix of models and perspectives.

QUESTIONS

What is the appropriate balance between structured mentoring/coaching activity and individual coachee agency?

To what extent should the context of the mentoring/coaching relationship influence the nature of the relationship between coach and coachee?

What processes best enable goal attainment? Is goal attainment, as opposed to self-knowledge, the primary purpose of coaching and mentoring?

What behavioural changes do we hope/expect to see in coachees/mentees and coaches/mentors?

What are the ultimate individual/organization outcomes that we hope/expect to see as a result of coaching and mentoring?

What is the relationship between behavioural changes (proximal outcomes) and the ultimate outcomes of coaching and mentoring (distal outcomes)? How might we understand and measure all of these things?

Are coaching and mentoring primarily one-to-one developmental dialogue or can mentoring and coaching take place one-to-many?

To what extent should coaching and mentoring be based on direct observation of performance by the coach/mentor?

To what extent should coaching interventions be focussed on understanding the roots of client problems?

To what extent is it legitimate to focus on solutions as opposed to issues and problems?

To what extent is mentoring and coaching needed in order to make effective life transitions?

How important is age/experience asymmetry in mentoring and coaching?

How important is it for successful coaching and mentoring that participants can relate to each other as peers?

To what extent is coaching and mentoring a two-way process? To what extent should coaching/mentoring be mutually beneficial to both mentor/coach and mentee/coachee?

What role does/should friendship play in coaching and mentoring?

What are the advantages and disadvantages of face-to-face mentoring?

What are the key factors which influence the effectiveness and strength of a mentoring relationship?

CONVERSATIONAL LEARNING

CHAPTER OVERVIEW

The chapter is about the power of one-to-one developmental dialogue. It explores the influence of the social context of learning and discusses as well as compares the 'linear' view of learning with the 'non-linear' view. We look at the non-linear nature of coaching and mentoring conversations and present and analyse a transcript of a live learning conversation. There are links in this chapter to the opposing views taken in research philosophy, mindset and gaze presented in Chapters 1, 2 and 4, showing how these viewpoints influence thinking and behaviour in practice.

INTRODUCTION

Within the wider business community there is a dominant rhetoric that change is just about the only constant in the twenty-first century developed world (Garvey and Williamson, 2002). This rhetoric has extended in recent times to suggest that the pace of change in organizational life, which is influenced by technological innovation, competitive pressures and political initiatives, has accelerated. Such is the dominance of this discourse that the implications of this fast-changing and competitive climate for people in organizations of all types and in all sectors are believed to be considerable. These implications have migrated into organizational policies for recruitment and selection, learning and development and health and safety. They manifest in learning and development and recruitment policies written with the assumption that the organization needs people who are able to:

- Adapt to change rapidly
- Be innovative and creative
- Be flexible
- Learn quickly and apply their knowledge to a range of situations

- Maintain good mental and physical health
- Work collaboratively.

In this climate, where the pressure to perform is increased, it is also crucial for employees to have 'strong and stable personalities' (Kessels, 1996a) and to be able to 'tolerate complexity' (Garvey and Alred, 2001). It is a very challenging list with elements not found in the competency frameworks so commonly promulgated by organizations! The notion of meaningful learning conversations holds a response to this climate and enables people to understand and appreciate the meaning of change for themselves.

METHODOLOGY

This chapter is adapted and extended from the publication which first appeared as Alred, G., Garvey, B., Smith, R.D. (1998) 'Pas de deux – learning in conversations', *Career Development International*, 3(7): 308–14. Here, we draw on some selected literature on learning and development philosophies, the importance of narratives and the social context in human development. We then present a transcript of a live learning conversation and analyse it using Megginson and Clutterbuck's (2005a: 32–6) concept of 'the levels of dialogue'.

RATIONALITY AND LEARNING

In association with the rhetoric of change, there has been a growing tendency in both the public and private sectors towards 'objectivity' in all work activities. Newtonian scientific method applied to organizational life has become a dominant preoccupation of managers (see Chapters 2 and 4). The exponential growth in performance league tables for organizations and performance objectives for individuals provides evidence of this (see Caulkin, 2006b).

As with the strong move towards the accurate, rational measurement of the performance of individuals and organizations, there is also a change in our understanding of the nature of rationality itself. The view of the kinds of thinking available to us is changing. 'Society is more rational, but it is a rationality of a limited kind' (Barnett, 1994: 37). It is sometimes argued (Habermas, 1974) that the most widespread current models of learning presuppose the impersonal, 'technical' mode of rationality. This mode of thinking aims to establish systematic bodies of generalized knowledge or explicit rules and procedures. It sets out to specify objectives and learning outcomes so that it becomes possible to judge success in teaching and learning if these outcomes or objectives are met. This approach lies behind current competence-based learning, referred to earlier in this chapter, which dominates the learning and development agenda in many organizations. This technical mindset towards learning is often accompanied by the strong inclination to think of learning as a linear activity (Bernstein, 1971; Habermas, 1974; Barnett, 1994). We have become so used to this that we no longer notice it, nor how it is only one, and perhaps not a very good, way of talking and thinking about learning. This view implies that, as we learn, we move along a straight line or that the learner moves up a kind of road or staircase. We may even be able to be hurried along this road or up the staircase or we talk of 'fast tracking' people. This may seem very logical for if we know the precise route that people take then (we might imagine) the most helpful thing we can do is accelerate their journey and get them to their destination as quickly as possible. Of course, we often do make progress in this way, such as passing a driving test, learning a new language, successfully filling a new role, but 'moving forward' is only part of the story.

The merits of this approach (in the context of a competitive climate) include the enhanced possibilities of accountability, quality control and the belief that we are accelerating the learning process. Despite criticism that concentration on outcomes is unduly technicist in approach, emphasis on outcomes does not preclude attention to process and relational aspects of learning (Jessup, 1991). However, the 'hegemony of technique' (Habermas, 1974) can only engineer what has been pre-specified (Bernstein, 1971). In other words, it gets us to where we want to go by the straightest and most direct route but it cannot develop our awareness of the different kinds of destination available, the speed of travel or the choice of route nor does it hold out any promise that in travelling we will be enriched. Consequently, this technical mode of rationality cannot be adequate to develop the learner in the fast-changing environment where he or she needs to be pre-eminently capable of collaborative working, flexibility, innovation, creativity and improvisation. It may actually be counter-productive as it has been argued that 'genuinely interactive and collaborative forms of reasoning' (Barnett, 1994: 37) or social learning are in danger of being driven out by technical or 'strategic' reasoning and individualism. This is one aspect of the way interpersonal relationships may weaken during times of rapid social change (Toffler, 1970).

There may be a way forward from the domination of the technical mindset. Garvey (1994c) has noted that despite the pressure for improved performance, linear and controlled learning there is also a strong desire for people in the workplace to reach out for the more human aspects of life. People seem to want to develop stronger and more supportive relationships at work to enable them to learn *by*, *from* and *with* one another to develop their knowledge and skills, enhance their performance and to assist them to progress their chosen careers. Clearly, mentoring and coaching can be associated with this dynamic and are another way of interacting and learning. It is no surprise that coaching and mentoring activity is growing right across all sectors of society. This desire for support and for improved human relationships among people at work fits well with Erikson's (1995) concept of 'generativity'. According to Erikson, if we are not 'generative' we can stagnate but by engaging with others in social interaction and dialogue and by developing others as well as being learners ourselves we may satisfy the 'generative' motive and avoid stagnation.

THE POWER OF STORIES

Another way of developing collaborative learning is through engaging in stories. The relationship between 'story' and learning is well established (Geertz, 1974; Daloz, 1986; Bruner, 1990). The main vehicle for 'story' is metaphor and it is through understanding the myths and symbolic representation of realities in a metaphor that a person may extract meaning (Morgan, 1986). While this can provide a positive vehicle for learning it may also be at the heart of conflicts between people. The differences between the protagonists may not be in their knowledge but in their understanding of the 'meaning' of the story, its language, metaphors and symbols. As raised in Chapter 1, Bruner (1990: 32) explores the importance of meaning and suggests that this is important to the practice of human psychology: 'Psychology...deals only in objective truths and eschews cultural criticism. But even scientific psychology will fare better when it recognizes that its truths about the human condition are relative to the point of view that it takes toward that condition.'

Bruner's (1990: 33) view is based on two points. First, it is important to understand how the individual's experiences and actions are shaped by his or her 'intentional states'. Second, the form that these 'intentional states' take is realized through the 'participation in the symbolic systems of the culture'. It is Bruner's belief that the interaction with the patterns inherent in the culture's 'language and discourse modes, the forms of logical and narrative explication, and the patterns of mutually dependent communal life' which shapes behaviour and attitudes. Consequently, we are not isolated individuals, nor are we rootless in response only to the present. On the contrary, we take meaning from our historical pasts which gave shape to our culture and we distribute this meaning through dialogue. It is Bruner's belief that 'meaning' is both individually and culturally constructed. So 'meanings' will inevitably vary and may be interpreted in the context of both the individual's 'intentional state' and the cultural frameworks from which he or she draws.

Coaching and mentoring conversations are one vehicle for such 'meaningful' dialogue and here, in our view, is the potential power of learning conversations to lead, shape and build changing attitudes, behaviours and performance in the workplace. We enact work through the story and an organization is only as good as its narrative allows it to be. This implies that there may be 'good' stories which help to shape a 'good' view of an organization but also 'bad' stories can equally become embedded as cultural norms. Bruner (1990: 97) suggests that a culture may be in conflict with itself and 'our sense of the normative is nourished in narrative, but so is our sense of breach and exception. Stories make reality a mitigated reality'. According to Bruner (1990: 97), conflict then is a product of:

1. Deep disagreement about what constitutes...ordinary...life.
2. When there is rhetorical overspecialization of narrative, when stories become ideological or self-servingly motivated that distrust displaces interpretation, and 'what happened' is discounted as fabrication.
3. Breakdown that results from sheer impoverishment of narrative resources.

The value of exploring story through conversation is in addressing these issues and in the ability of the conversationalists to develop new and alternative meanings so that a fuller picture is developed thus giving more choice of action. A conversation with a mentee or coachee may reveal that he or she 'knows this story already'. He or she is not encountering anything new, but may be helped to revisit and find new insights, understandings and meanings in old truths, such as the importance of team-building, or of maintaining distance *from* and perspective *on* work. With these topics we seem to be dealing with basic and apparently simple ideas, but in reality they are so complex, so deceptive in their simplicity, yet so important, that they have to be approached again and again from different angles.

The conversation can play a major part in learning for, as Bruner (1985: 23) says, 'language is a way of sorting out one's thoughts about things'. Discussion can help the learner to re-frame an idea, think new thoughts or build from old ones (Garvey and Williamson, 2002). The educational psychologist Vygotsky (1978) would agree because he viewed dialogic learning as a 'higher mental function'. This is because the engagement in ideas through dialogue externalizes the idea in a social context and enables new perspectives to emerge. These perspectives are then internalized and integrated into the individual's mental frameworks and functions.

THE SOCIAL CONTEXT

It is clear then that learning is also contextual and that the organizational context can influence the ability of those working within it to function (see Chapter 8). The notion of 'environments' put forward by Vygotsky (1978: 86) as the 'zone of proximal development' plays an important role in the learning process. He described this as 'the distance between the actual development level as determined by independent problem solving and the level of potential development as determined through problem solving...in collaboration with more capable peers'. The implication here is that a greater potential for enhanced understanding and learning is unlocked if there is guidance or collaboration through dialogue.

These notions have major implications for coaching and mentoring conversations and for how we organize for learning in the workplace. The influence and power of the social context in the learning process is not in doubt. As Bruner states (1985: 25), 'passing on knowledge is like passing on language – his [Vygotsky's] basic belief that social transaction is the fundamental vehicle of education and not, so to speak, solo performance'.

Lave and Wenger (1991) developed the idea of learning as a social activity within a social context in their notions of 'communities of practice' and 'legitimate peripheral participation'. Vygotsky saw learning as a holistic, continuous process which should be pursued until the issues are resolved or, in Kolb's (1984) or Jarvis's (1992) terms, with full consideration of the models of experiential learning. In Vygotskian terms, this means a 'unity of perception, speech and action, which ultimately produces internalization' (Vygotsky, 1978: 26). So, mentoring and coaching conversations have the potential to develop great insight, new thoughts and enhanced meaning within the social context of the discussing pair and at the same time, the social context of the organization.

NON-LINEAR CONVERSATION

Non-linear learning and meaningful conversation are natural bedfellows. However, conversations take place in any number of situations, and while all share a common factor of involving at least two people talking, they may in fact serve a variety of purposes, of which non-linear learning is only one. For example, many of us have fallen into conversation with a stranger when travelling, both parties being in transit. This can be an occasion for more expansive talk, or less inhibited talk, than when in a familiar context. Unexpected things can emerge: we can be surprised at what we are ready to share with a stranger, and such 'brief encounters' are sometimes remembered with fondness and appreciation (Simmel, 1950). The contrasting situation of talk over a meal among intimates in a domestic setting can be similarly valuable as a space to explore, to touch on matters that really matter, to connect the mundane with the fundamental, in short, to learn in a non-linear way. Any one conversation may serve a number of purposes.

Mentoring and coaching conversations are associated with the development of both the affective and the rational (see Chapter 1). These conversations assist in the development of the human qualities such as trust, openness, honesty and integrity as well as support the notions crucial to workplace learning such as the enhancement of skills, applications from training and understanding through experiential learning (Daloz, 1986; Garvey, 1994c). Coaching and mentoring can bring together those who view learning as a means to an end, such as improved effectiveness and efficiency, and those who emphasize the wider psychosocial (Kram, 1983) contexts in which people are regarded as 'ends in themselves'.

In their book *Techniques for Coaching and Mentoring* Megginson and Clutterbuck (2005a) offer seven levels of dialogue. A conversation in the office, for instance, may be prefaced with some 'social dialogue' aimed at establishing a social connection in a friendly manner. This could lead to 'technical dialogue' where the focus is on clarifying existing levels of knowledge about work policies, procedures and systems. The conversation may develop into a 'tactical' level of dialogue which is aimed at discovering practical ways to deal with the issue in hand. It could become 'strategic' where the purpose is to take a wider perspective and to put the immediate challenges into context. Over time, the dialogue could develop into creating the conditions for 'self-insight' where the learner gains an awareness of his or her hopes, fears, thinking patterns or emotions. Consequently, the insight may develop into 'behavioural dialogue' aimed at bringing together the understanding from the other levels to affect change. The final level of the seven levels of dialogue framework is the 'integrative' where the conversation is likened to a dance as both partners take the lead in turns. Moving from one level to another is not a linear progression but a deep-seated transformation of the nature of the conversation.

CONVERSATION AS A DANCE

In a mentoring or coaching conversation, the learning is often non-linear as the two conversationalists explore and probe ideas and come to conclusions or new viewpoints.

As an illustrative example, here is a transcript from an integrative mentoring conversation. This is put forward to highlight, not so much the content of the conversation but more the process of mentor and mentee talking together and what the mentee learns from it.

The mentee has recently been promoted within his organization. He talks about the nature of the new job, the changing relationship with his line manager and an aspect of his personality. The conversationalists know each other well and they have talked before. Their relationship and shared understanding enable the conversation to be respectful and purposeful. Knowledge is assumed and hence to an observer may appear understated, but both parties recognize its significance as the conversation proceeds. They explore the themes of the conversation, getting closer to new learning, refining understanding and meaning, as they go. There are repetitions, restatements of themes and variations in pace and the balance of support and challenge. The conversation has two distinct sections and hints at a third. The first is an exploration led by the mentor, the second is a refocussing based on a different understanding of the mentee's situation and the third is movement towards action (Alred et al., 2006).

At the outset the mentor mentions that he has observed a slight change of behaviour in the mentee. Normally, the mentee is very open about all aspects of his life. In taking on this new role, it seems to the mentor that he has been uncharacteristically reticent.

Extract from a Live Mentoring Conversation

Mentor: Can I take you back to this week, and the start of your new job. Usually, I know what's happening in your working life, and I usually know what's happening in your personal life, because you're very chatty – you share a lot. But this week, it's a big new beginning and you've said how you would have liked your boss to show some interest. I wonder if you could say a bit more about that. It seems like a quiet start...

Mentee: Yes, a quiet start...um...previously, he's been very supportive, but this week he's been very busy with other things, with another colleague actually. He says you have to manage him *(laughter)*. When I was in charge of the last area, he would leave me to get on with it and I would feed him information from time to time. But this new job is different.
The mentor intuitively senses that there is an issue to be explored. He leads gently.

Mentor: It sounds like there is something you want from him?
The mentee is challenged to move in this direction and brings the conversation onto a well-trodden issue.

Mentee: Er...I think I would like more information...I think there's this other issue which comes up...that he suffers from 'last minute-ism', in time management, and you know what I'm like with time management. You know, if it's not in the diary three months ahead, I find difficulty with it really. For example, there is a very important meeting today that I was just told about on Wednesday. Well, I'm sorry, there's no way I can go to it...*(laughter)*...so there's that issue.
The mentor follows by opening up the issue.

Mentor: That's his style...

Mentee: Yes, yes...worries me a touch...

Mentor: Really? He is somebody you are having to work to...yes...and that's a problem for you...?

Mentee: Yes, generally he's very good, the 'last minuteism', it gets a bit close for comfort, and personally I find that very difficult. I like a more planned future.
The mentor maintains momentum by offering a suggestion.

Mentor: You're usually very upfront with people. Have you thought about going to see him to discuss it?
After some hesitation, the mentee stays in step.

Mentee: I think I should, although...I've not really thought about it...*(pause)*...I think...*(pause)*...yes, I do need to go and see him and say, 'That meeting was important and you knew it was coming up, would it have been possible to have let me know more in advance?' With a lot of things, the administrator has put in place some of these dates and we now have them. And I think he needs to learn some of that...
The mentor now moves the focus from the manager to the mentee/manager relationship.

Mentor: This issue has come more to the fore this year with the shift to your new role as director. It's something to do with the last job being less important than the new one and here you are with a high profile. And it means you've got a different sort of relationship with him.

Mentee: Well, it's bigger business, it's worth a lot of money, in the picture of things, the last job is worth peanuts really, actually, in financial terms, whereas this one is worth a lot of money to the organization.

Mentor: So the stakes are higher?

Mentee: Absolutely.

The mentor holds the line.

Mentor: This relationship with your boss is perhaps more important than it's been before…is it?

The mentee begins to look at things differently.

Mentee: I think it is. (*Pause*) I just wonder, just sometimes, I wonder whether it's *me* that's got the problem with this time management business…um…

Mentor: It's bit of a running joke, isn't it…?

Mentee: It is really. (*Laughter*)

The mentor stays with the theme, leading the conversation and challenging.

Mentor: I have a simple man's diary…(*laughter*)…you…have a different sort of diary…

Mentee: Absolutely…absolutely, (*laughter*)…and you seem to survive all right (*laughter*)…um…

Mentor: So is that another issue…?

The conversation takes a significant turn.

Mentee: I don't know…but I wonder if, personally, it's a bit of an obsession. I think the busier you are the more you need to be organized. My view of time is…(*pause*) fundamentally,….Well…it's a negotiable thing and something around which you have choice…but I don't think everyone sees it like that (*laughter*)…

Mentor: Well…?

Mentee: I don't think he sees it like that. I think he feels he has a right to my time on request.

The mentor seems to feel that this is a significant moment so, rather than probe further, he feels it is time for some consolidation through summary.

Mentor: Interesting, I'm conscious that we've been talking for some time…I wonder if it would be useful for you to summarize…

The mentee, to his surprise, is given responsibility to lead.

Mentee: You want me to do that?

Mentor: You start and I'll chip in…

Mentee: All right…well, I suppose the first thing is the issue of the past, what went on then, but I don't…that's gone now, that was tense but I got out of that responsibility…so in a sense that was quite satisfying. But it wasn't like frying pan to fire, it's a new thing opening up. What I have now in terms of budget well that's a bit nerve racking. And then there's…(*pause*)…then there's the time management issue…um…which is…I'm not sure whether it's my problem or his. Either way, we've got to sort it out. And I think that's probably the key issue. When people are busy you've got to sort out some sort of organization around that.

The mentor takes back the lead and the conversation becomes steps towards action.

Mentor: So when we take this further, we'll pick up these issues. You're in the early, very early stages, the first days of the new responsibility…

Mentee: Yes.

Mentor: And working on the relationship with your line manager is a priority…

Mentee: Yes, I think it is, I think you're right, and I think I shall tackle that…although, I've always got on well with him…

Mentor: Yes.

Mentee: I don't have a problem with that. Because the stakes are a bit higher, the relationship is likely to be a bit closer.

The mentor reflects back the mentee's words.

Mentor: On the other side there's what you've described as being obsessive about time management. Perhaps it will be helpful to explore that more, so that you can get clearer about it, and that may help you with your manager.

Mentee: Yes, because it does create tensions. Last minute things create tensions for me, because my sense of responsibility says I should be doing that, and my sense of time management...which is 'my time and we negotiate' – thinks – I'm not going to be there because I've already made previous arrangements. So that's complicated. Feelings of guilt, I suppose (*laughter*) are around.

The conversation is coming to an end. The mentor ensures they end as a pair, looking ahead to the next conversation.

Mentor: So we've explored what the new responsibility is like and two issues, one to do with your line manager and one more personal. I wonder if that is a suitable place to stop.

Mentee: I think it is. I mean, what's it done for me is draw out this time management issue which...(*pause*)...I think it does have the potential to be significant and it does have to be resolved. Before we started this, I didn't really know where we were going to go. There was a concern there and I think I've clarified what that concern is.

Mentor: Can we agree to pick that up next time?

Mentee: Yes, that will be useful.

CONCLUSIONS

There are at least two stories inherent in this conversation. One story is the mentee's story that planning and organization are important. There is also a fairly sophisticated story about autonomy and independence versus compliance and interdependence between the mentee's manager and the mentee. Both these stories present potential problems for the mentee, the manager and the organization particularly as the financial stakes are quite high and the mentor is working hard to achieve 'self-insight' and 'behavioural change' in the mentee.

This example also serves to illustrate non-linear learning and the conditions that promote it. The conversation starts in a 'social' way and moves through 'tactical', 'technical', and 'strategic' quite quickly. Prompted by his new role, the mentee revisits issues he has addressed before. Time management is a perennial issue and here the idea that it is an 'obsession' is new and this is conversation at a 'self-insight' level. He states explicitly that he didn't know at the outset where the conversation would go but it has been productive, leading to insight, clarification and a commitment to action. Following a linear model, the mentor could have proffered these outcomes himself by giving advice and thus holding the conversation at a 'tactical' or 'technical' level. However, with a complex subject like time management, advice would be inappropriate at this stage. The mentor could have moved the conversation into a 'strategic' level but, instead, he initiated a non-linear conversation. The mentee provided the content and the mentor facilitated a process of criss-crossing the issues, looking at them from different angles, gently prompting the mentee to take risks, such as voicing a criticism of his line manager and admitting to an 'obsession'. In this way 'self-insight' develops. This conversation is also about the culture of the organization. The topic of time management is often influenced by the behaviour and values of those who lead. So, 'last minuteism' is the way the manager behaves and this is at odds with the mentee's behaviour. The 'self-insight' here presents the mentee with choices so that the next level of conversation at future meetings may be within 'behavioural change' but this may take some time to action and establish.

When the mentor asks the mentee to summarize, it is a further challenge to the mentee to lead the process, as well as explore the content. This pushes the conversation to an 'integrative' level. The mentee is learning about specific issues and about the non-linear conversation. He is learning to learn, and what he has learned is of considerable value both to himself in developing Vygotsky's 'higher mental functions' and to his organization in terms of collaborative working and adjustments in behaviour towards others. The conversation is also helping to maintain stable mental health by examining the meaning the mentee attributes to his behaviour and the behaviour of others. The mentee could quite easily become stressed if he fails to understand his manager's behaviour and fails to consider adjustments in his own. There is also potential for misunderstanding in this example leading to potential conflicts as the manager's and the mentee's meanings about time are differently constructed.

The Future

As we move to a future where learning conversations may become common in everyday life and work, there is a challenge to engage not only in learning conversations *that* work, but in learning conversations *at* work. A further challenge is to those who wish to 'manage' others in a changing dynamic in the workplace. The old methods of purposeful planning, systematic arrangement, command and control, status and hierarchy may now no longer be the best approach when learning, knowledge exchange and development are the key business drivers. These values may need to give way to greater autonomy, experimentation, exploration and the genuine facilitation of learning as a process that adds value. This requires space and time for different kinds of conversation and new conditions to enable people to perform to their best. The greater the desire to strictly control the conversation, the less it produces true creativity, freedom of movement and expression – valued attributes in the new business model of the twenty-first century. These are found in organizations that encourage learning through conversation.

QUESTIONS

Are we too shy, inexperienced, constrained, discouraged or lacking in opportunity to have more non-linear conversations in the workplace than we may currently do?

Have we forgotten how to engage in learning conversations?

If managers have conversations with colleagues already, who holds the agenda and what form does the conversation take?

How might we encourage people to have learning conversations?

If we change the way people talk, does this change the culture and have an impact on business performance?

PART II

INFLUENCES ON COACHING AND MENTORING

POWER IN COACHING AND MENTORING

CHAPTER OVERVIEW

In this chapter, we discuss the concept of power in coaching and mentoring. We believe that power is a key concept that permeates through all units of analysis in coaching and mentoring. First, we introduce an established typography of power and then present and critically discuss three established examples where power influences coaching and mentoring. We then draw the themes together and raise some key questions about power in coaching and mentoring.

INTRODUCTION

Throughout the book so far, we have argued that it is important to move beyond a technical-rational approach to coaching and mentoring. We have emphasized the importance of seeing coaching and mentoring schemes as human systems, often operating within larger human systems, i.e. organizations and societies. A key concept that permeates through all units of analysis in coaching and mentoring – the conversation, the relationship, the management triad (e.g. coach, coachee, manager), the organization, and so on – is that of power. This is for two main reasons.

First, power is a central concept in organizations, and therefore in organizational theory. Power is used to explain relationships between people within organizations and organizational structures; it is also used more widely to explain relationships between organizations, societies, countries and regions. Coaching and mentoring relationships are inevitably located within a given context, e.g. organizational schemes, mentoring engagement schemes and therefore power has relevance.

Second, it is often said that 'knowledge is power' (we explore this notion later); coaching and mentoring, whatever their nature, are often intended to enable some sort of exchange of knowledge, wisdom, understanding between their participants, so inevitably power will be involved. Further, coaching and mentoring are often associated with transition, development and growth. Therefore, it is inevitable that, as people grow and develop (often at different rates and times) this will alter the power dynamics between them. It is therefore important to try to understand power and the extent of its impact.

So, what is power?

Jackson and Carter (2000: 76), in their textbook on organizational behaviour, define power as 'the ability to get someone to do something that they do not particularly want to do'. This ability to influence behaviour seems to be a key part of most descriptions of power as a concept (see Bloisi et al., 2007 for a more detailed discussion of the various theories of power in organizational theory).

In our view, coaching and mentoring are essentially voluntary in nature and this value position is rarely explored. Power is often explained by referring to sources or bases of power and one of the best known of these frameworks is French and Raven (1962). They argued that power can be understood as being one of five sorts:

- Reward power – the ability to provide rewards such as promotions, pay rises or developmental projects.
- Coercive power – the ability to withdraw or withhold the rewards mentioned above or to make life difficult or unpleasant for those who do not comply.
- Legitimate power – derived from someone's formal authority or position within an organizational hierarchy.
- Expert power – derived from being perceived to hold knowledge, experience or judgement that others value but do not yet have.
- Referent power – based on personal qualities, i.e. likeability, being respected, charisma.

Clearly, this raises some interesting initial questions. If we take the first two categories of reward power and coercive power:

> What implications does this have for a manager who is trying to coach someone whom they also line manage?
> How honest and open can the subordinate be in a relationship when they know, or perceive, that their coach has the power to influence their career?

Turning to the impact of legitimate power on the matching process:

> Does this mean that all coachees and mentees vie for the most senior person within the scheme because they represent the best chance for career progression?

Moving on to the expert power category:

> What implications does this have for empowering the coachee to aspire to acquire this expertise?
> Do coachee's perception of the value of their coach change as they begin to acquire more knowledge and expertise?

Referent power is also a key issue and relates to issues of dependency:

How likely are you to end coaching and mentoring when the powerful person you are working with makes you dependent on them?

METHODOLOGY

Our approach in this chapter is to use an established typography of power, present some interesting and contrasting case examples and critically discuss these by employing three models that relate to power found in other literature on the topic. In particular, we employ McAuley's (2003) model of transference to help understand some power dynamics within some specific relationships, power in discourse and the concept of power bases. Our overall purpose is to raise key questions.

CASE STUDY: BEECH AND BROCKBANK (1999) ON POWER/KNOWLEDGE AND MENTORING

Perhaps the best way of exploring some of these issues is via a case study. Beech and Brockbank's (1999) article provides an excellent account of how power, knowledge and different understandings of mentoring play within a mentoring scheme in the British National Health Service. From a study of 35 mentoring pairs, they identified four pairs to focus on in their journal article. From these eight open-ended interviews, the researchers identified four main categories of data:

- The relationship and psychosocial functions.
- Management style.
- Power/knowledge.
- Career functions.

With the first pair, they examine a relationship between a line manager and their subordinate. In terms of the power and knowledge issue, we note that the mentor (referred to as Judith) paid relatively little attention to the knowledge transfer aspect of their relationship, preferring to focus on the psychosocial (Kram, 1983) aspect of the relationship. The mentee (known as Hannah), however, placed much more emphasis on knowledge transfer as being an important part of mentoring. Consequently, as the relationship progressed, Hannah's perception of Judith's 'expert power' decreased, as Hannah's own knowledge base grew. Beech and Brockbank (1999) also use transactional analysis (Berne, 1964) to explain Judith's strong need to fulfil a nurturing parent role with Hannah. This contrasts with Hannah's account of the relationship. Hannah rejects the closeness of the relationship. Beech and Brockbank describe this as 'the typical embarrassment of a child who is over-nurtured by an over-involved parent' (p. 13).

In French and Raven's (1962) terms, power does seem to be an issue in this relationship. The power seems to revolve around different understandings of what the mentee wanted and was getting from the relationship in terms of expert power.

Judith's account suggests that she was trying to minimize the effect of her legitimate power within the organization and, indeed, reward power and coercive power do not seem to be a feature of this on-line mentoring relationship. However, this contrasts sharply with the relationship between Juliet and Harry.

In this relationship, Juliet is Harry's line manager but reward power and coercive power are very noticeable in Juliet's account of the relationship. She refers several times to her power to influence Harry's career adversely. Beech and Brockbank (1999: 19) confirm that this is also Harry's perception. Although Harry is conscious of the reward and coercive power displayed by Juliet, he, like Hannah in the previous pair, questions the expert power of his mentor.

Jane and Hazel's relationship (the third pair) seemed to operate from an adult–adult position in Berne's (1964) terms and seemed not to suffer from some of the problems of the other relationships referred to in the study. This may have been because Hazel was not being line managed by Jane at the time when the mentoring study took place, though she had been, prior to that. We note that, although Jane (the mentor) sought to play down her knowledge, that knowledge was nevertheless important to Hazel; again, the 'expert power' seems pertinent here.

In Jackie and Hillary's case (pair four), Jackie had used her legitimate power to promote Hillary within the organization and, in her view, had invested in him. Despite achieving promotion, Hillary did not acknowledge Jackie's contribution to his development. Instead, Hillary started to question Jackie's knowledge and ask if it was of use to him anymore.

Discussion

Clearly, there are a number of patterns in this case study. First, the power dynamics are particularly significant when the mentor has some direct control over the mentee's future in terms of rewards and punishment, i.e. reward and coercive power. Second, power and perceived knowledge do seem to play an important part in determining how 'powerful' a mentee perceives their mentor to be. Of course, it is important to recognize that this may well be a function of the particular study and the individuals involved. However, the findings do seem to resonate with the power model found in McAuley (2003).

McAuley's model (see Figure 7.1) looks at the role of transference and countertransference in mentoring. Transference is a form of projection or enactment of previous relationships. De Vries and Miller (1984: 8) argue that transference happens within a relationship when an individual, often unconsciously, treats that relationship as though it were an important relationship from the past. Phillips (1995: 2) states that transference is the 'unwitting recreation and repetition of earlier family relationships'.

Within mentoring and coaching relationships there is the possibility that the mentee or coachee may project or enact a significant previous relationship with their mentor or coach. Countertransference occurs if the mentor or coach responds to the projection. This could be either positively and supportively or negatively. Either response has the possibility of creating either positive or negative inappropriate behaviour within the mentor.

McAuley (2003: 21) argues that 'the ambivalence in mentoring – the manner in which it is poised between more humane organizational practice but also supports the notion of management – creates a number of tensions'. He goes on to argue that an understanding of transference would help in understanding and perhaps dealing with some of these power tensions.

Figure 7.1 shows ways in which transference issues can have an impact on a mentoring relationship. At the start of the four mentoring relationships in Beech and Brockbank (1999), there is clear evidence that there was positive functional transference on the part of all mentees towards their mentors. They appeared to have respect for their mentor's expertise and process skills. Similarly, there is some evidence (with the probable exception of Juliet) that mentors were exhibiting positive functional transference towards the mentees, in that they were happy to be associated with their development. However, as the relationships deteriorate, we can see evidence of the mentees 'sucking the mentor dry and then complaining about their incompetence' (McAuley, 2003: 14) or dysfunctional negative transference. Furthermore, in Juliet and Harry's relationship, we can see evidence of negative dysfunctional countertransference on the part of Juliet. She seems to demonstrate a destructive tendency towards Harry, the mentee.

What appears to have happened, following Beech and Brockbank's (1999) analysis, is that mentees developed in their understanding and expertise whilst they were working with their mentors. As a result, all mentees reported a perceived reduction in the disparity of knowledge, expertise and understanding between them and their mentor. Their response to this perception was to begin to withdraw from the mentoring relationship and to question the quality of their mentor; in other words, the expert power that had attracted them to the mentor in the first place had, in their eyes, began to diminish. This deliberate withdrawal served to protect them from any psychological damage as the mentoring relationship deteriorated. Unfortunately, this was not the

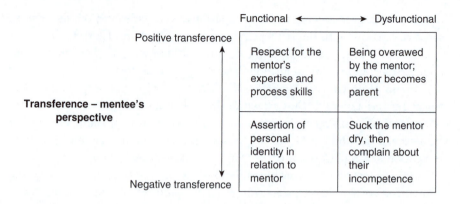

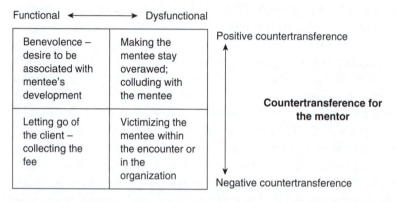

Figure 7.1   Transference and countertransference in the mentor–mentee relationship

Source: McAuley, J. (2003) 'Transference, countertransference and mentoring: the ghost in the process', *British Journal of Guidance and Counselling*, 31(1): 11–23, p. 14. Reprinted by permission of Taylor & Francis Ltd, http: //www.tandf.co.uk/journals

case for the mentors who were left confused and with a sense of unfinished business, for the most part, despite their apparent powerful positions due to their legitimate hierarchical power as well as the reward and coercive power that many of them could have used towards their mentees.

An understanding of the mentoring process itself seems to have been missing among the participants. In particular, there appears to be little awareness of Levinson's (1978) work on adult development. This work highlights age related transition stages in human development. Levinson, probably the first writer in modern times to acknowledge and highlight the contribution of mentoring to adult development, was interested in the question, 'What happens psychologically as we grow older?' He noted that adult development is made up of a series of transitions where our thinking patterns and value systems change (also noted by Jung, 1958; Erikson, 1950, 1995; and Sheehy, 1996) as we grow older and a mentor can assist with these transitions. Had participants been aware of this, it may have prompted them to see their mentoring partner in a different light. For example, mentors might have recognized that it is normal for mentees to want to separate from their mentors at certain stages in their development and this is a helpful thing for them to do. They may have taken steps to: (a) work with the mentee's negative functional transference to encourage the mentee to establish their own expert power in relation to that of the mentor; or (b) worked with their own negative functional counter-transference so as to enable them to let go of their mentee in more deliberate fashion to minimize the damage to them as mentors.

Unfortunately, the lack of this understanding, the power dynamics implicit in hierarchical managerial relationships within organizations, coupled with the power dynamics within mentoring conversations, led to an unsatisfactory outcome for most of those involved in the programme.

CASE STUDY: MENTORING IN THE BIG SIX ACCOUNTING FIRMS

Dirsmith et al.'s (1997) account of mentoring within the so-called Big Six accounting firms (pre-Enron) also provides some insights into how power manifests itself in mentoring. In this study, the researchers undertook 180 interviews in two phases. They found two key mechanisms present in these organizations: management by objectives (MBO) and mentoring.

Mentoring in this context was focussed around career progression as opposed to psychosocial support (Kram, 1983). Dirsmith et al. (1997) argue that mentoring was broadly informal and imply that, at least partly, mentoring became important in these organizations because 'MBO was found to be ostensibly mute on organizational politics' (p. 13). Also, MBO was mainly organizationally driven in its focus and did not really address itself towards individual firm members. MBO was, therefore, perceived as technical and being about 'looking after the numbers'. Mentoring, by contrast, was predominantly a political discourse, aimed at individual firm members. Dirsmith et al. (1997: 15) summarize it as follows: 'Largely off the record and enunciated among trusted people, the mentoring guidance and advice could be highly specific and "gritty", covering the protégé's relations with clients and key partners, the business aspects of the firm, the protégé's appearance and behaviour and the politics of practice.'

However, despite this apparent disparity between MBO and mentoring, Dirsmith et al. (1997) point out that the two discourses were connected. This was because many of those within the firms understood the role of 'a good mentor' to be one of 'looking after the numbers' of their mentee; in other words, defending and interpreting their performance against classic MBO targets: realization rates, client billings, time budget averages, revenue and profit per partner. Those who had mentors that would perform these roles for them were known as being 'on the bus' towards partnership or greater power. A fascinating feature in this study is that mentoring in this context benefits the mentor by enhancing their power base. Again, Dirsmith et al. (1997: 18) summarize this as follows:

> Mentors successfully sponsored protégés through the promotion process found themselves better connected with the new cadre of partners than non-mentors, which stabilised their own social network. Furthermore, practice office managing partners who had served as mentors often proved disproportionately effective in gaining promotions for their office's managers, so much so that they 'exported' many new practice partners to other offices and thus extended and further stabilised their own social networks.

In other words, mentors and their protégés both have a great deal invested in the mentoring relationship.

Discussion

This account, similar to the previous case study, draws our attention to a number of issues that relate to power in coaching and mentoring.

First, it is important to recognize the importance of language. For example, in Dirsmith et al.'s (1997) account, the person being helped to find promotion in the mentoring dyad is referred to as 'the protégé'. If, following the lead of Foucault (1979), we explore the genealogy of that term, the work protégé comes from the French verb *protéger*, which means 'to protect'. In the *Oxford English Dictionary*, protégé is defined as being 'a person under the protection, patronage, tutelage of another'. This definition of the term very much describes the mentoring process within Dirsmith et al.'s study. However, the terms 'mentee' or 'mentoree' do not necessarily carry those associations and these terms are much more common in European writing than the US (for an in-depth discussion of mentoring and coaching in the US see Chapter 14 by Dawn Chandler).

In our view, the terms protégé and mentee, as well as the term 'coachee', imply passivity. They suggest that the person referred to is a passive recipient of the help whereas much of the modern literature emphasize the importance of dialogue and of two-way learning. Downey (2003) tackles this issue by preferring the term 'player'. This is perhaps a link to the sporting roots of coaching.

Megginson, et al. (2005: 131) discuss the use of the term 'client' to describe the learner or mentee in a mentoring scheme in Engineering Co. and states: 'This has confused and misleading meanings. This term implies a customer–provider relationship and seems to be born out of the 'customer-led' concept [in Engineering Co.]. However, whilst the term itself may have been an attempt to alter the existing relationships within Engineering Co., mentoring is not a customer–supplier relationship.'

The word 'client' has become common in the literature on coaching. This positively acknowledges the interaction as being a business one where 'the client' is someone who pays for a service. Whereas the mentoring arrangement described above was voluntary and internal to the organization. The use of the term 'client' does seem to equate coaching and mentoring with other 'professional' services such as lawyers, psychotherapists and accountants for example. However, as Hawkins and Smith (2006) point out, there are a number of different ways of seeing clients. They talk about there being three clients:

- The person in the room.
- The organization or network of which they are a part.
- The purpose of their joint endeavour (serving customers and other stakeholders).

Again, this notion of multiple clients is seen in Dirsmith et al.'s (1997) account with individual mentoring firm members engaging with three clients:

- Their mentees and their development issues.
- The firm, as represented by the MBO discourse.
- Other stakeholders, i.e. senior partners, customers.

All of these different clients have an impact on the power dynamics both within the organization as well as within the mentoring dyad itself. This is also present in the following coaching intervention.

CASE STUDY: THE SUCCESSFUL ADVENTURE OF A DOWNWARDLY MOBILE EXECUTIVE (BLATTNER, 2005)

In this case study, Blattner (2005) presents an account of his own executive coaching work with his client, Terry. Terry is presented as a fairly senior executive who is experiencing some problems with 'lack of professional fulfilment'. In power terms, it is interesting to note the issues Blattner chooses to focus on and chooses to play down or leave out.

Blattner (2005) says very little about himself and why Terry might have chosen to come to him. In fact, all he says is that 'a colleague referred him' (p. 3). At this stage, Blattner gives no indication of who the colleague is or what being 'referred' means. However, in his author's description, Blattner refers to himself as 'a psychologist-consultant-coach with PAS International Ltd'. Upon searching for Blattner on Google, we found that he is listed as an Illinois-based psychologist (http://www.psychologyinfo.com/directory/IL/illinois-directory_15.html). This may or may not indicate a referral from a psychologist – Blattner does not tell us.

His biography is phrased in such a way that is intended to emphasize Blattner's expert power as a consultant, describing him as having '25 years experience as an organizational consultant and executive coach' and being 'highly versed' in doing this sort of work. Organizational consultancy and executive coaching would appear, rather like in Dirsmith et al.'s (1997) study, to involve two different units of analysis – the organization and the executive respectively. However, Blattner (2005) does not engage in any attempt to differentiate the two areas of work; indeed he seems to deliberately conflate them. For example, he says (p. 3) that 'as consultants, we still do not know how the process of coaching actually works' but does raise the question as to why organizational consultants should engage in executive coaching.

The use of language in this article is interesting, particularly when it comes to his description of his own interventions. These are often framed as 'suggestions' from the coach. For example, Blattner (2005) 'suggests' that he and Terry agree to a three-month coaching contract with a view to reviewing it after that. In the second session, he suggests that Terry completes a questionnaire. This appears to be a psychological instrument for assessing Terry against four measures: dominance, influencing, steadiness and compliance. It is only after this is completed that Blattner asks Terry to identify goals for the next three, six and 12 months.

As to the issues not discussed in this article. First, it is not clear why Blattner asks Terry to sign up for three months. Why not two weeks, four sessions or 10 sessions? Second, it is not clear why Blattner has chosen to use a self-reporting psychological instrument to evaluate Terry. Why this one and not another one? Why use one at all? Third, the scores that emerge from the instrument are taken, uncritically, as being representative of Terry's actual behaviour, as is illustrated from the example below (p. 4): 'Also, the scores provided some feedback regarding Terry's behavioural style. Some of the positive findings indicated that Terry was people orientated – building confidence in others; he was service orientated – a dependable team player, and he was cordial and helpful when dealing with new clients or customers.' The discussion in the article omits any evidence from anyone, other than Terry, that this is how others perceive him. Nevertheless, Blattner and Terry then use the data to agree on Terry's goals. The chronology of this process is interesting. Terry agrees to paid coaching for three months, then completes a self-assessment, then agrees the goals. Notwithstanding our questioning of the ubiquity of goals in coaching (see Chapter 10), it is not clear as to the basis on which Terry agrees to pay Blattner for three months. On what basis is Terry making that decision, when, as implied by Blattner, Terry is not clear about what he wants out of the coaching until session three? Furthermore, although Terry is presented as someone with significant legitimate power, he also seems very amenable to Blattner's 'suggestions' as compared with our mentees in the mentoring case studies examined.

As the coaching progresses, we hear about Terry's ups and downs and his frustrations with his new boss and his anxieties about his position. Notice, however, that, despite the fact that Blattner is a self-styled eminent psychologist, there is no examination of transference and countertransference in Blattner's account of the relationship even when it seems to be particularly merited. For example, on p. 10, Blattner recounts how he felt that Terry 'had just wanted me to roll out a formula, give him the answers and that would be that'.

However, Blattner recounts how he 'resisted that approach and responded by repeatedly reframing his questions and asking thoughtful and clarifying questions in return'. It seems reasonable to assume that Blattner was working with Terry's transference, in putting him in the role of expert, which had started to move towards being positively dysfunctional in nature (see Figure 7.1). By being aware of his own potential positive dysfunctional countertransference in wanting to remain being seen as the expert, Blattner appears to have avoided this danger in the service of the client. However, despite Blattner's use of Daniel Goleman's work on emotional intelligence and a demonstrable awareness of important phases in managing the relationship – e.g. on p. 12, he talks about arriving 'at a place to start working on closure for our coaching session' – the account is noticeably bereft of any emotional challenges within the coaching relationship.

Discussion

Blattner's account of this coaching relationship and our previous discussion of language draws our attention to an important aspect of power in coaching and mentoring that we have used several times already, that of 'discourse'. McAuley et al. (2007: 265) describe discourses in the following way: 'Discourses are sets of ideas and practices that condition our ways of relating to and acting upon particular phenonema; a discourse is expressed in all that can be thought, written or said about a particular topic, which by constituting the phenomena in a particular way, influences behaviour.'

If we apply this understanding to writings on coaching and mentoring, we could argue that the 'gaze' or mindset of the writer influences how people coach and mentor. In particular, following Jackson and Carter (2000: 66), a dominant or powerful, legitimated discourse determines 'who can say what, where – and why'.

The arguments made, particularly by postmodernist writers, for example Gutting's (2005) overview of Michel Foucault's work, is that writing about something is inevitably a powerful activity – as the Prophet Mohammad said, 'The ink of the scholar is more powerful than the blood of the martyr'. Referring back to Blattner (2005), we can see how he uses his power as the author of the text to convey certain impressions about coaching. Blattner decides that, despite his training as a psychologist, he has chosen not to use psychological constructs in order to talk about his relationship with Terry. Blattner's (2005: 3) position on his own article is that it 'offer[s] some insights into one process and to create or stimulate ideas for the professional currently engaged in such activity'.

However, an alternative reading of this text is to see it as a sales document. Blattner is presenting himself as writing for 'the professional' and hence associating himself with that professional discourse. Furthermore, he chooses to represent himself as a process expert making suggestions, but, nevertheless, hinting that he has an overall plan for Terry – using the term, phases, presents these developments as milestones along a journey that he has travelled many times before. Consequently, we believe that Blattner wishes to play up Terry's seniority and his desire for development and stretch but seeks to minimize or play down the view that Terry is in an emotional crisis and, in particular, that this is not played out within the relationship with Blattner. Instead, Blattner is using his power as the author of the text to present himself as a senior expert who works with other senior people in an organized way that has good personal outcomes in both personal and professional domains. He seems to distance himself and his work from being therapeutic and moves towards developmental language. And, like all good sales testimonials, he even has the client, Terry's, endorsement at the end! However, the discourses that remain silent or subdued are those of Terry's wife, his boss and his work colleagues – we only ever hear from Blattner or an edited version of Terry's 'voice'.

CONCLUSIONS

In this chapter, we have used three main frameworks: bases of power, transference and discourse analysis to look at the issue of power within coaching and mentoring. We have raised some important issues about coaching and mentoring when seen through the lens of power. To summarize, the power relations between coaches/mentors and their coachees/mentees are influenced by a number of different factors.

First, and most obviously, the impact of line management power relations on coaching and mentoring. As shown by our case studies, this can serve to influence mentee/coachee engagement with the process by either establishing collusion (see Dismith et al., 1997) with the manager in terms of the use of legitimate power to enhance the career progression of the mentee/coachee, or cause withdrawal from the process. Our discussions in Chapters 1, 3, 5 and 6 suggest that trust is a key component of the coaching and mentoring process. Adding the notion of power to the trust condition means that if coachees and mentees feel restricted in their openness with their coaches or mentors, due to managerial or hierarchical relationships, then the process is likely to be limited in the extent to which it can be successful.

Second, and related to the first point, it appears that the line management relationship can often crowd out the psychosocial aspect of mentoring (Kram, 1983) in particular, but can still be helpful for both parties in terms of career progression. However, this appears to be dependent on both parties in the dyad understanding the purpose of the process and their role within it. This was not the case within the NHS case study (Beech and Brockbank, 1999) where a limited understanding of the mentoring process appears to have contributed to psychological damage for the mentors and withdrawal and lack of satisfaction for the mentees.

Third, the statement that 'knowledge is power' appears to hold some water in terms of the evidence considered here. In each of the case studies, the coach or mentor's expert power was a critical feature of the process. Correspondingly, as the asymmetry in terms of knowledge and expertise between, in particular, mentor and mentee begins to reduce, the mentee's perception of the expert power of the mentor begins to diminish. However, how this is handled in the mentoring and coaching dyad is critical to the outcomes.

McAuley's (2003) analysis of transference and countertransference is useful in that it offers us a conceptual framework for understanding and anticipating the various traps and challenges facing us in coaching and mentoring relationships. Indeed, although Blattner (2005) does not use the terms (for reasons we will explore below), there is evidence that he did use these ideas within his coaching intervention with Terry, which seems to have helped Terry develop.

Fourth, all of the analysis above leads us to recognize that, although thinking about individuals having, or possessing power may be a useful analogy, to some extent, power is relational. The work of Foucault (1979) and others (see Gutting, 2005 and McAuley et al., 2007) helps us to recognize that power resides not in individuals but is co-created in the relationships between people. Key components of that co-creation are the various discourses that are created around coaching and mentoring. It is important to recognize, following Jackson and Carter (2000), that the dominant discourses that emerge are inevitably power laden and are concerned with who is able to say what to whom, when and why. In these different case studies, it is easy to see how the writer has certain purposes and agendas, be they academic, financial or a combination of these. One of the advantages of deconstructing discourses and developing a genealogy (as we do in Chapters 1 and 2) of coaching and mentoring is to recognize that it is possible to draw very different and often contradictory conclusions from a piece of writing and much depends on the lens used to view it through.

Finally, we should recognize that we ourselves, as writers of this text, are choosing to privilege certain discourses above others in this book. Because of our mutual background, areas of interest and power-interests in aspects of coaching and mentoring, we cannot hope to escape from the same challenges and criticisms that we have posed to others in this chapter and throughout the entire book. Clearly, we are seeking to influence the dominant discourse of coaching and mentoring and our own status within it as a result of writing it but hopefully in a way that helps others become aware of those challenges and choices as a result.

The Future

We should recognize that, as coaching becomes a more commonplace activity, issues of power, voice and discourse will become more important. Coaching and mentoring can seem attractive because there is the possibility of emancipation from dominant forms of control and oppressive power relationships. However, this does not mean that coaching and mentoring are immune from such power issues – far from it.

International professional bodies, like the European Mentoring and Coaching Council (EMCC) or the International Coaching Federation (ICF), and national bodies like the Mentoring and Befriending Foundation (UK), will increasingly need to work with the power dynamics. For example, at the 2008 EMCC UK conference, there were more than twice as many papers using the term 'coaching' as the term of reference. We conclude from this observation that the current popularity of the term 'coaching' may be crowding out the positive contribution of the mentoring discourse. The impact of this is not yet clear but will increasingly become an issue over time.

QUESTIONS

Who or what is driving what is talked about/discussed in a coaching/mentoring relationship?
What is the impact of these influences?
What might be being denied/avoided in your coaching or mentoring scheme?
Who is being empowered/disempowered in your coaching and mentoring work?

MULTIPLE RELATIONSHIPS

CHAPTER OVERVIEW

Coaching and mentoring conversations are social interactions facilitated in specific contexts for a variety of purposes. This chapter explores the idea of multiple coaching and mentoring relationships and considers this in the context of the knowledge economy and the consequential implications on organizational structures and practices.

INTRODUCTION

It would be difficult to conceive of any economy which was not driven by know-how. According to Garvey and Williamson (2002), all economies are knowledge economies and they always have been. Clearly, many different factors fuel economic progress but it is the development of ideas that enables progress; for example, in agriculture, the seed drill and the tractor, crop rotation methods and contour ploughing, in manufacturing and transport, the steam engine and the internal combustion engine, and in electronics, the valve, the transistor and the microchip. These advances are the products of learning processes facilitated in environments suitable for learning. As discussed in Chapter 6 and as many other writers have suggested (see Rogers, 1969; Habermas, 1974; Vygotsky, 1978; Bruner, 1990 and Lave and Wenger, 1991), learning is a social activity and people learn through, by and with others. Therefore, organizational structures and practices play an important role in creating and developing such environments.

Kessels (2002) argues that a knowledge-productive environment is an essential requirement for a work-based organization to be able to operate in a knowledge economy. Nielson and Eisenbach (2003) support this view, citing Pfeffer (1995), and suggest that 'knowledge is the only meaningful resource in today's economy...people within which that knowledge resides become the primary sources of competitive advantage'.

Clutterbuck (1998) describes a range of one-to-one dialogic partnerships that could contribute to knowledge work. Garvey and Alred (2000) suggest that mentoring activity in the workplace offers potential to develop a knowledge-productive environment. Rosinski (2003: 245) suggests that a coach is a 'knowledge transferer' and Bowerman and Collins (1999) that coaching is a vehicle for knowledge transfer. These views suggest that developing people through coaching and mentoring to support and facilitate others becomes an important consideration for active participation in the knowledge economy.

METHODOLOGY

In this chapter, we critically discuss some literature related to the concept of the knowledge economy, developmental and social networks. The chapter starts with a discussion of changing employment trends. We then go on to look at the notion of multiple coaching and mentoring relationships. Following this, we apply the concepts of complexity and social network theory to the discussion. Finally, we examine a new notion of social organization for learning put forward by Williamson drawn from his unpublished notes on communities of discovery. This chapter raises some key challenges for coaching and mentoring as well as organizational design.

CHANGING EMPLOYMENT TRENDS

Higgins and Kram (2001) note four important changing trends in employment in the US:

- Changing contractual arrangements.
- Technological change.
- Changing organizational structures.
- Increasing diversity.

Changing Contractual Arrangements

These relate specifically to the changing nature of the psychological contract, influenced by:

- An increasingly competitive environment.
- A strong trend towards outsourcing.
- Increasing organizational restructuring.
- Globalization.

Technological Change

Technological change influences career development and links to both the developing notion of 'knowledge workers' and the associated changing requirements of workplace skills. Here, general competency development is giving way to more specific competency development which suggests the creation of more 'expert' environments at work. Garvey and Williamson (2002) also observed this trend towards the 'expert' environment in the workplace.

Changing Organizational Structures

Organizations are tending towards changing structures to facilitate:

- Faster action.
- Flatter hierarchies.
- Flexible working.

Higgins and Kram (2001) noted that these changes in the US provide both threats and opportunities to employees. As stated in Chapter 6, in this climate, where the pressure to perform is increased, it is also crucial for employees to have 'strong and stable personalities' (Kessels, 1996a) and to be able to 'tolerate complexity' (Garvey and Alred, 2001). The opportunities offered may be for a new, personalized approach to learning and development as new networks and relationships open up in the new environment.

Increasing Diversity

Higgins and Kram (2001) point to the increasing diversity of organizational membership. They cite Thomas and Gabarro's (1999) work on black and white managers and show that successful black executives develop strong multiple developmental relationships drawn from multiple sources both inside and outside the workplace in preference to a single mentor. Krackhardt (1992) argued that strong links to others in a network are important for building trust and are shown to be particularly helpful in uncertain and insecure times (Krackhardt and Stern, 1988).

These trends outlined above are also observed and supported in the UK through the CIPD's paper 'Managing change: the role of the psychological contract' (2005) (http://www.cipd.co.uk accessed 17/07/07).

We believe that coaching and mentoring activity offers a positive contribution in these circumstances outlined above but there are some changes in the way coaching and mentoring is conceptualized.

Multiple Developmental Relationships in Coaching

In preparing this chapter, it became clear that the material available on multiple relationships in the area of coaching and mentoring is limited. Some of the developmental network and social network writings link their ideas to mentoring but very little links to coaching. We suggest that there are three main reasons for this.

First, as observed throughout this book, the coaching literature is fairly new and under-developed.

Second, the rise in interest in coaching (in the UK at least) is mainly linked to external coaches. The CIPD's learning and development survey (2007) shows that 64 per cent of voluntary-sector and 88 per cent of private-sector businesses offer external coaching to executives. This is set against 65 per cent of respondents claiming that only a minority of them train their managers to coach and only seven per cent completely agree that coaching is part of a line manager's job. This demonstrates the bias towards the use of external coaches on an individual basis and much of the published material focusses on one-to-one external coaching relationships. A further implication is that within an organization, if the focus is on external coaching, the opportunities for creating developmental networks reduce.

Third, where coaching is an internal organizational process, it is most often associated with performance improvement (CIPD, 2007) rather than specifically learning and development. Although performance can be associated with learning, performance coaching by managers on their staff raises agenda ownership issues. Within the context of the knowledge economy abilities such as 'time management, relationships, communication skills and sharing what you know, problem solving, creativity, emotions, metacognitive skills and a capacity to reflect upon behaviour and experience' (Alred and Garvey, 2000: 262) as well as 'flexibility, adaptability, creativity and innovative thinking' (Garvey and Alred, 2001: 526) are generally agreed as the desirable attributes of knowledge workers. In a performance coaching situation, within a line function where the agenda is either shared or with the coach, the main aim of the conversation is often compliance and obedience to organizational or team goals. This 'compliance mindset' does not sit well with the behaviours and attitudes needed in a knowledge worker. As established in Chapter 3, enabling robust and critical thinking is essential if a true learning environment is to become established. Most coaching literature holds the view that the coachee's agenda is paramount or crucial – this is also the case even in some specifically performance-related coaching writing. There is clearly a tension here and McLeod (2003: 166), for example, states, 'I may have to set the scene in the corporate context...Only then will we go to the issue that they have brought to the session.'

One exception is the paper by Bowerman and Collins (1999). In their paper, the main purpose of the coaching network was to develop a knowledge development and sharing environment. In developing this coaching network within Canadian businesses, they note some interesting features:

- An emphasis on cross-functional relationships.
- Individuals to work together on the basis of learning needs.
- Mutuality.
- Skills development for both coaches and performers.
- Linking individual and organizational outcomes.
- Seeking continuous development opportunities through opportunities to apply the newly acquired skills.

The programme was established with an underpinning humanitarian and liberal philosophy which employed Lievegoed's (1993) humanitarian perspective on development, Flores' (1999) on interpretations of language work, Argyris' (1977, 1986) concept of 'undiscussables' and 'skilled incompetences' and Revans'(1983) views on action learning. Within the coaching network, there were multiple definitions of coaching which tended to relate to the learning requirement of both parties. This, we view as normal. All too often organizations are tempted by the lure of simplification that they misunderstand something as complex as coaching and fail to realize its full potential by trying to reduce it to something simple.

In this scheme, seniority was put to one side and relationships could be constituted with the senior person being in the 'performer' role. This status inversion is very difficult to achieve and requires a visionary leadership and a quality of humility on the part of business leaders. (See Chapter 4 for an example of status inversion with the Expert Patient Mentoring Scheme in the UK Health Service and Chapter 7 on the notion of 'expert power'.)

A number of controls were put into the process. These included a time boundary of 20 weeks, formalized reflection sessions and just-in-time skills workshops as appropriate and according to need. Limited evaluation data exists to date and there is no longitudinal aspect to this paper. However, the authors believe in the potential of coaching networks.

MULTIPLE RELATIONSHIPS IN MENTORING

Many recent conceptualizations of mentoring have positioned it as an exclusively one-to-one relationship with those in learning alliances (Levinson, 1978; Clutterbuck, 1992) engaging in the practice of having a single or perhaps, a primary mentor. However, Garvey and Alred (2001), Higgins and Kram (2001), and Burke et al. (1995) suggest that many people, particularly in their workplaces, are in fact part of a 'learning network' with mentoring and coaching being among many other developmental roles. Higgins and Kram suggest that, in the past, we have simply been 'studying different types of mentoring' (2001: 266).

This observation is illuminating, particularly for the points made in other chapters in this book about the similarities and differences found in coaching and mentoring. Higgins and Kram (2001) classify these different types of mentoring as roles performed by the 'mentor' and offer the following typography:

Entrepreneurial – those relationships with high developmental network diversity and high developmental relationship strength.

Opportunistic – those relationships with high developmental network diversity and low developmental relationship strength.

Traditional – those relationships with low developmental network diversity and high developmental relationship strength.

Receptive – those relationships with low developmental network diversity and low developmental relationship strength.

They suggest that these various roles provide 'an important new lens through which to view mentoring at work' (Higgins and Kram, 2001: 264).

Clutterbuck and Megginson (1995: 237) present a model with the learner at the centre emphasizing that the mentor is one of many who can make developmental alliances. The crucial point in both these ideas is for the learner to manage this network.

Burke et al. (1995) throw some light on the importance and impact of interpersonal networks in the workplace. They build upon Kram's (1985) idea of 'relationship constellations' in mentoring and look at a range of 'supportive' relationships for both men and women both inside and outside of the organization. Burke et al. (1995) note that the participants (in the main in middle to senior management positions) in their study found a range of career support both inside and outside the work environment. Those who described their work environments in positive terms indicated:

- Greater career and job satisfaction.
- Better organizational integration.
- Reduced intentions to leave.

Interestingly, they noted that men and women who reported a greater percentage of males in their outside networks also reported greater satisfaction in their career progress. They also noted that those participants with more family dependants reported greater organizational commitment. However, they were unable to find any linkage between the structural nature of their participants' interpersonal networks and a wide variety of work or career outcomes. Their explanations for this finding are as follows:

1. It is unlikely that interpersonal networks affect work and career outcomes.
2. Interpersonal networks may be more significant at earlier stages of a career than later.
3. The effects of interpersonal networks, although present, are modest but may be dependent on other work setting characteristics.

It is our view that point 1 is contrary to other social network research findings (see, for example, Cross and Parker, 2004). Additionally, the participants in the sample were all in early or mid-career and therefore this may explain point 2. However, point 3 relates well to Garvey and Alred's (2001) assertion that the form mentoring takes within an organization may indeed be dependent on the cultural characteristics within that organization.

While offering a helpful perspective, Higgins and Kram's (2001) and Burke et al.'s (1995) work does not illustrate the complexity of either the subject under investigation or the changing dynamic of organizational life as articulated at the start of Higgins and Kram's (2001) work. While the Higgins and Kram (2001) typography of networked mentoring relationships helps provide a framework for discussion, it only provides a limited 'snapshot' in time. Clearly, interpersonal relationships both inside and outside of the workplace are many and varied. Therefore, attempting to isolate variables and consequently draw cause and effect conclusions as well as precise definition are impossible tasks. Rather, it is more appropriate to view Higgins and Kram (2001) and the Burke et al. (1995) research as 'layers' from which we can start to draw a range of meanings about the idea of networks of learning.

A COMPLEXITY-INFORMED PERSPECTIVE

As raised earlier in this chapter, simplification in management has its appeal but social processes like coaching and mentoring are inherently complex. Clifford Geertz (1971) offers us alternative perspective on social systems by suggesting that they are better understood in terms of a 'thick description' (Geertz, 1971). Geertz explained that a rich description is a term for the systematic exploration *of*, an interpretation *of*, and the search for meaning in social action. Consequently, other insights may be gained from a complexity-informed perspective.

We make a distinction between 'complicated' and 'complex'. If we give a kitten a ball of wool to play with, it will make a complicated mess with it! However, it would be possible, given enough time, to unravel the mess. With complexity, on the other hand, it is not possible to unravel the mess. All we can do is attempt to understand small, localized parts and keep exploring to understand how the localized parts interact with other parts. At the same time, as our understanding grows, further complexities appear. Complexity is ongoing and continuous. There is no solution only temporary 'holding positions'.

Garvey and Alred (2001) argue that mentoring activity is complex and the organization in which it is operating is also complex or as Stacey (1995) suggests in a 'bounded state of instability'. Here they suggest that mentoring is analogous to Boolean algebra. Boolean algebra is often modelled using a series on networked, interconnected light bulbs. As the different switches are flicked, the bulbs illuminate in different and unpredictable patterns, some bright and some dull. 'A light bulb in a Boolean array makes a difference because it is part of an open system, it is well connected, responds unambiguously to other light bulbs and sends clear messages' (Garvey and Alred, 2001: 524).

In a human developmental network, the system rests on similar qualities in that a good learner is well connected with an array of strong and weak connections with each participant offering different perspectives, insights, skills and knowledge. The learner draws on this network to further their learning but, in turn, they may help other members of their network to develop and change. There is a natural symbiosis here, rather like the bee visiting flowers gathering pollen for its own survival whilst fertilizing the plant for its continued life.

This is similar to the perspective on mentoring first described in Homer's epic poem *The Odyssey* (see Chapter 1). In the poem, Telemachus, perhaps the first mentee, had several 'mentors' in his network. Some of the relationships in his network were longer term and strong partnerships while others were shorter term and less strong. Some were opportunistic while others were more formalized, almost appointed. Each, however, provided something different and unique to aid his development.

Mullen (2007: 129) noted in relation to student mentoring that members of a developmental network often have multiple and interchangeable roles. She suggested that those who are developmentally aware actively seek to support others as well as seek support for themselves. Another set of layers may be found in Garvey and Alred (2001) when they suggest factors such as power structures (see Chapter 7), organizational culture, management style and the 'dominant logic' of an organization affect the nature and form of mentoring. This may also be the case in the influence of social networks on career progress.

SOCIAL NETWORKS

Cross and Parker (2004), in their work on social networks, conclude that 'well-managed network connectivity is critical to performance, learning and innovation' (2004: 10). Their findings suggested that when activities and decisions are focussed primarily on the boss, or if a team is poorly networked, performance is significantly reduced compared with well-networked and more loosely controlled groups. They also noted that neither the use of technology nor significant individual expertise alone created high performance. Rather, high performers in the petrochemical, pharmaceutical, electronics and consulting industries were consistently part of larger and more diverse personal networks. More importantly, in the context of learning, their research demonstrated that 'whom you know has a significant impact on what you come to know, because relationships are critical for obtaining information, solving

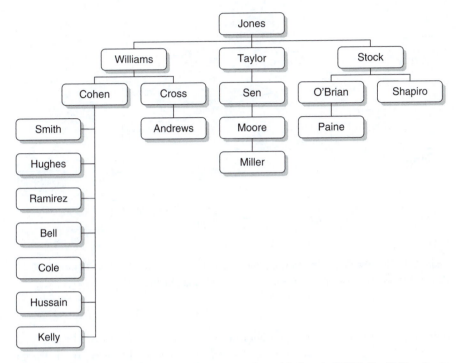

Figure 8.1   Formal structures. Adapted from Cross, R. and Parker, A. (2004) *The Hidden Power of Social Networks*. Harvard Business School Press: Boston. p. 5.

problems, and learning how to do your work' (2004: 11). Furthermore, in no cases explored in their research did they find that the use of technology or a knowledge management system outweighed the significance people placed on their personal network for learning.

Cross and Parker (2004: 5) illustrate a social network by comparing it with an organizational structure chart as shown in Figure 8.1. Using Social Network Analysis, this translates as shown in Figure 8.2, where Cole is clearly the centre of the network and it is likely that through him most of the information flows. If Cole were to leave the organization, a knowledge gap would appear. It is particularly interesting that Jones, the boss, is not networked very well although he is networked with Cole and therefore has access to the key player and his networks. There is a lesson here in that organizational hierarchies do not necessarily present the sources of 'social power' within an organization. Additionally, if this business wanted to bring about change, the key player to work with is Cole. If Cole agrees and accepts the change, then others will as well. This is relevant if, say, a developmental network approach was to be developed in this business.

To illustrate, in a recent discussion with an organization wishing to develop coaching it became clear that there was a fear of uncertainty and difference. The organization in question is large, growing, multinational and

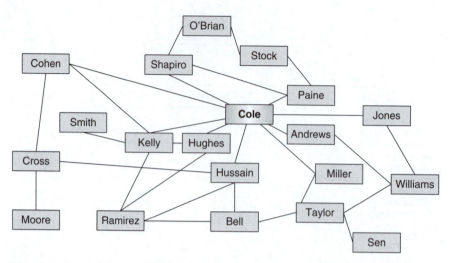

Figure 8.2 Informal networks. Adapted from Cross, R. and Parker, A. (2004) *The Hidden Power of Social Networks*. Harvard Business School Press: Boston. p. 5.

complex. The issues raised by coaching in one country are not the same in another. Management attitudes to coaching are also different in different countries. Therefore, to try and impose a coaching model (with the assumption of one best way) is asking for problems. They anticipated issues of definition, skills, culture, meaning and acceptance. In their uncertainty, the HR managers in this group were seeking simplicity and practical steps – an understandable but not a sensible position. Eventually they agreed to a unifying definition but accepted localized variation in implementation. The definition was not about such platitudes as 'we are all singing from the same hymn sheet' but, rather, diversity and complexity are natural and normal in human systems. Perhaps this statement challenges managers to develop a new level of sophistication in thinking about organizations, particularly in a knowledge economy.

CONCLUSIONS

Bringing all these above ideas together, in the context of a coaching and mentoring developmental network, the layers of complexity may be found in, for example:

- The numbers of people involved
- The network's scope and purpose
- The roles adopted within a developmental network

- The nature of the organization's business
- Cultural considerations including attitudes and values
- The views taken on the purpose of mentoring and coaching
- The ownership of the developmental agenda
- The skills and processes employed.

In practical terms, living with or tolerating complexity is important to organizational progress. The natural desire to control and simplify needs to be moderated in order to allow for difference, disagreement, challenge and openness. Taken together, it seems that extensive social and developmental networks are important to human development and progress, particularly in the context of a knowledge economy. If this is the case, then there are clear challenges for organizational structures, management practices and in the organization of coaching and mentoring.

The concept of the coaching and mentoring culture (outlined in Chapter 3) provides some insight into how to achieve this. Additional help may be found in Lave and Wenger's (1991) 'situated learning' and 'communities of practice'. They refer to learning as a social activity being a form of 'participation'. The consequences of situated learning manifest in relationships with other members of the organization, for example through engagement in the organization's social practices, by contributing to the achievement of the goals and aspirations of the organization, and in the ways in which people relate to their concept of *self* within a social context. The notion of Lave and Wenger's 'community of practice' relates well to the idea of developmental networks where the 'person' of the learner is emphasized. This is similar to the value placed on the learner in mentoring and coaching relationships. A prerequisite of this kind of learning environment is that: 'Learners are engaged both in the contexts of their learning and in the broader social world within which these contexts are produced. Without this engagement there is no learning, but where the proper, wholesome and full engagement is sustained, learning will occur' (Alred and Garvey, 2000: 266).

Cultural, mindset and practices are therefore very important simply because an organization can make it more or less possible by its actions that learning can occur. Traditional hierarchies, simplification of complexity and a 'tell' approach to learning do not lend themselves to a developmental network culture.

The Future

The concept of 'communities of practice' is not without its problems. As first raised in Chapter 3, the tendency for 'defensive and cult-like reactions' in groups is great. Groups often create a power base of those who are 'in' with a desire to keep those who are not 'in' out! Cultures enable this to happen through cultural rituals, language, assumptions, symbolic displays and narratives. A community of practice may have similar tendencies and thus openness to new ideas and creative innovation may become reduced. An alternative concept is a 'community of discovery'.

Community of Discovery

To be creative, innovative and able to change requires new thinking, the discovery of new ideas and new ways of working. The challenge, therefore, is to find the ways forward for people to discover these. Clearly, we cannot learn about things that have not yet been discovered but we can learn about how to make discoveries and encourage learners, enquirers and innovators to experience their learning as discovery. A community of discovery is a philosophical position with practical implications.

The Known World

We thank Bill Williamson and Stuart Martin for introducing us to the concept of communities of discovery. We draw from Bill Williamson's unpublished notes for some of this section.

In a meaningless world, human beings have a strong desire to attribute meaning. Human attempts to do this may help to explain the tendencies to reductionism and simplification, as discussed earlier. Religion, culture, science and the arts also provide a means for people to create meaning.

No one human has the knowledge to understand all there is to know about creation, evolution and the structure of both the material and the social worlds. Consequently, human discoveries have been collective, social achievements. As Sir Isaac Newton observed, 'I have seen further because I stood on the shoulders of giants.' However, we contend that what there is to know or what is potentially knowable is not there already waiting to be discovered. However, it is through a sense of discovery that we will create and transform everything we currently claim to understand. The known world is not something that is just given; it is a world constantly being discovered.

What it means in practice differs from one person to another and these differences amplify across cultures and through different periods of history. Such differences are the subject of comparative history, anthropology and cultural studies. To understand the many ways people have constructed their worlds, we need to discover how to map out the different *ways of knowing* (see Peat, 1995; Pickstone, 2000) from different cultures and societies. We also need to explore those differences to reveal the subtlety and complexity of the interaction between experience and worldviews, social position and ways of knowing, circumstances and beliefs. This task requires us to understand these interactions at different levels:

- Whole culture level.
- Organizations and other groupings within their level.
- Individual level.

Additionally, we need to understand how we come to know how to think within the frameworks of different cultures, social setting and the complexity of work. This involves at least two key questions: How do people learn the fundamental categories of thought that bring coherence to the worldview of their society? How are people able to use these categories as a *grammar of understanding* and interpretation that enables them to live in and to adapt to their world in ways that enable them to bring order and coherence to change and uncertainty?

These issues are central to that domain of inquiry known as the sociology of knowledge where, unfortunately, there has been both a concentration on political and ideological beliefs and a failure to consider how human beings actually assemble meaning in their lives through learning.

Finally, we need to enquire about:

- Where new ideas come from?
- How people come to change their thinking?
- How, through that, their worlds change?

These really would be discoveries!

The Applications of the Concept of Communities of Discovery

These points may seem at first very abstract, but they are, in fact, very practical. If we seek to understand the learning and development needs of any group of people in any organization, we have to find credible answers to the kinds of questions raised above. For example, suppose a company, like the one discussed earlier in this chapter, wanted to develop multi-developmental networks. Using the themes cited above, we can ask the questions:

How do people in an organization perceive and understand coaching and mentoring?
How does coaching and mentoring fit into their *way of knowing* about the world?
What explains the differences in knowledge of coaching and mentoring competency among them?

How far are such differences a product of their previous experience of coaching and mentoring?

How does the prevailing work culture shape attitudes to coaching and mentoring?

How can members of the organization best be helped to think about engaging in coaching and mentoring in their organization?

None of these questions has answers found in a file or provided by a consultant. The answer to each would have to be discovered through analysis, reflection, dialogue and experimentation so that members of the organization can share their views, learn from one another and continue to discover new ways of engaging in coaching and mentoring conversations. Either organizations can be managed in ways that nurture discovery or they can be left just to get on with their work. The difference between the two explains why some companies, projects, institutions and organizations are innovative and successful and why others are not.

Given the competitive pressures of change in the global economy, these are not matters that can be left to chance. The *necessary* conditions of successful innovation include:

- Investment.
- Expertise.
- Leadership and management.
- Diversity of knowledge and experience, culture and background.

These break down into many more discrete qualities and actions including:

- Extensive social and developmental networking.
- The development of appropriate reward systems.
- Product and service development.
- Marketing.
- Benchmarking.

The *sufficient* conditions for success include subtle factors such as:

- A commitment to learn on the part of members of a group.
- Extensive communication and dialogue.
- A diverse culture of excitement about change and ideas.

Above all, there has to be:

- Curiosity and a commitment to and delight in discovery.
- Determination to live in the world of ideas.
- Toleration of complexity, a celebration of success.
- Recognition that not all is controllable.
- A sense of mutuality in the learning process.

When there is a prevailing sense among members in a group of belonging to a community where new ideas are valued and acknowledged, these conditions will be met. We describe such communities as *communities of discovery*.

QUESTIONS

How do people learn the fundamental categories of thought that bring coherence to the worldview of their society?

How are people able to use these categories as a *grammar of understanding* and interpretation that enables them to live in and to adapt to their world in ways that enable them to bring order and coherence to change and uncertainty?

How do people in an organization perceive and understand coaching and mentoring?

How does coaching and mentoring fit into their *way of knowing* about the world?

What explains the differences in knowledge of coaching and mentoring competency among them?

How far are such differences a product of their previous experience of coaching and mentoring?

How does the prevailing work culture shape attitudes to coaching and mentoring?

How can members of the organization best be helped to think about engaging in coaching and mentoring in their organization?

E-DEVELOPMENT

CHAPTER OVERVIEW

Increasingly, we are using electronic media to make social connections between people. As well as the more established conventions of telephones and electronic mail, additional modes of communication are becoming available via electronic means. For example, the use of blogs, chat rooms and other social networking facilities such as My Space and Facebook. All these have recently emerged to complement the use of personal websites. New applications such as Skype, for example, provide alternatives to conventional telephone calls and integrative technologies, such as Blackberries, enable users to link email, text messages and video conferencing together.

In this chapter, we investigate the growing use of electronic media used to make social connections between people. This may include the use of email as well as dedicated coaching or mentoring software designed to facilitate developmental relationships. We take a critical look at the form the developing technologies are taking and consider some practical issues about the impact of these innovations on coaching and mentoring.

INTRODUCTION

As Headlam-Wells et al. (2006: 273) point out in their work on E-mentoring, it is 'a relatively new and under-researched field, particularly from a European perspective'. As a result, the descriptions of E-coaching and E-mentoring are generally confined to talking about the use of email in an asynchronous manner to fulfil many of the functions of coaching and mentoring described thus far in this book. Indeed, our own research in this area (Megginson et al., 2003a, 2003b) is essentially focussed on schemes that used email as the predominant mechanism for the delivery of mentoring. However, given the increase in the variety of media available, we need to make our starting point for E-development a little more inclusive. Initially, we will use the term E-development to refer to any coaching or mentoring process where the main mode of coaching and mentoring uses electronic means to connect people. This includes telementoring, video conferencing, Skype, text, email and other mechanisms that use the internet.

As is the case with many areas in mentoring and coaching, there is much more published research material that has come from the mentoring literature than the coaching literature. Indeed, the literature does not generally recognize the term 'E-coaching'. However, it seems reasonable to argue that many of the advantages and disadvantages of E-development apply equally to coaching initiatives as mentoring ones, particularly as much of discussion and comparison of such processes are between face-to-face interventions (common to both coaching and mentoring) and electronic ones.

METHODOLOGY

In this chapter, we draw on selected research and other findings to identify some of the issues and challenges of E-development. We introduce a taxonomy of E-development to help develop thinking and we present two studies of E-mentoring in order to raise some key questions. We also look ahead to the future and raise some further challenging questions about the future of technology-based coaching and mentoring.

EXPLORING E-DEVELOPMENT RESEARCH

In Megginson et al. (2006), Kate Kennett writes an account of her E-mentoring relationship with David Clutterbuck (pp. 216–19). Kennett draws on this experience and identifies a range of issues for E-mentoring. One issue is as follows: 'all being delivered in *writing*, this process leaves a recorded trail of thoughts to which I can regularly return for further reflection. In this respect, I have found that E-mentoring has a definite advantage over face-to-face contact, for which an excellent memory may be required to recall an accurate account of a conversation' (Megginson et al., 2006: 216–17).

Where transparency and accountability might be required, in, for example, legal work, professional ethics or in work with vulnerable adults or children, the benefit of a record of the content of a conversation can be particularly important. However, Kennett also sets this against the potential loss of richness that a face-to-face developmental conversation may provide:

> Virtual mentoring inevitably does not offer the wide range of communication and information that is available in face-to-face mentoring, depending as it does pretty much solely

on the written word. I think that this lack of opportunity to observe the mentor in action, 'read' his non verbal messages (and he mine), and sense and hear complex intonation in the communication has affected the potential richness of the mentoring relationship. (Megginson et al., 2006: 218)

Kennett is offering a different meaning to the idea of capturing or recording the content of a conversation. Despite the arguable efficiency gains from using email for developmental 'conversations', the processes of summarizing and paraphrasing what the learner says in a face-to-face conversation can be particularly powerful. Karl Weick's (1995) question, 'How do I know what I think until I see what I've said?' seems to resonate strongly with the above point. Email, in particular, is less effective in capturing the richness of a conversation and cannot convey much about the tone of voice or body language. This presents both challenges and opportunities for the coach or mentor who is working with the written word rather than the spoken.

Hamilton and Scandura (2003) offer an opportunity when they argue that not having the social and visual clues can minimize the impact of 'status and social cues' such as gender, ethnicity, age and other interpersonal factors that can influence the learner's perception of the help that they are being given. They suggest that, by removing these features, the mentee is able to focus on the message rather than the messenger. Hamilton and Scandura (2003) also argue that E-mentoring by email can help by making the mentoring more accessible to more people (due to its ability to overcome geographical barriers and asynchronous nature). Because of these advantages, they argue that E-mentoring can increase the available pool of mentors as well as their diversity (which may be crucial in some schemes). In summary, they make the following claim:

A mentor is a guide, role model, counsellor and friend. As long as these functions are being performed, the mentor's organizational location in relation to the protégé is immaterial to the success of the E-mentoring relationship...Whilst research on E-mentoring is just beginning, initial concerns regarding the lack of face-to face interaction and a decrease in the richness of communication may not be as much of an issue as initially assumed. (Hamilton and Scandura, 2003: 400)

We offer a cautious note here. Hamilton and Scandura's (2003) article is not research based (although both are noted researchers). Furthermore, O'Neill and Harris's work (2004) in telementoring in education suggests that, in terms of scheme design and facilitation, the particular demands of a non-face-to-face programme should not be underestimated. They suggest that E-working requires specific skills from the mentors and the organizers of the scheme.

Thus far, we have identified a number of possible advantages and disadvantages of E-development. We will now look at some schemes and interventions in more depth to try to develop a richer picture of the E-development process.

MENTORSBYNET – AN E-MENTORING PROGRAMME FOR SMALL TO MEDIUM ENTERPRISES

Megginson et al. (2003a) is an evaluation of an E-mentoring project for the Small Business Service in the South East of England. The project's aim was to develop and grow the skills, knowledge and confidence of SME owner-managers with a view to helping them succeed. The participants were entrepreneurs or small business managers. The pilot for this project lasted for over three months and was delivered entirely by electronic means. This included the support, a web-enabled on-line tutorial with four modules on mentoring and evaluation.

The research method used for the evaluation involved pre- and post-surveys. These surveys examined factors such as the perceived experience of the programme, programme outcome, satisfaction with contact frequency and satisfaction with on-line training. These measures were similar to a comparable Australian study (abbreviated to APESMA) and this Australian study was used as a benchmark for the UK evaluation. We summarize the key findings below:

- 96 per cent of mentees and 80 per cent of mentors described their E-mentoring experience positively. This compared favourably to the APESMA study where only 82 per cent of mentees described the experience as a positive one, whilst the mentor response was similar to APESMA at 80 per cent.
- 91 per cent of mentees and 84 per cent of mentors indicated that they would participate in a similar programme at some time in the future.
- Over 60 per cent of mentees and over 70 per cent of mentors cited convenience, flexibility and ease as the major benefits of email-based mentoring while 30 per cent of mentee and mentor responses indicated there is an element of impersonality about this type of communication.
- Over 50 per cent of mentees and mentors indicated that they were planning to or thinking about continuing their relationship after the conclusion of the pilot.

Discussion

This scheme touches on several of the emergent themes that we have identified in our opening remarks in this chapter. First, as Hamilton and Scandura (2003) suggest, the experience of being mentored (irrespective of the mode used) seems to have resulted in a positive experience for those involved overall. However, as Kate Kennett (Megginson et al., 2006) suggested, the lack of face-to-face contact was an issue for at least a third of the participants. Other aspects of the feedback were also interesting. For example, there was a significant disparity between what participants expected to receive and what they actually felt they got out of the programme. Prior to mentoring, 95 per cent of mentors had expected to gain some personal development whilst only 54 per cent of them felt that was what they had in fact received in the post-evaluation survey. Similarly, 90 per cent of mentees had expected specific benefits in terms of improved business practices, whereas only 44 per cent of them felt that they had received that.

We have to treat these findings with some caution because the pilot involved only 87 people with a 50 per cent response rate for mentees and 59 per cent for mentors. Also, there is no way of examining whether the participants' own assessment of their development is accurate. Nevertheless, as in face-to-face mentoring and coaching, these findings do draw our attention to the importance of contracting and development processes in terms of setting realistic expectations of what the mentoring can or cannot achieve. Although this was included in the on-line tutorials, this raises some questions about whether it is possible to engage with mentoring skills development without some aspect of experiential learning (see our discussion of coach and mentor development in Chapter 11).

E-MENTORING AT HULL UNIVERSITY

Perhaps the most sophisticated study and analysis of E-development that we have come across was at Hull University in the UK. This is presented in Headlem-Wells et al. (2006). The paper is based on two research programmes. 'Empathy–Edge', one of the programmes, was a study involving 122 volunteers (all women) who were matched into pairs. The participants were mainly drawn from the Yorkshire region of the UK but approximately a third were based in London. It took place over a seven-month period and resulted in 96 per cent of all mentors and 78 per cent of all mentees saying they would take part in future schemes as a result. The scheme is a very interesting one due to a number of features as follows:

- Training was offered in on-line communication techniques.
- A face-to-face meeting was set up for all pairs at a regional briefing seminar.
- Hands on sessions were set up to train participants to use the E-mentoring system.
- E-moderators were introduced to provide a supervision function to participants.
- Photographs of participants were taken at the briefing seminars and uploaded to the site so that each person's picture was available to their partner as they talked on-line.
- The event was officially wound up at the end of seven months.

The E-mentoring system in this study appears to be designed for purpose and transcends a simple email based system. It included features such as instant messaging, public and private discussion areas, and organized on-line meetings, as well as resources such as mentoring guidance, links to other mentoring information and a help desk. However, despite these mechanisms and resources, Headlem-Wells et al. (2006: 378) found that 'a "blended approach" where a variety of communication media was used, was reported at both evaluation points as most frequently adopted'. This suggested that many people had extended their mentoring relationships beyond the boundaries of E-mentoring, although there was strong evidence that the site was widely used.

Discussion

If we compare the Hull programme with the MentorsByNet programme there are several differences. Within the Hull programme, the scheme organizers clearly recognized that there are some advantages and disadvantages to E-mentoring. They used a mixture of approaches, recognizing that, for some, electronic meetings may be important in terms of widening their experience and interaction whilst honouring the privacy and intimacy of the dyad. Due to the relative sophistication of the bespoke programme at Hull University, the platform used to deliver this was able to offer flexibility around these interactions. The relatively managed approach taken by the organizers in the Hull scheme appears to be another key element that made a difference to the successful outcome. For example, they organized a number of 'E-tivities' – on-line activities that were useful to participants. In addition, the scheme organizers thought through the issue of support for participants and created E-moderators. The E-moderators blended the role of supervisor with scheme facilitator and the management structure of the programme appears to have the potential to offer support to the participants via the central project team.

In terms of the contracting issues raised, there appear to be a number of features that are pertinent here. In the Hull study, 58 per cent of the mentors and 66 per cent of mentees felt that they had achieved what they had hoped to, compared with 54 per cent and 44 per cent in response to similar questions in the MentorsByNet project. Although direct comparisons between such studies are crude at best, there may be some grounds for suggesting that, in Headlam-Wells (2006), the scheme organizers managed the expectations of E-mentoring better. There is some support for this point. For example, from the finding that 88 per cent of mentors and 78 per cent of mentees said that they would take part in an E-mentoring programme again. There were similarities (albeit more dramatic in this study) to the MentorsByNet scheme in terms of the impact of mentoring, as shown by the following excerpt: 'The proportion of mentees who agreed that they "know what to do to develop professionally" showed dramatic improvement – from 19 per cent to 71 per cent. The proportion of mentees who agreed that they knew what they needed to do to improve rose from 39 per cent to 66 per cent.' (Headlam-Wells et al., 2006: 381). These findings seem to indicate that mentees became clearer about the actions they needed to take for their future direction. The

Advantages	Disadvantages
Often diminishes visual status cues, for example, ethnicity, gender, age	Diminishes opportunity to pick up on one or more sources of information, such as body language, tone of voice, facial expression
Can break down geographical barriers to coaching and mentoring	Being easy to make, E-development relationships can also be easy to break
Can increase pool of available coaches and mentors	Removal of context for the coach/mentor can make it more difficult to pick up on what is not being said/shared
Can break down time pressures on participants – convenient, easy to access in short, more sessions	If contracting is not carefully managed, it is easier to develop unrealistic expectations about the regular relationship
What is said is captured, recorded and can be referred back to	If the process is predominantly electronic, experiential learning can be more difficult, which may militate against learning

Figure 9.1   E-development – advantages and disadvantages

following mentee's quote from the MentorsByNet Study (Megginson et al., 2003a: 8) seems to echo this:

> What the mentoring programme has done has 'enforced' delivery of a business plan, enabled prioritisation of different business opportunities, given me a clearer focus on what resources I need and given me more confidence in my own business abilities. The results of the mentoring programme are the birth of another business with two more waiting in the wings.

Here we suggest that there is more evidence that, in the eyes of a mentee at least, mentoring and coaching offers greater clarity and self-awareness about the future. Of course, we would expect this in effective face-to-face coaching and mentoring relationships as well.

E- DEVELOPMENT: MOVING THE DEBATE FORWARD

In Figure 9.1, we have summarized the main advantages and disadvantages of E-development (which is predominantly E-mentoring) based on our own research and other selected studies to date. It is clear that there is a shortage of good-quality published research and development in the area of E-development.

Following Ensher et al. (2003), we see three broad archetypes of E-development within coaching and mentoring:

1. Pure E-development – this is where all aspects of the coaching/mentoring are done using electronic means including recruitment, selection, development, matching, conversation, support and evaluation.
2. Primary E-development – this is where the majority of the coaching and mentoring activity is done using electronic media but interspersed with some face-to-face meetings.
3. Supplementary E-development – this is where the use of electronic media for coaching and mentoring activity is seen as a useful add-on or additional aspect of the process but is not central to the scheme or process.

The majority of this chapter so far has focussed on primary E-development but, using Figure 9.1, it is our view that most coaching and mentoring programmes fall into the supplementary E-development category. It is also our view that the majority of all coaching and mentoring relationships – be they formal or informal – are in the supplementary E-development category. This is simply because, as we argued at the start of this chapter, electronic media has become a central part of many people's lives. Inevitably, whatever the starting point for the relationship, participants in coaching and mentoring relationships will create and develop ways of interacting with each other, using a variety of methods. Although the core interactions – the substantive aspect of the relationship – may be face-to-face meetings, it is increasingly likely that these things will be followed up and supplemented with phone calls, emails, text messages and other ways of maintaining and developing the relationship. Similarly, if the starting point is E-development, unless there are significant temporal, geographical or other boundaries that prevent it, it is likely that face-to-face meetings will become part of the relationship at some point, even if the relationship remains a primary E-developmental one overall.

In our view, there are relatively few pure E-development relationships but it is important to point out that it is more helpful to conceive of E-development as a continuum (see Figure 9.2). This illustrates that, whilst the majority of coaching and mentoring relationships fall into the supplemental category, this is a broad category. Following the logic we have put forward, nearly all coaching and mentoring relationships will fall into this category.

It is hard to imagine a coaching and mentoring relationship where some aspect of the activity – recruitment, selection, and so on – is not done using electronic media. Therefore, we introduce the idea of 'low tech' coaching and mentoring. This is where, although some aspects of the coaching and mentoring are arranged on-line – arranging meetings by phone or email, for example – the fundamental, substantive coaching and mentoring work is done in a face-to-face work.

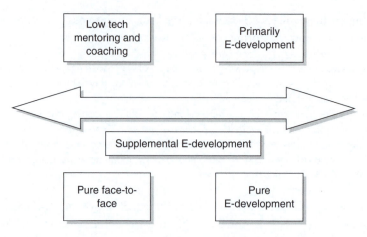

Figure 9.2   A conceptual map of the E-development continuum

There are two main reasons why coaching and mentoring may be low tech. The first reason is technical capacity. This may include, either lacking access to the equipment or a lack of competence in using the equipment (this one will be explored later). The second reason is a more complex one. We have made the point several times in this book (see Chapters 1, 6, 7 and 8) that we see coaching and mentoring as extensions of normal human activity. For many (Zuboff, 1988), electronic media has the potential to isolate us from other human beings by replacing face-to-face contact with machines. Organizational behaviour, as a field of study, has a long history of studying these phenomena and writers comment (see Hislop, 2005) on how technology can lead us to become alienated from ourselves and our work. Hence, for some, coaching and mentoring, with its traditional emphasis on rich, face-to-face interactions, may be inherently human in essence. Therefore, for them, E-development may represent the antithesis of what they most value in human relationships and their 'low tech' approach may be more about personal choice than a lack of capability.

Because there are no hard and fast rules about where one category starts and another ends, there is, as shown in Figure 9.2, an overlap between supplementary E-development and both the primary and low-tech categories on the continuum. Further research into coaching and mentoring schemes may reveal yet more distinctions and differences.

There is, however, a further important issue to consider, if we accept the premise that most coaching and mentoring is moving to become part of supplementary E-development processes. Much of the research into coaching and mentoring so far, with the exception of those studies that are focussed on primary E-development programmes, has helped us to develop significant understandings around the conversation (see Chapter 6 for evidence of this). However, much of our practical understanding about what works comes from research conducted at a time when coaching and mentoring was much more towards the pure face-to-face end of our continuum. Therefore, much of what we know about the effective frequency of meetings, duration of meeting required and so on, was developed before many of the newer uses of technology became ubiquitous. This raises some important questions which we present in the key Questions section of this chapter.

CONCLUSIONS

Overall, E-development is an under-researched activity. The research that is published tends to be about E-mentoring schemes and there are few published accounts of E-coaching. The research we have examined seems to suggest that E-development will inevitably play some part in most coaching and mentoring activities.

In this chapter, we have examined some of the issues and challenges with E-development but acknowledge that it is a growing trend and have put forward a simple taxonomy for thinking about this area. It is our view that, as time goes on, the generation that has grown up with the newest technology will increasingly find it natural to incorporate it into their way of working. This will mean that we will need to add to our understanding of the impact of such mechanisms, develop appropriate protocols for their use and recognize their inevitable impact on our understanding of coaching and mentoring as an activity.

The Future

E-development is the most future orientated of all the chapters in this book. This is because currently there is insufficient research or experience of how to use the 'newest' of new technology within coaching and mentoring. However, there are already signs of where this might go. For example, one of us was recently invited to 'meet up in Second Life' to discuss a possible coaching intervention. Our sense is that this was an unusual request but it may not be long before this becomes more common place. Our prediction is that, although E-development will play an increasingly bigger part in coaching and mentoring activity, in the main it continues to be a face-to-face process. However, the ability to capture conversations electronically may mean that each session will have a more lasting impact as it could be 'returned to' repeatedly. One possible effect of this may be to reduce the number of sessions that is typical of a coaching intervention. In other words, if recorded sessions enable coachees and mentees to notice more nuances and patterns, and to become more self-aware more quickly, then they may not need as much face-to-face input from the coach or mentor.

Our prediction is that E-developments will also extend into training, development and the supervision of coaches and mentors. Not only will E-development influence the content of these helping interventions, it will also affect the mode of delivery. This will present, as we have suggested, challenges and difficulties for coaches and mentors but it also opens up another realm of possibilities for the field.

QUESTIONS

If we accept that coaching and mentoring participants will increasingly use E-development to some degree or other, what impact will this have on face-to-face meetings?
What is an appropriate and effective length of an E-development conversation using email? Half an hour? Six months? A year?
What is the optimum blend of face-to-face and E-development activity and to what extent is this contextually driven?
If we acknowledge that coaches and mentors make contact with their coachees or mentees outside face-to-face meeting, what implications does this have for organizational evaluation of the efficacy of such schemes?

THE GOAL ASSUMPTION: A MINDSET ISSUE IN ORGANIZATIONS?

CHAPTER OVERVIEW

This chapter examines some of the issues raised when introducing coaching or mentoring into organizations. It builds on the pragmatic discussions in Chapter 3 on creating a coaching culture and on the theoretical considerations on power in organizations in Chapter 7 and resonates with the issue of 'objectivity' in learning raised in Chapter 6. We focus on and debate the concept of 'goals' within coaching and mentoring, raising six key questions as a basis for our discussion. We discuss the belief that setting goals seem to be a taken-for-granted assumption about good practice, particularly in coaching but also in mentoring. In this chapter, we look at alternative possibilities to 'goals' and ground these in our own research as well as other perspectives that relate to our findings. Finally, we turn to the organizational implications of these issues and show how these implications illuminate a number of key organizational practices in the use of coaching and mentoring. This chapter is research based.

INTRODUCTION

The discourse on 'goals' has practical implications for how individual coaching and mentoring relationships are conducted, and it also serves as a window opening a view onto many of the questions we seek to ask about organizational issues that surround the practice of coaching and mentoring.

There is a strongly established norm that working with goals is at the core of effective coaching. Indeed it is embedded in the coaching process model GROW. This practice is less firmly established in the literature of mentoring, but nonetheless it is discernible. Our research suggests that 'goals' are not necessarily everyone's preoccupation and those that do not subscribe to the dominant discourse of 'goals' still have a sense of direction and intent in their work and lives.

In Chapter 7, we discuss the issue of power and in this chapter we argue that the discourse of 'goals' is a power issue that raises some important questions about the way in which people interact and communicate within organizations.

Garvey and Alred (2001: 523) state:

> Mentoring is an activity that addresses a combination of short, medium and long term goals, and concerns primarily 'ends' as well as 'means'. Hence, mentoring is severely challenged in an unstable environment. It may become focused exclusively on short term goals, disappear or be displaced by friendships between people sharing a common difficult fate (Rigsby et al., 1998). Mentoring may slip into the 'shadow-side' (Egan, 1993) where it has the potential to be both destructive or add value.

Drawing on Kantian philosophy, in which treating people as a means to an end is morally wrong, whereas treating people as ends in themselves is morally appropriate, the above quotation stresses the social context as an influence on mentoring forms and highlights a problem associated with short-term goals – 'shadow-side' (Egan, 1993) behaviour. According to Egan, 'shadow-side' is what happens unofficially in an organization. It is about conversations and actions behind the scenes and away from the overtly managed. We have mentioned the dominant discourse of compliance and obedience in organizations in Chapters 6, 7 and 8 and one consequence of this is 'shadow-side', which has the potential to influence coaching and mentoring agendas, collusion, spontaneity and authenticity in organizational life. This is the basis of this chapter.

METHODOLOGY

The above generates, for us, the following organizational questions:

- Who dictates the agenda?
- Whose interests do the goals serve?
- Whose model of reality is privileged?
- How can the impact be measured?
- How can the usefulness of coaching and mentoring be focussed?
- How can collusion be controlled?

We address these questions through the lens of 'goals' and begin with a consideration of the place of goals in coaching and mentoring by drawing on our field data collected via a survey and four focus group discussions with over 50 coaches and mentors. We then examine the implications of this perspective for the questions listed above.

GOALS

Most training and education bodies involved in coach or mentor development have encouraged their students to help coachees to set goals (Megginson and Clutterbuck, 2005a: Chapter 2), and we have emphasized the importance of coaching schemes having an organizational goal (Clutterbuck and Megginson, 2005: Chapter 4). In this, we have followed thought-leaders such as Downey, 2001; Whitmore, 2002; Berg and Szabó, 2005; and Grant, 2006a. Both Grant and Whitmore have been specific, and the others have at least implied, that goal setting is the very essence of coaching. It is probable that this view of development came from the ideology of management by objectives (MBO), advocated by Drucker (1955, 1989) in the US and by Humble (1971) in the UK. Some consider the goal view as a dismal, reductionist, mechanical perspective that potentially corrupts behaviour, for example see Caulkin (2006a). In Chapter 6, in the context of learning, we position the goal argument as an objectivity-driven perspective and offer the alternative perspective found in the notion of non-linear conversations.

Reflecting upon our own practice as coaches and mentors, and upon research into planned and emergent learning (Megginson, 1994, 1996), we wonder if the goal-setting ideology reflects lived practice and presents the whole story of conversational learning. The literature on quality management is interesting on this point. Johnson and Bröms (2000), for example, confirm our concerns about targets at the organization level. They argue that goal-free improvement led to Toyota's 20-year steady growth of profit and volumes and that focussed financial targets led the big three US auto manufacturers into constantly recurring trouble.

Another interesting perspective comes from studying mountain climbing and applying the lessons from there to management. *Destructive Goal Pursuit: the Mount Everest Disaster* (Kayes, 2006) is an account from a business researcher of how the high-altitude expedition business can be a metaphor for the practices of some business executives in generating dependency and justifying the present suffering by fanatical devotion to a future desired state. And, of course, in the popular media on every side there are articles about the UK government's obsession with goal setting and targets, with warnings about how destructive and distorting of behaviour this is (for example, Caulkin, 2006a).

A closer examination of academic and business journals in coaching and mentoring reveals a mixed picture. Megginson and Clutterbuck (2005b: 1), for example, state that, 'effectiveness depends on coach and learner having a common understanding of success'. Much coaching research (see, for example, Parker-Wilkins, 2006), takes goals for granted and describes their achievement using measures of return on investment. Others use goals to measure skill development. An example of skill development as a measure is a study by Smither et al. (2003). This work is also interesting in that it introduces another theme found in our survey, namely that coaching gets people into the habit of setting goals. They found that those who were coached were more likely to set goals and that this led to improvements in their 360 degree feedback rating. Evers et al. (2006) also showed that goal-setting behaviour is an *outcome* of coaching. So, these sources indicate that coaching itself socializes coachees into the received wisdom of goal-setting.

There are, however, sources (Ibarra and Linebak, 2005) that argue that goals are not central to transformation, but a strong focus on an issue is what makes a difference. Taking the argument a step further, Hardingham (2005) says: 'The coachee may have achieved all the goals set out at the start of the relationship, but ... how can we be sure that in the long term those goals turn out to have been the right ones?'

Spreier et al. (2006) make a full-frontal attack on goal setting. They highlight the destructive potential of overachievers in a way that is reminiscent of Kaye (2006), referred to earlier. However, they see coaching as an *alternative to* goal setting, in a way that contrasts with the literature advocating goals.

So the jury is still out in the literature on coaching about the plusses and minuses of goals. The advocacy of goals is stronger in the books on coaching than it is in equivalent mentoring books where there is an emphasis on the mentee's dream (Caruso, 1996). We now turn to what we discovered in our survey of coaches' and mentors' views about goal setting.

THE DARK SIDE OF GOALS – DATA

Overall, the literature seems ambivalent on goals. In response to this, we gathered data from a sample of over 50 experienced coaches and mentors about their use of goals. Initially, we used a semi-structured questionnaire and then ran four focus groups to examine the data's meaning. We give a summary of the main themes and examples of verbatim quotes from respondents (italicized) below and note that the respondents made both positive and negative comments about goals. We focus on the respondents' reservations in an attempt to redress the widespread assumption that goals are an unequivocally good.

Themes

Organization Issues

Seeking to Serve Organization Goals at the Expense of Client Goals

Goals are determined by the most powerful stakeholders, i.e. the coachee/manager/leader. They don't necessarily reflect the interests of people in the wider system (e.g. frontline workers) affected by coachee's decisions.

Personal goals – the emergent can turn out almost unintentionally to fit with the organization...

Goal setting can be profoundly destructive of the coaching process...but companies do need to have objectives for their investment in coaching. This is an ambiguity coaches have to manage in the contracting process.

Gaining organizational commitment often requires goals to 'appeal' to the positivist decision makers. We believe that conflict in goals between sponsor, coach and client diffuses motivation and creates confusion.

Setting Goals as an Unconsidered Routine

Doesn't correspond with my [coaching] training but does with my non-directive/Rogerian training – and that makes a lot of sense to me.

Inherent Issues about Structured Processes
Don't Reflect Changing Nature of Life and Complexity of Work

Goals spur for action. There are situations where 'relax', 'just be' or 'let go' are important. Not to make goals/actions the key issue requires extra attention.

In some cases clients don't respond to being tied down to a specific goal.

In this situation I frame the goal in a way that is more acceptable to them, giving them freedom to take action or not. My experience is that they outperform the 'goals'.

Background as relationship counsellor and action learning set facilitator.

I think that my belief that it can be very useful to start from a place of confusion, for which the only goal might be to find clarity about what the named goals might be, leads me to be confident that there is no need to have a precise goal to start off with.

It's an unknowable world...

Goals may distance us from connection with action/desire/focus, etc.

Goals focus on what is perceived to be important at the expense of what is interesting.

Coach Issues
Satisfying Coach's Need for an Illusion of Control

I think goals are an aspect of my personal preferences for clarity and control. There are other ways which I fear I have not explored.

Am I a goal junkie?

Client Issues

Clients May Not be Ready to Set Goals

Coachee may not be ready for goals setting – resistance might slow the process down – need preparedness, maturity, confidence to set goals.

If I am in transition, I can't commit.

Goals don't work with people who are not in a positive place. They reinforce discomfort.

Whenever I press someone about their goals for coaching, I find that they'll give me something because they feel obliged to meet my expectations that they should have a goal. Whatever they say at this point is almost never what they really want to work on.

It is also possible to find clients who have moved beyond goal setting (Megginson, 1994).

Superficial – Client Avoids the Deeper Issues

Do goals act as a crutch/excuse to avoid what would be painfully beneficial?

Perhaps the only goal is to do what is best for the client at the time. That may or may not include setting goals.

Goals can limit what is covered and prevent broad development of the person or prevent getting into deep and difficult issues that require a nuanced entry following lengthy dialogue.

ORGANIZATIONAL IMPLICATIONS OF LITERATURE AND OUR RESEARCH FINDINGS ON GOALS

The organizational issues that we address include:

- Who dictates the agenda?
- Whose interests do the goals serve?
- Whose model of reality is privileged?
- How can the impact be measured?
- How can the usefulness of coaching and mentoring be focussed?
- How can collusion be controlled?

Who Dictates the Agenda?

In most assignments involving an external mentor or coach there is an organization stakeholder: the scheme organizer, an HR development executive, a member of senior management, who has a more or less clear perspective on what the coaching or mentoring is for. They may say that it is for driving change through the organization, to unleash performance, or to engender creativity in the achievement of organizational objectives. However this perspective is expressed, it represents a significant constraint on the autonomy of helper and helped. The coaching or mentoring pair may get round this constraint, but in that very act they are giving attention to the issues that the promoter is interested in (see our discussion of Dirsmith et al., 1997 in Chapter 7). The ownership of the agenda is not a simple issue. Clearly, many have claims, perhaps the way forward is to raise and discuss these multiple perspectives within the one-to-one relationship with a view to arriving at a deeper understanding, the creation of more options for action and more rounded decision making.

Whose Interests do the Goals Serve?

We were surprised in our own research how often thoughtful coaches acknowledged that goals helped them to manage the ambiguity of helping. They didn't necessarily see the goals as helping the client, but rather they gave the coach an opportunity both to limit the discussion to topics acceptable to power holders, and to the kind of issues which the coach felt they were resourceful in addressing. This returns us to the question of agenda and raises a challenge to the dominant discourse found in coaching and mentoring that the learner's agenda is paramount. Perhaps goals actually serve the coach's perception of their own performance?

Whose Model of Reality is Privileged?

The practice of goal setting can be located within a discourse of atomism (for further discussion of this process, see Chapter 13 on standards and competencies). By this we mean that goals help to divide up the world into manageable chunks. Our experience is that many clients address complex situations as a whole rather than looking through the optic of this skill or that competency. They can be socialized into changing their view to focus on competencies but only at the cost of deadening their perception of the issues and of marginalizing the relevance of the coaching or mentoring to their core concerns.

HR functions have advocated the use of competency models because it provides them with a common language for managing HR processes from recruitment and selection through appraisal and performance management to discipline and redundancy. Another model of reality is the one embodied in SMART goal setting, which suggests that if people have an unambiguous target then they will unquestioningly work towards it. At a deeper level lies an almost entirely unchallenged assumption that growth is a good thing (especially economic growth), that the current situation is unacceptable and must be improved. The three main UK political parties, and virtually all private and public companies espouse this view. In terms of popular culture, TV schedules are full of 'reality' programmes where goal setting is an, often explicit, essential part of the process. UK TV programmes such as *Grand Designs* and *Property Ladder* combine property development with self-development. There is much talk of bringing one's dream to life, creating an ideal home. The underlying assumption is that there is a desired or ideal state and that this can be arrived at via careful project planning and hard work.

So, the atomistic skills of competency models, the specification and compliance implied in SMART goal setting, the growth orientation of political rhetoric and the dream fulfilment of property TV programmes are all partial models of a taken for granted reality. In coaching and mentoring conversations all such assumptions can usefully be deliberated upon, so both parties can make conscious choices about what they want to achieve or be.

How can Impact be Measured?

As we discussed in Chapter 4, evaluation tends to focus on return on investment or, failing that, on the development of specified and standardized competencies. Both these measures can be described as nomothetic rather than ideographic. By this, we mean that they are set along the same lines for everyone, rather than being crafted for and by each individual in the context of their own understanding of their unique situation. As a one-to-one relationship, coaching and mentoring seems ideally suited to ideographic measures, but they are often subordinated to a nomothetic measuring stick by other parties wishing to control what may legitimately be discussed in the privacy of the development dyad. The concept of non-linear conversations, discussed in Chapter 6, is relevant here. By hurrying, often in a straight line, towards a goal, we may miss the richness of the learning that comes from the journey itself.

How can the Usefulness of Coaching and Mentoring be Focussed?

Goals dominate the UK public sector and translate into an obsession with targets, action plans and the paraphernalia of performance management or measurement (see for example, Caulkin, 2006a). They promote action which appears productive but which often fails to achieve a meaningful outcome. They can be an outward form, often substituted for the thing that they are meant to be part of (for example, a well thought-through purpose to which one is committed). Other cases of this are organizational policies or position statements (on the environment, diversity, etc), the production of which becomes an end in itself and a substitute for having embedded commitment to sustainability or equality throughout the organization. The concept of the rational and pragmatic manager raised in Chapter 3, which dominates modern business life, seems at odds with the professed qualities and behaviours outlined in Chapters 3, 6 and 8 that seem necessary for high performance in a knowledge economy:

- Adapt to change rapidly.
- Be innovative and creative.
- Be flexible.
- Learn quickly and apply their knowledge to a range of situations.
- Maintain good mental and physical health.
- Work collaboratively.
- Have 'strong and stable personalities' (Kessels, 1996).
- Be able to 'tolerate complexity' (Garvey and Alred, 2001).

Coaching and mentoring activity do seem to have the capability to make a useful contribution to these abilities, but this would require a shift from the rational pragmatic towards a more holistic and complexity informed perspective of the workplace.

How can Collusion be Controlled?

Can goals be used to sublimate, or repress, uncomfortable unconscious impulses? The protagonist in William Golding's *The Spire*, who, as Dean, drives forward the construction of a cathedral with a huge spire, even though the foundations are not secure. It becomes clear in the novel that the spire is a symbol of his unadmitted lust for the builder's daughter. In terms of goals, it represents the use of outward busyness as a distraction from difficult unconscious material. Both coaches and mentors and their clients can engage in the busyness of goal setting at the expense of digging a bit deeper into difficult issues. This tendency is reinforced by the organizational context that legitimizes goal achievement as the prevailing *modus operandi*. Additionally, while a goal may promote activity it may, like the Dean, distort behaviour. If a police officer has a goal for the number of arrests per month, there is more than one way to achieve it! We suggest that it is not a case of being for or against goals but, rather, goals need to be assessed honestly and with full knowledge of their complexities. A focus on goals only, without consideration of the attitudes and behaviours required to achieve them, simply invites negative collusion and distortion. Coaching and mentoring offer real and tangible opportunities for deep understanding of attitudes and behaviour, which in turn offers the prospect of:

- Improved ethical decisions.
- Changing these attitudes and behaviours.
- Transformational learning and development.
- Enhanced and informed strategic choice.
- Improved relationships and less conflict.

The depressing picture is one of continued collusion in rational pragmatic, dehumanizing management.

CONCLUSIONS

The above research evidence and the literature suggest that goals are indeed an organizational mindset issue. Coaching and mentoring are pervasive phenomena in contemporary organizations. They can serve goals of surveillance (see Chapter 7) and soft HR control (Legge, 1995; Jacques, 1996) or they have the potential to emancipate. Jacques (1996) warns against suggesting, rather simplistically, that a one-to-one relationship can free an individual from the thrall of organization and societal control; however, they do hold out the possibility of 'articulating different possibilities and implications that exist *within* these relationships' (p. xviii). How it is played out in any particular context will depend, in part, on how the participants in coaching and mentoring activity engage with goals, purposes and issues of agency and ethics.

The Future

It seems to us that major organizations are going through a phase of having the centre of the organization (often represented by the HR function) take control of the agenda for coaching. This is increasingly being done by careful centralized selection of a pool of executive coaches, who will honour the company agenda and help clients to work towards it. Similarly, organizations are appointing more full-time internal coaches, who are even more directly controlled in the service of the corporate agenda. It is hard to predict how long this trend will continue. We see a tension between, on the one hand, the focussing benefits of control and, on the other hand, the energizing advantages of liberation and personal responsibility.

QUESTIONS

Who should influence the coaching/mentoring agenda? How?
What is the place of goals in coaching and in mentoring? Whose interests do they serve?
What are the underlying assumptions embedded in coaching that influence the model of reality that is privileged?
How can and should the impact of mentoring and coaching be measured? How can the impact be focussed?
How can collusion in coaching be recognized and addressed?

PART III

CONTEMPORARY ISSUES IN COACHING AND MENTORING

SUPERVISION

CHAPTER OVERVIEW

In this chapter, we discuss the issue of 'supervision' in coaching and mentoring. Although this is a relatively new term in coaching and mentoring, it is a growing area of interest. We explore the reasons for the explosion of interest in supervision as well as examining the different approaches, functions and roles that supervision can play. Some argue that there is a recent demand to professionalize coaching and mentoring and that this has created this need. Others, for example paying clients, are considering issues of quality control and competence. A further driver for supervision is the training or development of coaches and mentors. A central issue here is, as Gibb and Hill (2006) ask, what is the subject discipline we draw on to inform the education of coaches and mentors? They suggest:

> Understanding the nature of knowledge construction can help move us beyond a contest among favoured prescriptive models to situating theory and action in an integrative and inclusive framework for reflective practice. And it may also help guide both teachers and learners, writers and commentators, away from the traps of exchanging or mistakenly criticising unexamined preferences, and into debates where issues and matters, both critical and empirical, can be engaged with to the benefit of a broad and growing community. (2006: 53)

This chapter takes a critical look at some of these arguments.

INTRODUCTION

Following on from Chapter 7, we can identify a dominant discourse that is beginning to emerge about coaching and mentoring supervision. One of the drivers for supervision has been the general professionalization of the industry (see Chapter 13 for a review of this). Organizations such as the European Mentoring and Coaching Council (EMCC) and the International Coach Federation (ICF) now require their members to engage in supervision.

Related to this first point, there is greater pressure coming from individual and corporate paying clients for coaches and mentors to be quality assured. Supervision has become one way in which clients can be more confident that they are dealing with a competent professional and perhaps take reassurance that another professional monitors their work.

METHODOLOGY

First, we discuss Berglas' and Bluckert's work with the question – should a coach or mentor be 'psychologically minded' or 'psychologically trained'? We then examine two models of supervision, one drawn from the coaching literature and the other from the mentoring literature, and critically consider their application in practice. We conclude by presenting our own position on supervision and argument for an ongoing developmental model.

DEVELOPING COACHES AND MENTORS – KEY ISSUES

The literature on coaching specifically raises the importance of what Lee (2003) refers to as 'psychological mindedness'. Bluckert (2006: 87) describes this as 'people's capacity to reflect on themselves, others, and the relationship in between' and he suggests using an understanding and awareness of psychological processes to do this. Lying behind this point is a debate that continues within the coaching and mentoring field – do you have to be a trained psychologist, counsellor or psychotherapist to be effective and safe as a coach or mentor? This debate seems critical to this whole area as it determines the approach and content to coaches' and mentors' training.

Berglas (2002) advocates that coaching, in particular, is something that should only be done by trained therapists. However, his position does not seem so clear-cut, as the quotation below illustrates:

> My misgivings about executive coaching are not a clarion call for psychotherapy and psychoanalysis. Psychoanalysis, in particular, does not – and will never – suit everybody. Nor is it up to corporate leaders to ensure that all employees deal with their personal demons. My goal, as somebody with a doctorate in psychology as well as serving as an executive coach, is to heighten awareness of the difference between a problem executive, who can be trained to function effectively, and an executive with a problem who can best be helped by psychotherapy... (2002: 89)

Although Berglas is a coach himself, he is nevertheless deeply suspicious of those who coach without an understanding of psychological issues. In particular, he argues that such coaches without an understanding of psychology have a narrow focus on behavioural issues and find difficulty in recognizing the value of other perspectives. Whilst Bluckert's (2006: 92) tone is more measured, he too is a strong advocate of the psychologically minded trained coach as the following quotation suggests:

> In the near future I believe we will see greater attention to the psychological development of the coach as a response to the growing awareness and acceptance in the field that psychological mindedness is one of the key higher-level proficiencies of executive coaching.

In fact, it is difficult to find anyone in the literature who will overtly demur from the view that it is helpful and probably essential that coaches and mentors have some awareness of psychological processes. However, the key questions appear to be: how much is enough and who should decide?

Bluckert's (2006) approach to being psychologically minded as part of coaching is to recognize that a key part of this is being aware of oneself and one's emotions so that they might be employed to help stimulate greater awareness in the client. Interestingly, this ties in with Grant's (2007) research into the link between emotional intelligence and coaching skills training. In this study, Grant (2007: 258) claims that coaching skills 'are inextricably related to emotional intelligence', as 'to move through the goal-focussed coaching cycle, individuals have to be able to regulate their thoughts, feelings and behaviours so that they can best achieve their goals'. Grant's (2007) study was also interesting as it shed some light on coach training. He compared the outcomes from two modes of coaching training; one over 13 weeks and the other over two days with a three-week break in the middle. He summarizes his conclusions below:

> The main implications of these findings are that, whilst short, intensive programmes may improve participants' goal focused coaching skills, organizations seeking to deepen the impact of 'Manager as Coach' training programmes and improve the underlying emotional intelligence of participants should use a spaced learning approach over a number of weeks... (2007: 257)

It would seem that a more extended learning experience helps coaches make the necessary connections with their own thoughts, feelings and behaviours but also that this is possible to achieve by following a 'rigorous process of reflection, questioning and mutual support within an adult learning context' (Grant, 2007: 257).

This seems to fit with Bluckert's (2006) conclusions drawn from his own practice. He makes an important distinction between psychological training and psychological mindedness: 'Psychological training in an academic sense does not necessarily generate psychological mindedness as it may hardly touch on the awareness development of the student' (p. 92).

Whilst it is difficult to argue against the view that an awareness of psychological processes and one's own responses are important, psychological training – even that which is psychologically minded in nature – need not be the only route to self-awareness. As we found in Chapter 1, self-awareness, according to Caraccioli (1760), is achieved through a process of:

- Observation leading to...
- Toleration leading to...
- Reprimands leading to...
- Correction leading to...
- Friendship leading to...
- Awareness.

Returning to current times, Du Toit (2006: 53) suggests, 'In order to develop self-awareness the individual must have access to honest feedback...' And Garvey (2006) suggests that self-awareness is developed through a thorough exploration of an individual's story.

Our own approach to mentor and coach development has several strong connections with Bluckert (2006) and Grant (2006) but perhaps has the strongest connection with Hawkins and Smith's (2006: 92) approach. This we reproduce in a condensed form below.

As coaches and mentors ourselves, as well as experienced higher-education lecturers, our philosophy is summarized using a slightly adapted form of Hawkins and Smith's (2006) core principles as follows:

1. Focus on self-awareness using experiential learning processes.
2. Teach theory only when experiential learning has started.
3. Learn iteratively by raising learner awareness of development need and quickly have an opportunity to put it into practice.
4. Use intensive feedback in small groups where learners work with each other as peers.
5. Teach basic skills in a way that brings them to life – demonstrations, illustrative stories, engagement and learners reflecting on their own lived experience.
6. Real play – using real unsolved issues for learners – not role-play, which uses scenarios of case study issues from the past.
7. Long periods of practice (which are supervised) which follow on from initial training in which learners establish their own connections between self awareness, skills, theory and their experience of practice.
8. Challenge existing patterns of behaviour that may be unhelpful when coaching and mentoring.
9. Genuine belief in the learner's potential and ability to learn and to recognize that the learner's ability may exceed that of the teacher.

Like Hawkins and Smith (2006), our view of adult development recognizes that following a predominantly didactic model of teaching runs the risk of alienating experienced people who feel that their experience is denied. In addition, our view is that this approach is compatible with Bluckert's (2006) approach to psychological mindedness. We do not believe that approach is exclusive to those with a psychology, therapy or psychotherapy background. Now that we have established some core principles and ideas around development, we move to the issue of supervision.

WHAT IS SUPERVISION?

As Bluckert (2006) quite rightly points out, although supervision has a strong tradition within the helping professions (see Hawkins and Shohet, 2006 for a review of this literature), it does not really feature in the coaching and mentoring literature until after the year 2000.

Hawkins and Smith's (2006: 147) definition of supervision is: 'the process by which a coach/mentor/consultant with the help of a supervisor, who is not working directly with the client, can attend to understanding better both the client system and themselves as part of the client–coach/mentor system, and transform their work'.

Barrett (2002: 279), based on his mentoring research, considers supervision as being 'on the processes that occur between mentor and mentee during an interaction'. Bluckert (2006: 109), on the other hand, considers coaching supervision as being a 'time and place to reflect on one's work either with a senior colleague, in a led group, or with a number of peers' with the purpose of helping 'to make greater sense of difficult and complex work assignments and to gain more clarity going forward'.

Whilst there are differences in terms of emphasis and focus between these two positions, there does seem to be a consensus that coaching and mentoring supervision is a process that has its primary focus on the supervisee's practice as a coach or mentor. We define supervision as: *a process whereby the supervisee (who is a practising coach or mentor) is helped to make greater sense of their coaching and mentoring practice, with the goal of improving his or her practice as a result.*

HAWKINS AND SHOHET'S (2006) MODEL OF SUPERVISION

Perhaps Hawkins and Shohet (2006) offer the most useful and most widely known model of supervision. This is also examined in Hawkins and Smith (2006) (see Figure 11.1). In this model, known as the seven-eyed model of supervision, there are seven process areas to help focus the supervisor. We summarize these below:

1. The Coachee/Mentee – known as 'the client' in this model. Here, the supervisor helps the supervisee to focus on the client and to pay attention to what they bring. As Hawkins and Smith (2006: 162) put it, it 'is almost impossible to do quality supervision on a particular client until that client has – metaphorically speaking – entered the room'.
2. The Interventions and strategies used by the supervisee when with the client – here, the supervisee is encouraged to focus on the interventions they have made with client, in terms of tools, techniques, models and frameworks, and is invited to consider other options.
3. The Relationship between the supervisee and the client – in this mode, the supervisee is encouraged to reflect on their relationship and invited to consider why the client has

chosen to work with them and what they see the relationship as being like. This starts to bring the transference and parallel processing issues that might be playing out in the relationship – Hawkins and Smith suggest that the interplay between mode 3 and 4 is important, for this reason. Also, the supervisor brings 'the relationship' as another stakeholder to the conversation, thus encouraging the supervisee to pay attention to the dynamic between themselves and the client.

4. The Supervisee – in this 'eye', the supervisee is prompted to reflect on their own feelings and issues and how the client affects them. Key to this process is the supervisee's countertransference (see Chapter 7) – the supervisor plays an important role in helping the supervisee to become more self-aware and therefore enables them to make choices about how to respond to the client.

5. The Relationship between the supervisor and supervisee – the supervisor uses the supervisory relationship itself as data for shedding light on how the supervisee and client might be relating to each other. In particular, the supervisor helps the supervisee to recognize parallel processing within the supervisory relationships, which mirrors the dynamic within the coaching/mentoring relationship with the client.

6. The Supervisor – in this mode, the supervisor uses their own feelings and responses to the supervisee as data. In doing so, the supervisor is (a) offering feedback to the supervisee based on what they feel that they are 'picking up' from the supervisee, so as to give additional perspective for the supervisee to explore, and (b) modelling a process that the supervisee may try with their clients.

7. The wider context in which the work happens – includes the social, cultural, political and economic worlds of influence, as well as the professional codes and ethics, organizational requirements and constrictions and relationships with other organizations involved. Here, the supervisor is helping the supervisee to acknowledge that there are a number of wider contexts and stakeholders to consider.

This model shows that, however experienced a coach or mentor may be, there is a need for another to keep an eye (or seven!) on the factors that influence their ability to help others.

Despite this, we feel it is also important for a coach, mentor and supervisor to have some understanding and awareness of pertinent organizational and sociological constructs in order to frame these 'eyes' appropriately.

THE MERRICK AND STOKES (2003) MODEL

This part of the chapter is adapted from an article by Merrick and Stokes (2003). In this article, they draw on their experience of designing and developing mentoring schemes to offer a framework for mentor development. Like Hawkins and Smith's (2006: 139) framework, this connects supervision needs with various developmental stages for the mentor. Hawkins & Shohet's (2006) work is primarily written for those working in the helping professions whereas, Merrick and Stokes (2003) write from a mentoring practitioner perspective, with a scheme design audience in mind.

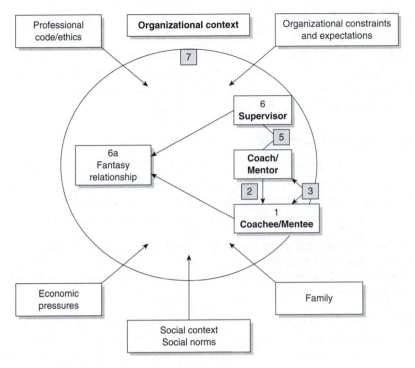

Figure 11.1   Supervision in the organizational context
Hawkins, P. and Smith, N. (2006) *Coaching, Mentoring and Organizational Consultancy: Supervision and Development*. Maidenhead: Open University Press. Reproduced with the kind permission of the Open University Press Publishing Company.

Merrick and Stokes' (2003) categories for mentor development are as follows:

- Novice Mentor.
- Developing Mentor.
- Reflective Mentor.
- Reflexive Mentor.

We consider these in relation to mentor development and the implications for supervision.

The Novice Mentor

A Novice Mentor is someone who may be new to mentoring, with little or no experience of mentoring in practice. This does not mean that they are untrained or unskilled, but that they have relatively little experience as a mentor of participating in a live, dynamic human mentoring process. They may have been mentored themselves or used mentoring skills in their work but may not have thought of themselves as a mentor before. As a result, such a mentor may have development needs that are different and distinct from more experienced mentors. For instance, they will need to become familiar with the protocols, aims and objectives of mentoring within their particular scheme. They will therefore need help and support in defining or refining their approach so that it is consistent with their scheme. Clearly, they will also need help in gaining access to the various existing theories and models of mentoring.

Implications for Supervision

At the Novice Mentor stage, a supervisor needs to ensure that the mentoring is operating congruently with the aims of the scheme. This closely resembles Hawkins and Shohet's (2006) management/normative function of supervision. This is a quality assurance or auditing function and it has two main purposes:

- To check the mentor's ability as a mentor, i.e. that they are using the key skills of acceptance, empathy and congruence with their mentee.
- To bestow what Feltham (1995) calls the 'aura of professionalism' to ensure scheme credibility in the eyes of its sponsors.

Within organizational schemes, where supervisors may be organizational members, this affords the supervisor the opportunity to intervene to avoid any damage to the mentee as well as to the reputation of the programme. This intervention is likely to be indirect by helping the mentor to rectify or repair any damage done. It may also be direct where the supervisor may need to intervene personally – this is where the role of supervisor and scheme organizer may be conflated. This conflation can create difficulties and a conflict of interests (see Megginson and Stokes, 2004 for a discussion of this).

The Developing Mentor

In one sense, all mentors could be developing and continuing to learn. However, in this context, the Developing Mentor is someone who has some experience of mentoring 'under their belt' and understands the 'rules' within their particular context. They can use a well-known mentoring model or process (e.g. Kram, 1983) that they can use within a mentoring conversation and they will have an awareness of some of the skills and behaviours required by an effective mentor. However, this knowledge and repertoire of behaviours is basic and their comfort zone as a mentor is still fairly limited and confined to a small repertoire of behaviours.

Implications for Supervision

At this stage, the Developing Mentor needs to start to identify other ways of mentoring to expand their effectiveness as a mentor. The supervisor may therefore need to pay more attention to supporting the mentor in their process development and in recognizing the dynamics within a mentoring relationship. This closely resembles what Hawkins and Shohet (2006) refer to as the educative/formative supervision role. The supervisor will need to model some of the behaviours involved to help the mentor acquire these skills and may indeed coach them specifically in these areas where appropriate.

In this stage, the supervisor needs to support the mentor to identify a mentoring process that is effective for them. The supervisor needs to help the mentor to understand the different phases and stages of the process and the application of the necessary skills.

Both gaining an awareness of the boundaries of the relationship and the skills needed is particularly important for the Developing Mentor. Mentors who are able to participate in a comprehensive programme of mentor training may have gained much of this knowledge on the programme, but not necessarily had the time for practise. They may be in the situation of practising their skills in their real-life mentoring relationship. Alternatively, perhaps, they may have received minimal training to become a mentor initially. The supervisor needs to explore these development needs with their supervisee and help them to identify ways of fulfilling them.

The meetings may be part of a course of pre-arranged meetings and the supervisor is looking for a level of development, which might be recorded formally.

The Reflective Mentor

The Reflective Mentor is someone who has a fair amount of experience as a mentor and has successfully extended his or her repertoire of skills beyond that of the Developing Mentor.

They are probably aware of most of the different approaches to mentoring theory and practice. They may have developed an awareness of context and their own identity as a mentor within the mentoring community. They now have both the experience of mentoring and of supervision so they can critically reflect on their own practice to develop their skills and understanding of different mentoring approaches. They may draw insights from other mentors, their supervisor and from other helping professions.

This process may have begun within the Developing Mentor stage but in this stage it becomes central. It is distinct from the Developing Mentor stage in that the Reflective Mentor would have had the chance to reflect on some of their experience as a mentor through the lens of their supervisory discussions. Hence, the Reflective Mentor is someone who has begun to take some responsibility for thinking about and directing his or her own development as a mentor. They may also have started to incorporate ideas developed within supervision and elsewhere into their mentoring practice.

Implications for Supervision

One of the important aspects of effective supervision for the Reflective Mentor is that the supervisor is able to demonstrate empathic attention and insightful reflection to the mentor. Mary Cox writes: 'What I want from my supervisor is intelligent listening, experienced reflection, realistic mirroring, perceptive confrontation and a sense of personal warmth and humour' (in Feasey, 2002: 141). This development function is a combination of Hawkins and Shohet's (2006) role of Educative/Formative support. It is through reflecting on and exploring the supervisee's work, the supervisor focusses on developing the skills, understanding and ability of the mentor they are supporting. Therefore, there are two changes in focus here. First, the supervisor is focussing more on the mentee and the 'work' of the mentor whilst at the same time encouraging the mentor to begin to recognize how the mentor's own experiences (including those as a mentor/supervisee) are beginning to impact upon their mentoring work. Second, the supervisor is supporting the mentor to develop his or her own internal critically reflexive capacity.

The Reflexive Mentor

The Reflexive Mentor is someone with considerable experience as a mentor and may also be a mentor supervisor. They have developed sufficient self-awareness, with the help of their supervisor, to reflect critically upon their own practice and to identify areas for their own development, as well as being more competent in detecting and using their own feelings within mentoring conversations to inform their practice. They are, however, astute enough to recognize that there is a need to continue with their development and to understand the dangers that lie in complacency and a rigid approach. In this sense, the Reflexive Mentor needs supervision to assure the quality of their helping skills and to prevent blind spots or damage being done through arrogant or careless interventions.

Implications for Supervision

For the effective supervision of a Reflexive Mentor, the supervisor would need to be a highly competent, flexible and experienced mentor themselves as the range of supervision required might range from very gentle support when a problem occurs, as a 'spot mentoring' transaction or conversely adopting a strong critical position in order to challenge the potentially complacent supervisee. As a result, the frequency of supervision may differ, depending on the needs of the supervisee. For instance, Feltham (1995) refers to a highly experienced psychotherapist Arnold Lazarus who does not use regular supervision:

> I probably ask for help or input from others mainly when I run into barriers or obstacles or when I feel out of my depth. If things are running along smoothly, why bother, but if there are some problems that make you feel lost or bewildered, or when you feel that you are doing OK, but could do better, why not bring it to the attention of somebody else, and discuss the issues? (Dryden, 1991: 81)

Discussion

As suggested above, the models presented above offer two different approaches to the idea of supervision. Hawkins and Shohet's (2006) approach has its roots in models of psychotherapy and counselling and presents the supervisory process as a complex and sophisticated one. Merrick and Stokes' (2003) approach draws on Hawkins and Shohet's previous iterations of their model but seeks to develop supervision against four archetypes of mentors, with different support needs due to their different stages of development. Hawkins and Shohet's model is particularly helpful in illuminating the supervisory process for the supervisor, in that it gives a conceptual framework to guide supervisory practice. Merrick and Stokes' (2003) model, reminiscent of situational leadership models, may be more useful to the supervisee and to the scheme organizer in understanding what sort of support needs (and indeed what sort of supervisor) might be helpful at certain points in the mentor or coach's development.

We have not yet explored in any depth the appropriateness of the term 'supervision' in the context of mentors and coaches. Hawkins and Shohet (2006) acknowledge that many discourses inform the word 'supervision', for example psychotherapy, counselling, education, social work and management.

Earlier in this chapter, we commented on Bluckert's (2006) observation of the dearth of supervision discourse prior to 2000. It is almost as if, as coaching and mentoring have moved towards professionalization, there came with it a need to delineate clear channels of progression and development for coaches and mentors. Furthermore, within this profession, more experienced coaches and mentors needed to differentiate themselves from less experienced coaches and mentors and to create a role for themselves as senior members of such a profession. Unfortunately, this meant that there was a lack of a framework and no language to achieve this, thus leaving a 'gap' in the coaching and mentoring discourse. It seems as if this gap in the discourse has been filled from the already established discourse and practices of psychotherapy and counselling. We believe that this discourse provides a useful way of understanding and working with coaches, mentors and their development. But there is a risk. When a discourse becomes dominant within a social group, its members may cease to challenge or question it and this can blind the members to alternative perspectives.

Kennett (2006) offers an alternative discourse in her unpublished Master's thesis. She questions whether supervision is an appropriate term to use and ponders whether the term 'reflective practice' (Schön, 1991), with its emphasis on developing professional practice and reflection in action, is a better model. Others, like Wild (2001), have preferred to use terms like 'coaching the coaches' or 'meta-mentor' to suggest that there is no substantive difference between coaching a client or mentoring a mentor. Another part of the discourse that seems to get subdued by the dominant discourse of supervision is the idea that a mentee or a coachee is skilled in the process (see Stokes, 2007 for an account of the skilled coachee). This idea has important implications for coaching and mentoring development programmes in general.

The problem with 'supervision' as a term is that it, like coachee and mentee, is passive. This militates against the learner as active participant in a learning dialogue at the same time as maximizing the power of the supervisor in relation to the supervisee. It plays down the possibility that the supervisor is learning as much *if not more* than the supervisee and gives privilege to the all seeing eye of the supervisor, particularly in Hawkins and Shohet's model (2006). We can see how the normalizing of supervision via such mechanisms as coaching and mentoring professional bodies (see Chapter 13) and by other professional bodies such as the Chartered Institute of Personnel and Development (CIPD) in the UK (see Hawkins and Schwenk's (2006) work on this) have almost given a moral authority to those who are being supervised. In less than a decade, we appear to have gone from a place where supervision was hardly mentioned to a place where those who do not have supervision are deemed unprofessional.

Given that we have used the work of Foucault and touched on discourse analysis already (Chapter 7), it is tempting to draw power-related parallels again here. Gutting (2005: 72) argues that Foucault was critical of the modern psychiatric profession's rejection of the mad on moral grounds. He suggests that Foucault saw madness as a human alternative to normality or even a meaningful challenge to what was reasonable or normal and there was a 'conceptual exclusion of the mad from the human world'. Are we seeing the beginning of a similar totalizing discourse in coaching and mentoring, where those who are not supervised are deemed 'unfit to practice' and morally inferior to those who are 'responsible' enough to be supervised on their practice?

Hawkins and Schwenk's (2006) CIPD-commissioned research suggest that we are not quite there yet. Despite over 80 per cent of respondents saying that supervision was important, the following quotation is surprising (Hawkins and Schwenk, 2006: 1): 'A striking revelation, though, is that far fewer (less than half) of all coaches actually do have coaching supervision and less than a quarter of organizations that use coaches provide any form of supervision for them.'

What does this say about supervision? Hawkins and Schwenk's study (2006) is the only small-scale study commissioned by a professional body and it can therefore not claim to represent the whole coaching and mentoring community. Nevertheless, it does seem to provide some support for the argument for the disciplinary power existing within the coaching and mentoring community where members have a clear sense of what 'ought' to be done. However, what is not clear is why there is a disparity between espoused theory and theory in use (Argryris and Schön, 1996) in the supervision discourse.

Why do so few people have supervision or organize it for others when so many see it as valuable? Hawkins and Schwenk's (2006) data suggests that this is because there is a lack of understanding about what supervision is and how it applies to coaching and mentoring. It may also be because, for some coaches and mentors, their modes of reflecting on their practice do not resemble the one-to-one supervision model that is common in the literature. In our experience, coaches and mentors use other mechanisms to reflect on their practice to gain new insights and to improve their skills. These include:

- Academic courses.
- Short courses.
- Action learning sets and Open Space events.
- Scheme gatherings and get togethers.
- Action research or participating in evaluation exercises.
- Group supervision.

We are not suggesting that all or even any of these are necessarily equivalent to one-to-one supervision or equal in terms of depth and breadth of coverage. However, we are suggesting that it may be premature to suggest that people are not engaging in reflection on their practice simply because they say they are not in one-to-one supervision.

CONCLUSIONS

We will conclude this chapter by articulating our own position on supervision and the development of those involved in coaching and mentoring.

As coaching and mentoring become more commonplace and an accepted part of organizational life (and of wider society), it is natural that those involved in it as clients, practitioners and purchasers want to see the quality of what is being provided increased. One way of doing this is to pay more attention to developing the skills of coaches and mentors via properly designed coaching and mentoring programmes. Like Bluckert (2006), we believe that coaching and mentoring development programmes need to raise awareness, in coaches and mentors, of their own impact and developing psychological mindedness is a key part of that. In addition, we agree with Hawkins and Smith (2006) that this needs to be coupled with an understanding of organizational and societal context. We therefore need to add organizational mindedness and sociological mindedness to the capacity of the effective coach or mentor. Like Bluckert (2006), we have come across plenty of coach-managers who do not understand enough about the organizational context, and plenty of psychologically trained coaches and mentors who do not have sufficient self-awareness, as well as the other way around. Therefore, we do not believe it is necessary to be a psychologist or a former CEO to work with a senior executive; both of these backgrounds – either together or separately – may be helpful in working with such a person but do not guarantee success.

We firmly believe that engaging in a rigorous and challenging process regularly with the support of skilled colleagues is helpful and necessary. This process could be paid one-to-one supervision in the way that Hawkins and Shohet (2006) describe it, or support could be gained by a skilful integration and use of a variety of different means of challenge and support from a range of mechanisms. Also, we believe that such support and challenge should be extended and encompass all those involved with a coaching and mentoring intervention and not just designated 'supervisors'. Of course, this is not always possible given the usual constraints on time, money and people.

A good coach or mentor is a critically reflective one. We do not believe that it is helpful to have an unquestioning, uncritical dominant discourse that only legitimates one-to-one psychologically driven supervision. However, we do believe, like Gibb and Hill (2006) cited earlier, that it is preferable to have challenge and disagreement around what is appropriate support and development for coaches and mentors.

The Future

In his book on relational coaching, De Haan (2008) raises some interesting questions about supervision. In particular, he asks whether formal supervision is substantially different in quality or effectiveness when we compare it with informal support. Our prediction is that the concept of supervision will come under increased critical scrutiny. As we have discussed in this chapter, there are already those who question the usefulness of the term 'supervision', given its strong associations with management, control and links with psychotherapy. As more becomes known about what effective support for coaches and mentors looks like, we predict that there will be an increase in demand for group supervision processes, like action learning sets, which are likely to be cheaper (shared costs) and which expose the coaches and mentors to wider range of perspectives and other avenues for support.

QUESTIONS

What support are you currently getting for your coaching and mentoring practice?
To what extent does that support enable you to be both psychologically and organizationally minded?
What power dynamics are present within your current mode of coaching/mentoring support?

COACHING AND MENTORING AND DIVERSITY

CHAPTER OVERVIEW

This chapter takes a critical perspective on the issue of diversity and its relationship to coaching and mentoring. Diversity presents perhaps the biggest challenge to humankind; it is a complex subject, one that, in an organizational context, can be dealt with in various ways. We attempt to explore these variations through the lenses of 'tolerance' and 'acceptance'. Coaching and mentoring offer an opportunity for individuals to explore the concepts of 'tolerance' and 'acceptance' and thus move forward to a new diverse future.

INTRODUCTION

The term 'diversity' has many meanings; for example, on strategic, policy or philosophical levels it may relate to:

- Multicultural philosophies.
- Political agendas.
- Business agendas.

Multicultural Philosophies

The notion of multiculturalism is an ideology based on the assumption of inclusiveness regardless of the diverse cultural and religious backgrounds of people in a particular society. Within an organizational setting, multiculturalism may be seen as a 'proactive and systematic process' (Dass and Parker, 1996: 384).

Political Agendas

Diversity, as a topic, could relate to a political agenda where policies are aimed at developing tolerance of people from different backgrounds. In the

UK, governments of all persuasions and organizations participate in policy making in relation to diversity issues.

Business Agendas

Diversity could also link to broad business agendas where the business tactic is to encourage diversity of employees to better serve a heterogeneous customer base.
  On a more individual level, diversity could relate to:

- Race or cultural difference.
- Nationality or regional difference.
- Gender.
- Sexual orientation.
- Age or marital status.
- Political viewpoints.
- Religious views or ethnicity.
- Disability as well as health issues.
- Socio-economic difference and family structures.
- Values.

Clearly, there are many diverse positions on the subject of diversity.

METHODOLOGY

First, we discuss the meaning of diversity and examine current philosophies and practices found in organizations. We then present a new case example of where one-to-one dialogue is used to support an organizational approach to diversity. This is discussed critically. This chapter links to many of the themes already established throughout this book and we signal these in the text. We conclude the chapter by raising some challenging questions.

CURRENT APPROACHES

According to Dass and Parker (1996), in the practice of human-resources management in the workplace, diversity is an important issue. Organizations tend to take three main approaches to diversity:

- Emergent and episodic.
- Programmatic.
- Strategic multiculturalism.

Emergent and Episodic

Organizations may develop an emergent and episodic approach to diversity. This is often a senior management-led process to identify unmet or unfulfilled needs or problems with the organization. At other times, incidents occur or examples arise from other levels within the organization that require actions.

An organization adopting this approach may engage trainers to facilitate diversity training aimed at sensitizing organizational members towards better communication and awareness of difference. Others create brief action learning sets to discuss common concerns and resolve problems.

While this approach can have a positive impact, it may also generate false and unresolved hopes by raising expectations which later cannot be met. Alternatively, it may be used as a precursor to more developed and prolonged diversity initiatives.

Programmatic

Some organizational recruitment approaches, in the pursuit of fairness, may attempt to neutralize difference by standardizing recruitment and selection processes. Other organizations may take a more affirmative approach by positively highlighting, nurturing and valuing difference. The programmatic approach is sometimes developed from the episodic approach in an attempt to create an organizational development approach to diversity.

Strategic Multi-culturalism

The third level, according to Dass and Parker (1996), is a more strategic approach based on the positive philosophy of multi-culturalism. This approach seeks social integration and cohesion for long-term strategic progression. Dass and Parker (1996: 385) believe that this approach makes it more likely that honest expression of difference 'can lead to a synthesis of the conflicting perspectives to take advantage of the similarities as well as the differences within organizations'. They also argue that this approach is more holistic and balanced, and represents a more realistic position on the complexities of diversity.

Whilst it cannot be the case that the multicultural approach is the 'one best way' the other approaches listed above can lead to difficulties. For example, the more affirmative approaches outlined above can be switched 'on' or 'off' as the circumstances allow. With these approaches there is always the potential for 'lip service' policies supported by the assumption that more education and training is the way forward. Neither policies nor education and training necessarily alter the subtle ways in which people can be intolerant or find difference unacceptable. However, there is some evidence (see case example below) that the affirmative approaches can provide powerful and transformational learning experiences for people.

Set against this background it is interesting to note the UK Government's current position on diversity is somewhat confused. Whilst the rhetoric is in praise of diversity and has a multi-cultural philosophy, there is also a drive towards creating 'faith based schools'. This is opposed by teachers unions:

We question whether faith schools provide an environment for interaction between different faith communities...[and] why should schools nurture young people in a particular faith. Surely, the job of schools is to nurture young people as individuals and as responsible, compassionate global citizens, and the promotion of a particular religious viewpoint should remain the province of religious groups. (From a speech by Mary Bousted of the Association of Teachers and Lecturers, *Metro*, 10 September 2007: 2)

This is an important issue and relates to the now familiar concept of mindset raised in Chapters 1, 2, 7, 8 and 10.

At times, intolerance or prejudice is not only related to outward signs of difference, such as obvious disability, gender or skin colour but may appear as a communication problem. This is because language and meaning are also culturally specific and even if a common language is spoken, people talking from different cultures may misunderstand each other. As Bruner suggests in a range of his publications (see Bruner, 1985, 1990), language is also a vehicle for culture but individuals from different cultures in conversation with each other may process the common language through different cultural filters and reach different understandings.

Typically, misunderstanding may lead to conflict. For example, if a British person is asked by a Swiss-German-speaking person speaking English 'Did I upset you?' The British person may reply, 'I was a little taken aback.' The Swiss-German person may then say, quite understandably, 'What?' The British person actually means, 'Yes, you did upset me', but his or her cultural conditioning of politeness would inhibit such a direct response. However, the Swiss-German would, according to his or her culture expect a direct answer of 'Yes' or 'No', and is confused by the obscure British response. Although there is a small risk of conflict in this example, it does illustrate the potential for greater misunderstanding in other situations. It is not the actual words that matter; it is the cultural filter that may alter the meaning and this example may lead to a stereotype of 'British people are not straight and Swiss-German people are rude'. Clearly, this is not the case.

THE CHALLENGE OF MINDSET

Three philosophies which do not lend themselves to a diversity mindset are:

- Power and control over the many by the few.
- Newtonian concepts of cause and effect methodologies for improving efficiency and effectiveness.
- Tayloristic 'one best way' thinking.

Garvey and Williamson (2002: 194) go further with their views, written shortly after 9/11, when they state: 'The old frameworks for thinking about the global order of our lives, its political fracture lines, religious and ideological diversity and its sustainability in environmental terms, are all shown to be inadequate.' Clearly, 9/11 was an horrific act but the events which followed it can hardly be viewed as a change of such mindsets but rather an aggressive restatement of old approaches based on the lack of understanding of difference and 'west is best' thinking. We can conclude, from such a view, that the arguably natural human instinct of the 'intolerance' (see Back, 2004; Bhavani et al., 2005) of difference seems to be a major challenge right across all sectors of global society.

There are two issues here. The first is that 'intolerance' does not imply that the opposite concept – 'tolerance' – is any less problematic. What a dominant group may see as normal, a minority group may see as an aberration worthy of punishment or vice versa. Some may see the concept of 'toleration' as an acceptance or 'putting up with' an unacceptable custom or behaviour. Such a position could be seen as moral relativism and as such having dubious connotations. It is difficult also to separate tolerance from power. A dominant group may have more choice to 'tolerate' than a minority group. The minority may simply have to 'endure', 'suffer in silence' or 'put up with' a dominant group's perspective.

Alred and Garvey (2001: 526), in using the term 'tolerance', suggest that it has at least two meanings.

> One is about '...putting up with'. Tolerance in this sense implies that a person views situations as, simplistically tolerable or intolerable so that the very perception of a situation becomes part of what makes it more or less tolerable. This, we believe, chips away at the personal qualities and abilities that determine optimal performance.

The second meaning put forward by Garvey and Alred is '...closer to its etymological root [and means] "to sustain", to keep going and remain effective in prevailing conditions'. The second quote offers a more positive perspective and involves aspects of the Rogerian concept of 'positive regard' for difference. An alternative to 'positive regard' may be found in the concepts of 'civility' or 'pluralism'. These ideas include the notion of 'acceptance'.

The second issue is that 'instinct' is not underpinned with knowledge and therefore there is no understanding in an instinct. In essence, we seem to be returning to the issue of the 'objective' versus the 'subjective' as raised in Chapter 2. The ideas outlined above are deeply problematic because they involve both the rational (objective) and the emotive (subjective) aspects of the human brain. 'Acceptance' or 'tolerance' or any other concept in the context of diversity is a blend of the rational and the emotive. Many organizations attempt to 'manage' diversity and lever it for strategic or social benefit and this is a completely rational choice – it makes sense. However, making sense, as Bruner (1990) tells us in Chapters 1, 6 and 8, is a construction based on individual and societal narratives. People have within them a narrative line about themselves and about others. These narratives influence behaviour and by exploring an individual's narrative, understanding, tolerance and acceptance become possible.

In diversity, there are no easy ways forward but, in the context of learning and development, diversity is an essential characteristic of the creative process. It is not about 'putting up' with each other but more about creating genuine tolerance, acceptance and understanding of difference, living with it as normal rather than defining others by their differences and as outsiders. Bruner's (1990) view is that meaning is distributed through dialogue and here is the link to mentoring and coaching. Mentoring and coaching dialogue offers the potential to explore dominant narratives and meanings, develop understanding and to explore the emotive as well as the rational.

EXAMPLE OF DIVERSITY MENTORING AND COACHING: THE YORKSHIRE POLICE POSITIVE ACTION MENTORING SCHEME (PAMS)

Thanks to Inspector Simon Mellors of South Yorkshire Police for providing his support and essential information for this example.

The History

In 1948, the profile of a typical police officer in South Yorkshire was:

- Male (females kept office hours, were paid less and had no patrol function).
- White (black police officers were accepted from 1947).

The South Yorkshire Police Service was formed out of smaller forces in 1974 and, by 1981, the general profile of a police officer in South Yorkshire consisted of:

- Living in South Yorkshire Police Area.
- A minimum weight of 10½ stone (men) or 8½ stone (women).
- A minimum height of 5ft 9½′ (men) or 5ft 5½′ (women).
- Maximum age of 30 years (unless left military service within the last 12 months and under 40 years).
- Married or, if not, then living separately from partner.

This suggests that traditions and institutions in policing are discriminatory, sexist, racist, ageist, elitist and that the pace of change within SYP is very slow when compared to the rapid pace in the broader society. Although by 2007 these policies had changed, the dominant profile of a typical South Yorkshire police officer is still white, local and male. This does not reflect the current profile of the South Yorkshire population.

Background to PAMs

In 1993, a young black teenager was murdered on the streets of London. There then followed the MacPherson inquiry into the Metropolitan Police's handling of the investigation and one of the findings suggested that this police service in London was 'institutionally racist'. Following the publication of the MacPherson Report, considerable efforts were made in police services across the UK to identify and tackle this issue. In the South Yorkshire Police (SYP) the 'Race to Mentor Scheme' was developed with the primary aims of improving the recruitment, retention and career development of members of minority groups.

The mentors all received initial training in associated skills and subjects, such as counselling, problem-solving, learning styles, conflict management, coaching, motivation theory and action planning. Each mentor is an established employee of the organization, and brings his or her own individual experiences, skills and knowledge to enrich the scheme. They are a diverse group of people, recruited into the scheme for their desire to help, encourage and benefit others.

As a result of new thinking and changing legislation, this scheme has recently changed its name to the Positive Action Mentoring Scheme (PAMS). This is to position the mentoring services as part of a wider diversity agenda rather than ethnicity alone.

Positive Action

'Positive Action' is an umbrella term about balanced legal interventions aimed at addressing workforce representation in recruiting and selection activity.

In practice, 'Positive Action Mentoring' is for minority groups but does not assist the mentees beyond planning and preparation for any recruiting or selection procedures involved. Mentees must meet the same criteria, and undertake the same tests and filters within those selection processes as everyone else.

The Mentors

The Association of Chief Police Officers (ACPO) (2002), suggest the following definition of mentoring in a police environment:

> Mentoring is a private relationship between two individuals based on a mutual desire for development towards a specific objective. It is additional to other forms of development not a replacement. Mentoring is a non-directive relationship and more broadly focused, it is normally the student (mentee) who decides the areas that are causing them concern, or ones that require development.

ACPO also states that the relationship is usually a non-reporting one and does not infringe upon the organizational structures. They add, in line with the Clutterbuck and Megginson (1999) definition, that it has more chance of success if the two people are off-line.

Some of the mentors from the previous scheme have continued into this new arrangement but a new group of volunteer mentors has also recently attended a series of development workshops at Sheffield Hallam University.

The training primarily focussed on skills and processes and was delivered in the 'mentoring way' (Garvey and Alred, 2000). In this way, the participants were able to develop their own agendas for learning and in the final two sessions they directly influenced the development agenda in relation to their own practice.

Four broad types of activity make up the mentoring role. The first is listening and support by being a sounding board and willing to help explore the mentee's situation with empathy and understanding. This will also involve giving and receiving feedback and developing rapport and trust.

The second is by having organizational awareness the mentor is able to signpost the mentee to what is available and discuss with him or her how it might be accessed. Within this, it is not expected that a mentor will represent the mentee's interest or actively 'promote' her or him. It is also important that the respective line managers are aware that the mentoring relationship exits. However, the mentor does not override the manager's authority.

The third is to help the mentee to identify and work towards achieving his or her work ambitions. This may involve seeking opportunities and problem-solving activities.

The fourth is to help the mentee to acquire skills, knowledge and understanding, share experience, develop insights into the way things get done so that he or she can make more informed decisions.

There is no expectation on PAMS mentors to draw up a formal contract with their mentees but it is expected that there will be a discussion about the groundrules and boundaries of the relationship. These are determined by both parties.

Confidentiality is a key component of the groundrules but it is a difficult area and clearly has limits; however, experience has also shown that, in a police environment, keeping the relationship confidential is important. The alternative is to place the partnership in the public domain but this can create resentment among the dominant group who may speculate that there is an unfair advantage to be gained by mentoring. Some minority groups within the police service may fear that they could be perceived as substandard by the dominant group if they participate in mentoring. It is also important to understand that in a police environment total confidentiality cannot be guaranteed.

The feedback from the development programme was very positive but also included some surprise benefits. One such benefit was that some mentors had started to use the mentoring process in their daily work with the public and with colleagues and reported considerable positive changes in the nature of and outcomes of the conversations. Others were using the mentoring process in their personal lives. One key lesson was that mentors need mentees quite quickly after the development in order to maintain their energy and skill level. This confirms a long held assertion (see Garvey and Alred, 2000 and Megginson et al., 2005) that people get good at mentoring and coaching by doing it and by having a support framework to discuss their experiences. Overall, it is hoped that PAMS will deliver a range of benefits as classified by Garvey and Garrett-Harris (2005) for a range of stakeholders. For example, the mentees, mentors, SYP and perhaps the public as follows.

Mentee

- Enhanced skills.
- Clearer understanding of capabilities and prospects.
- Feeling valued.
- Improved communication in working relationships.
- More rapid and effective integration into new roles and responsibilities.
- Opportunity to acquire skills and insights not generally available.
- A wider perspective on which to base career decisions.
- Opportunity to develop broader networks.
- Facility to explore work and personal issues with a more experienced colleague.

Mentor

- Satisfaction from helping others.
- Being challenged from a fresh point of view.
- Becoming better informed strategically about the organization.
- Opportunity to hone new skills, or existing ones in fresh contexts.

South Yorkshire Police

- More motivated employees.
- Improved morale.
- A broader and deeper talent pool in the workforce.
- Increased ability to respond to, and be open to change.
- Breaking down of glass ceilings and employer-profile stereotypes.
- Improved representation of minority groups across different levels of the workforce.
- Capacity to withstand scrutiny and inspection.
- Improved performance on diversity-management issues.

The Public

A service which reflects the social mix in their communities leading to:

- Police officers who can understand their perspective.
- Police officers who can engage the public with a diversity perspective.
- Improved relationships between police and community.

Discussion

The above example highlights developments in one-to-one developmental dialogue focussed on minority groups. We could ask, is this coaching or mentoring? If there is a need for differentiation, we suggest it is both in that a skilled PAMS mentor may perform many functions. All of these functions may involve a blend of coaching and mentoring.

This scheme is not about offering preferential treatment. It is, however, similar to other such mentoring schemes, focussed on addressing inequality through personalized learning and development opportunities. The argument is that it is through learning that social challenges are addressed. Therefore, understanding provides the basis for tolerance and acceptance. This position is, to some extent, justifiable and is the core assumption made by those who support 'learning solutions'. If this is the case, there is a strong argument for such schemes to be focussed on not only the minority group but also the dominant group. If learning is necessary for the minorities to develop tolerance and acceptance, it is also a need for dominant groups. We could therefore consider such schemes as offering co-mentoring or co-coaching (see Chapter 5). This would mean that both parties in the co-relationship would need training. It is our view that schemes that focus on balancing power, or addressing injustice of some kind, have a long road ahead because the educational and communication challenges this raises are considerable.

We argue that the one-to-one approach in the diversity context is a good thing because it considers the individual and therefore potentially it reaches greater depth and has more impact. As in other contexts, the key is the relationship and its intent. PAMS has a clear intent and clearly focusses on relationship-building processes.

Clutterbuck (2002: 91) suggests that both parties need to:

- Respect and try to understand the differences.
- Identify the positive factors behind a different behaviour or viewpoint.
- Recognize the underlying common values, which the different behaviours address.

Drawing on Clutterbuck (2002), perhaps 'respect' could be substituted for 'tolerance'? For a powerful discussion of this point, see Žižek, 2008.

The Future

Overall, given the current tendency to religious, social, cultural and political polarization of difference in modern society, we believe that diversity is a major challenge to humanity but one which should be embraced. De Bono (1992) offers insight into polarization with his concepts of rock logic and water logic. Rock logic positions beliefs as right or wrong and therefore options are severely limited in this two-way system. Water logic is about flow and possibility. It is about where this might take us and therefore offers multiple possibilities. A key principle of coaching and mentoring is the generation of many options to work with and therefore they offer scope to develop multilayered perspectives on respect, tolerance and acceptance. Without intending to overstate, mentoring and coaching may offer a serious way forward for humanity and provide an alternative to the human tendency to simplify and polarize.

QUESTIONS

What is your organization's approach to diversity?
How can you make this approach sustainable?
How might coaching and mentoring offer realistic opportunities for a new order of things?
How might you operationalize coaching in mentoring for diversity?
What challenges do you anticipate and how might they be resolved?

COMPETENCIES, STANDARDS AND PROFESSIONALIZATION

CHAPTER OVERVIEW

In this chapter, we look at the debates around competencies, standards and the professional-ization of coaching and mentoring. Rather than adopting a position on these issues, we raise many questions and present a comprehensive list of the extensive opposing arguments.

INTRODUCTION

It is our view that the issues of competency, standards and professionalization in coaching and mentoring present a conundrum and indeed contradictory positions. Standards, for example, seem to be a basis for a higher and higher proportion of qual-ifications and curricula throughout the western world. These standards are increas-ingly based on competencies or learning outcomes. This approach seems to have become a dominant discourse and is rarely challenged. As discussed in Chapter 6, this is an example of linear thinking about learning and, as discussed in Chapter 10, it also relates to 'goal' assumptions applied in the context of learning and development.

The consequence of these discourses, as we have discussed in relation to other dis-courses is that they have become so loud and so embedded in professional bodies, universities and other providers' minds that alternatives become marginalized or worse, ignored and discounted and risk becoming wiped out by those who hold the loudest voices. This presents a problem for coaching and mentoring practice where, in the literature at least, individualism, variety, difference and complexity are cele-brated as a core values.

METHODOLOGY

Overall, this chapter addresses three main questions:

- Can and should competencies be used as a basis for describing the role of coach and mentor?

- Can and should standards be built upon these competencies?
- Can and should a professional accreditation be established on the basis of these standards?

We also raise other questions.

On competencies we ask, what, in their turn, are the competencies based upon? In some cases, it seems as if the basis is what providers currently do; but we could ask, what are these existing providers' competencies based on? This line of questioning takes us into the Discworld created by the novelist Terry Pratchett. Featured in most of his 26 books, the Discworld is an imaginary location which consists of a flat disc sitting on top of four huge elephants which are in turn standing on the back of an enormous turtle as it slowly swims through space. One of his characters believes that the turtle sits on another turtle which sits on another turtle and so on. With competencies, it's perhaps from here on down just turtles all the way!

On standards, we ask the question, do you accredit the programme or the individuals or both?

On professionalization, we ask, how much professionalization is needed and appropriate in the field of coaching and mentoring, and the requirements for a profession that serves its customers.

To address these questions, we start with a discussion on the issue of competency. We then explore the pros and cons of the competency based view. We repeat this process for standards and professionalization.

COMPETENCIES

Competencies emerged from the systematic training model of the 1960s. Systematic training identified skills and knowledge (and later, attitudes) as a basis for building curricula. In the 1970s, there was a move to replace these curriculum-based units of analysis with a work-based unit, the competence. This described something that an individual in a job was able to do. At that time in history, it seemed a significant step forward, and, we would agree that competencies do have a number of advantages. Before considering their dark side, we outline these below. Looking at the positive side of these issues, we make the case for competencies being based on research – illustrating this point by employing the European Mentoring and Coaching Council (EMCC) work in this area.

Arguments For a Competency Basis

Regulating the Wild West of Executive Development

Coaching has been described as the Wild West of executive development (Sherman and Freas, 2004). It is depicted as being populated by quacks and charlatans making unlikely claims based upon dubious methods, inadequately researched (see Chapter 2). We found in the early 1990s that corporate purchasers of coaching were crying out for something to happen to show them who were the sound coaches and who the fly-by-nights, among the dozens who were approaching each organization every week and offering their wares.

Ground Understanding of the Role on What Practitioners Do

Willis' (2005) research for the EMCC was perhaps the most thorough study of mentoring and coaching competencies undertaken anywhere. She developed her long list of over 900 competencies for mentors and coaches from the curricula of organizations that had produced detailed specifications to train coaches and mentors. This approach has the advantage of grounding the framework in current practice but, as discussed above and in Chapter 11, there is a risk that the dominant discourse of current practice has the disadvantage of not allowing for innovation and new emerging perspectives.

Creates Framework of Comparison

By bringing together differing frameworks on competencies, researchers have enabled the profession to see commonalities and contrasts between various approaches. This also contributes to developing a typology of roles such as executive mentor or career coach (see Chapter 5). They have also created a template that individuals can use in planning their professional development.

Validated by the Field

The EMCC framework was distributed to members and other leaders in the field who were asked to indicate which competencies they saw as core to their practice, which related to a particular approach or clientele they addressed and which were not relevant to their practice. In this way, patterns of competencies emerged that were doubly grounded in existing practice – first, from the competencies list that had been developed from existing curricula and, second, from the survey of experienced practitioners.

Arguments Against a Competency Basis

Atomistic

The practice of any reasonably high-level skill is conducted and experienced as an integrated whole. We illustrate this point with terms in the EMCC's competency framework (www.EMCCouncil.org) which might apply to one action by a coach or mentor. The coach or mentor, when they reflect back to their client what has just been said, may be showing 'empathy', and they could also be said to be demonstrating 'listening', 'feedback', perhaps 'assessment', 'learning theory', 'supporting independence', 'ensuring understanding', 'active listening', 'building and maintaining the relationship' and many other items from the detailed list of competencies. To break down what a coach or mentor is doing and to specify it in unambiguous terms could be flying in the face of practice as experienced by both helper and helped.

Monoculture

There is a question for the profession of whether a standardization of coaching practice would be a good thing or not. Coachees and mentees are hugely varied in what they can do and what they want, and standardizing the offering is not necessarily a desirable feature for those seeking help. Biologists remind us of the inherent instability of monocultures.

Mere Competence

Another concern about competencies is that they create a frame of mind where professionals seek simply to do a 'good enough' job, rather than to create their own kind of excellence.

Deficiency Model

Competencies and standards can lead to a 'training gap' orientation, focussing coaching or mentoring on what the client lacks. This seems a pity motivationally and it misses all kinds of opportunities. Fairbairns, an early critic of the gap mentality, argued that in organizations where 'we have little idea about what is coming next, maybe we should stop looking at training needs analysis to help us to decide what training and development programmes to run' (1991: 45). Solutions-focussed approaches (Berg and Szabó, 2005) offer a reminder that the deficiency model is only one perspective on coaching.

Competencies Degrade in the Context of High-Anxiety and Low-Resource Base

A shrewd observer of mentoring in the UK National Health Service, Ed Rosen, made the observation to us that when professionals are highly anxious – perhaps because of detailed surveillance, and under strong resource pressure, then the delivery of competencies can degrade. The professional is tempted merely to deliver what has been specified, even if it does not meet the emerging requirements of the situation.

In contrast to the idea of competencies, Richard Oliver's *purposive drift* offers another perspective (Oliver, 2006). He suggests coaches be clear about purpose, and open about what might turn up on the way: we should pay attention to making it up as you go along. Machine thinking and the claims made for it are a 'reassuring fiction'. 'We are smarter than we think, though more ignorant than we know' (2006: 23) and 'Our life work consists of identifying, maintaining, extending and amplifying our states of well-being' (2006: 24).

Oliver argues: 'Sense of well-being is our compass point. Purposive drift is a relationship between values, competencies and contexts. Focussing on your context and your interactions with it tells you both what you value and the competencies that you can bring to bear on it' (2006: 29).

Three good questions for coaches around purposive drift are:

- Can I change anything in my context to help it to contribute to my well-being?
- Is there anything I can change in my interaction with my context to make it contribute to my well-being?
- Do I need to move from this context to another to increase my well-being?

Conclusions

There are arguments for and against competencies. The arguments for are about regulating a chaotic market and understanding what it is that coaches and mentors are purported to do.

The arguments against are grounded in the contrast between the ambiguous nature of the world and the nuanced approach necessary to the performance of a high-level skill.

Our view is that some kind of competency framework has become necessary – especially for external coaches, and, this being the case, it is better that the competencies be grounded in thorough research and linked to accredited qualifications but at the same time, like good practice in mentoring and coaching, there is scope for review and development.

STANDARDS

Are standards possible in coaching and mentoring? This field is not an occupation with an overall model of theory or of practice. Comparison can be made with occupations like 'TA therapist', which have strong unifying theory behind them; or accountancy, which has national and international practices that dictate how it should be conducted. In contrast to this position, there are many ways of delivering coaching and mentoring.

How much desire is there to standardize practice? Are those who purport to be interested in setting standards driven to further the profession and to improve the service to users or are they seeking personal advantage in an ambiguous market place? There is a parallel with the World Boxing Federation – are we seeking to create a unified belt, to win the inter-professional competition for influence, to regulate out deviants or to improve standards?

Is the development of standards in mentoring and coaching likely to lead to a pass or fail mentality, or is it likely to contribute to open-ended development? Parsloe (1992) and Parsloe and Wray (2000) suggest it can do both, though we have argued (Megginson et al., 2006: 247) that there is a significant risk that the standard becomes the *de facto* maximum that training and education providers will aspire to. So, a paradoxical question is: do standards raise standards?

A related issue is whether the requirement in some standards' frameworks for 'flying hours' (or number of hours of practice) as a criterion are an example of 'misplaced concreteness' (see Chapter 1).

If you decide to follow the standards route, then a pragmatic question is: do you accredit the programme or the individuals or both? The EMCC has followed the route of accrediting programmes and strongly in the UK, and increasingly in other European countries, coach and mentor training providers are seeking accreditation. The International Coach Federation (ICF), on the other hand, focusses on individual accreditation and has built a substantial base of accredited members in the US (see also Chapter 14) and increasingly in European countries.

Arguments For a Standards Approach

Time of Purchasers in Dealing with Bids

One of the ways that the need for standards emerged within EMCC conferences and other gatherings was in purchasers from large organizations complaining about the time they had to spend in dealing with unsolicited bids for work from coaches. It was as if aspiring coaches were going away on a weekend course, and then stopping off at a service station on the motorway and going to a machine and printing off a business card claiming that they were a business coach. A perception arose that something had to be done – and the professional bodies saw accreditation as the way to go.

Creating an Efficient Market for Coaching Services

In an ambiguous market, there are greater transaction costs if product quality is hard to verify. These greater costs are borne in part by purchasers, who have to create bespoke processes to verify the quality of suppliers. However, the transaction costs also impinge on the suppliers.

First, the overall size of the market will be reduced by marginal purchasers deciding that the game is not worth the candle and opting out.

Second, the ambiguity creates costs for sellers of services as they may have to spend unremunerated time on bespoke selection processes (beauty parades) in order to obtain work. Reducing ambiguity makes the market work more efficiently – purchasers can ask: do you have ICF accreditation, or does your training as a coach receive the EMCC quality standard? And this could be all they need to ask because the profession has created standards for itself that are acceptable to the purchasers.

Customers can Judge Standards Easily

There are of course inherent ambiguities in answering the question: what is quality in coaching provision? However, for some purchasers getting a guarantee that a supplier is an accredited professional may be all the assurance they need. The Association for Professional Executive Coaching and Supervision (APECS) seeks to take the simplification process further by encouraging purchasers to become members and to allow the Association to do the selecting of coaches for them.

Arguments Against a Standards Approach

On the other hand, there are arguments against standards. These are arguments of principle rather than of practice, so the debate about the usefulness of standards can be seen as a tussle between pragmatists, who want order and to get on with the job, and theorists, who see the apparent rationality of standards as being spurious and as kowtowing to unacknowledged and unattainable needs for certainty.

Illusion of Control – Misplaced Concreteness

Many feel that if there are variable standards and opacity of performance in an occupation, then setting standards will resolve this problem. Critics of this view argue that standards related to mentor or coach training or alleged coach performance miss the point. Standards, to influence the improvement of coaching, need to attend to the relationship between the coach or mentor and their client. It is between our noses rather than between the coach's ears that the standard is established.

In practice, standards are located in an even wider forum than this – the context also dictates whether the experience is judged as being 'up to standard'. A mentor and mentee may both agree that the relationship was transformative and energizing for the mentee, but if the organization sponsor thinks it didn't meet the scheme agenda, or if the mentee's boss thinks that it didn't address their staff members needs as the boss perceived them, then it may become judged as a failed intervention. And what about the mentee's colleagues or staff? Or the mentee's customers? Or HR department? Or the government body funding the scheme? The boundaries that we put round the relationship, who is in and who is outside, will influence, perhaps markedly, how any one-to-one relationship is perceived (see Colley, 2003).

Credentializing the Passable

It is often said that, 'What's measurable gets measured'. When people enquire about a course from a training provider or an education establishment they often ask: but can you be sure that it will make me a better coach? Providers, to deal with such enquiries, focus on particular competencies or curriculum that seems to them to satisfy their potential clients. What they offer is a set of abilities and they say that to pass you have to demonstrate that you have these. But what about maverick coaches who want to use their own view of what helps? Or principled mentors who lodge their interventions in a view about what a just society might be like?

Providers of training have to be fair to all, so they are drawn into ensuring that there is a common template against which all will be measured. And then there is the question of marginally passable people. As external examiners and in our own institution we experience difficult cases where a course member's performance has been marginal – just about good enough to pass the course, but no more. Would you want to be coached or mentored by such a candidate? Probably not, but the credentializing process means that such people will inevitably be out there. No one wants to be operated upon by a brain surgeon who got 1 per cent over the pass/fail boundary, but lots of patients are operated on by just such people and the same principle follows for qualified coaches.

Lack of Coherence to Coaching and Mentoring as Activities

We have made the point that many professional bodies are held together by an extensive shared body of knowledge. In spite of the attempts by bodies such as EMCC and ICF, it is still the case that there is a huge range of ways of coaching and mentoring in all sectors of society. As this is the case, it makes setting standards more problematic than it would be for a more established profession. As pointed out in Chapter 1, both the literature and the market place are populated by people who see the practices of others as deeply flawed. For example: 'Don't go to a Gestalt coach, they mess with your head'; 'If you go for a business coach who isn't solutions focussed you'll spend all your time looking at problems'; 'Don't go to a mentor at all; they'll just dish out gratuitous advice.' This positioning is perhaps an inevitable consequence of the commodification of coaching and mentoring first raised in Chapter 1.

A Note on 360-degree Feedback

A very helpful short article on 360-degree feedback (Goodge and Coomber, 2007) argues that coaches using 360-degree feedback should focus on performance rather than on the data. This accords with our experience of using these tools. A crucial step is to identify the big goal, instead of getting bogged down in the minutiae. While working on this goal, Goodge and Coomber (2007) suggest that the coach helps the client to find ten options for action, especially attending to change processes, use of time, delegation, meetings, structures, jobs, relationships, information systems; and not just books, courses, learning from others. This is strong advice, as 360-degree feedback tends to be an HR intervention and therefore HR remedies are often recommended. Goodge and Coomber (2007) redirect our attention to learning and action in and through work itself, and away from the standards that lie behind most feedback frameworks.

Conclusions

Standards are a pervasive part of organizational life. They can do much less than is often claimed for them. Nonetheless, for many, they are a necessary part of developing an emerging profession of coaching or of quality assuring the social movement of mentoring.

PROFESSIONALIZATION

Is professionalization a convenient rationale by the proto-profession of coaching to help to raise prices, by restricting supply? Or does it regulate the 'dog eat shark' approach of commercialism? What happens to an occupation when it makes the journey from an unregulated group of practices to a unified profession? Will the insiders move closer to the centre, while the outsiders are pushed further out? The latter point is offered as a critique of communities of practice in Chapter 8 ('Learning Networks').

In coaching and mentoring we are dealing with a thoroughly amorphous cluster of interests and foci. The population varies according to:

Client group – the differences could not be wider: some executive coaches deal with the most senior levels in global companies; some social mentors deal with the most disadvantaged, demoralized and deskilled in our communities.

Level of skill – some line managers operating as coaches do so after a day or even less of training; some executive coaching organizations argue that to be a coach you need to first be qualified as a psychologist and then do extensive training after that.

Basis for helping skill – some executive coaches and small business mentors seem to think that having been in a senior position and having trod the same path as their clients that is all they need to function well; other executive coaches argue that therapeutic skills of a high order are needed. Even among this latter group there are many sharp differences – some feel that existential therapy is the answer, others adhere to transactional analysis, others Gestalt therapy; the list is endless.

We explore how much professionalization is needed or appropriate in the field of coaching and mentoring, and the requirements for a profession that serves its customers. What are the arguments for and against professionalization?

Arguments for Professionalization

Emerging Profession

Professionalization can be seen as a natural process that is followed by a huge range of occupations as part of their evolution. A body of knowledge is identified, it is codified and one or more membership organizations seek to defend the code and define the field. There are ancient professions – medicine, church, law – newer professions – accountancy, surveying, architecture – and proto-professions – coaching and mentoring, IT, facilities managers. According to this view, professionalization is a natural process and different occupations will flow along this course in a natural and somehow inevitable way.

Control of Poor Performers and Unethical Practitioners

Every membership body concerned with coaching and mentoring has a code of ethics and an ethics committee to oversee it. This interest in ethics seems to be unfeigned. The EMCC ethics committee at a formative stage conducted a survey of members and found a remarkably high degree of interest in and use of the ethical standards among members. When offering external coaching or mentoring, purchasers are pleased to know that those selling their services are bound by a professional code. It is very unlikely that the purchaser will need to invoke the code – and the sanctions that its upholders can apply are limited in proto-professions – nonetheless, purchasers report that it is good to know that it is there.

Reduce Burden of Assessment of Potential Coaches

As discussed above under the heading of 'Standards', there are money and time costs of not having standards, and professional membership acts as a useful first filter in assessing which coach or mentor a purchaser will use.

Enables Committed Professionals to Differentiate Themselves in the Market

Any rigorous process of entry to a professional body, if it does nothing else, at least separates those committed to the profession from casual or dilettante practitioners. And some years of study and reflection on professional practice is highly likely to create some improvement in performance in an overwhelming majority of cases, even if it can offer no guarantee in every individual so accredited.

Carried by a Public-spirited and Non-doctrinaire Body it can Prevent Partisan Advocates of One Particular Approach from Dominating the Scene

In recent years, our experience of EMCC has led us to the conclusion that without bodies like this the coaching profession could have been hijacked by people with a self-interested axe to grind. Psychologists would have been more tempted to claim that you have to be a psychologist to coach; retired executives would have had a louder voice calling for the T-shirt test (that you have to have been there to help others); and alumni of a particular school of coach training might have had a disproportionate traction on the market.

Arguments against Professionalization

Focus on Where the Big Bucks Are rather than Areas of Greatest Social Need

It is surely no coincidence that the biggest interest in the multiplicity of bodies involved in professionalizing coaching has clustered round executive coaching. There is an old joke that the answer to the question, 'What's the difference between a life coach and an executive coach?' is '£200 an hour'. In some quarters of central London the fee for executive coaching may change the punchline to as much as '£1,000 per hour'. By encouraging the development of a profession we might unwittingly marginalize those who work in unfashionable or badly funded areas of work, and this would be undesirable.

Self-interest of Providers

More generally, professionalization can be seen as serving the self-interest of their members and not focussing on the good of the wider community of customers, clients, purchasers and society at large. So, while professions may not do much harm, they attend to doing 'good' primarily for their members and only secondarily for others if this helps them to maintain their mandate from society.

Professionals are a Conspiracy against the Laity

George Bernard Shaw called all professions an organized conspiracy against the laity. This is the strongest case against professions in general: that they actively do harm to others by protecting the incompetent, defending the indefensible and preserving the mystery of the occupation from the prying eyes of outsiders who might question the taken-for-granted beliefs or dominant discourses of practitioners. A particular target of this attack on professions is the practice of members of the profession serving as judge and jury of behaviour in the profession. Cases of professional misconduct are handled universally by members of the profession themselves, and those outside the charmed circle may feel that their experience of the profession is given short shrift in the process.

Conclusions

Professions are seen as a pervasive feature of contemporary life, and so, it could be argued, coaching and mentoring need to get in on the game with everyone else. The case for this is supported by an austere vision for professions as the disinterested guardians of standards in public life. Standing against this argument for professions is the perspective that they operate largely on an agenda of self-interest. Reflecting on our own involvement with the coaching and mentoring profession, we see both these motives at work. Professionalization provides more education work for universities; it creates a climate where more people are likely to seek paid coaches and mentors. At the same time, we find ourselves impelled by a sense that we owe it to our clients and to the wider society to ensure that people who are licensed to coach and mentor abide by the highest professional standards and ethical codes.

THE INFLUENCE OF THE EUROPEAN UNION

The EMCC, the Association of National Organisations for Supervision in Europe and three national organizations (two German and one French) have jointly appointed a representative to explore how the associations could develop their strategic alignment in the European Union. The Bologna Process from 1999 has initiated close co-operation between universities in establishing a European system with standardized levels for Bachelor and Master's degrees. The Copenhagen Process from 2002 identified four priority areas for vocational education and development: strengthening the European dimension; transparency; recognition of competencies and qualifications; and quality assurance. Then in 2005 the European Parliament agreed a Directive on recognition of professional qualifications, and in 2006 a framework for joint platforms. In 2007, the Commission decided on the formation of a group of co-ordinators for the recognition of professional qualifications. Work in the EU has been undertaken on the development of vocational guidance and it is possible that developments in coaching and mentoring could be related to this established body of work. An argument for those involved in coaching and mentoring becoming active in the European dimension is that this will enable us to be masters of our own fate. One of the other issues for coaching and mentoring is whether a distinctive European framework is desirable and needed or whether it is satisfactory to follow a US-led framework.

CONCLUSIONS

To return to the three main questions we raised at the start of the chapter:

- Can and should competencies be used as a basis for describing the role of coach and mentor?
- Can and should standards be built upon these competencies?
- Can and should a professional accreditation be established on the basis of these standards?

This chapter, while focussing on standards, competencies and professionalization, has as an underlying theme the question of social order and how it is maintained in communities of practice and in organizations availing themselves of the communities' services.

Taking the first question, yes competencies can be used as a way of describing the role of a coach or mentor. The question of 'should they be?' is debatable with no clear answer.

To take the second question, standards could be built on a competency framework but again, the question of 'should they be?' is still a debate.

The third question raises some conflicting issues. We conclude that there are strong pressures to bring order to mentoring and coaching communities but perhaps this is driven by the dominant concept of the rational pragmatic manager first raised in Chapter 3. Whilst there is nothing wrong with this concept, several hundred years of research into learning and development also points to alternative ways of interacting with the world. The risk of the rational pragmatic dominating is the risk inherent in Tayloristic 'one-best way' practices which may be fine in a stable world but, as discussed in Chapter 13, diversity is a big challenge to humankind and a diversity-informed perspective embraces different and alternative views.

There are also persuasive arguments against a competency-based approach. These are based on both libertarian values and the search for innovation and impact from coaching and mentoring and a diversity mindset where difference is to be celebrated. The alternative is the logic of 'turtles all the way down' or the dominance of one power base over another. In the end the current state is based on 'you pays your money and you take your choice': but, is paying your money one way or the other a sophisticated and all-embracing position fit for the twenty-first century? Perhaps not.

The future

We see pressure for competencies, standards and professionalization growing in the future, thanks to the combined interests of suppliers, purchasers, educators and regulators. We dream of a world where people have a more nuanced approach than this and negotiate their wishes between each other as free and responsible citizens. Is this going to happen? At our university the number of people wanting to come on our competency-grounded, EMCC-standard-approved, professional Master's course is increasing year by year. On the other hand, in recent years we have met a growing trickle of people coming to us and saying, 'Is there any way of studying this subject in a coaching way, where I negotiate the curriculum to meet my idiosyncratic needs, and where I do only what will be useful to my practice?' We are developing ways to encourage and work with this trickle of people. Will the trickle become a flood? We hope so, but we are not holding our breath.

QUESTIONS

For coaches and mentors, from where do you draw your professional credibility?

Is it the credentials of courses or professional membership?

Or is it your need to be on a purchasers' approved list of preferred suppliers?

Or is it the references that your past clients give you?

What do they themselves say about the process and effects of working with you?

What do the people you work with and their customers say about the effects of the coaching or mentoring?

For purchasers of coaching in organizations, one of the big questions is: is it better to use proprietary-selection processes for external coaches or go for some industry standard?

Is the extra work involved in coming up with your own standards worth the benefits of customization?

In one case in the public service in the UK, a department of state (the Department of Work and Pensions) has used the same list of external coaches as another public body (the National Health Service Institute) – for you to do this would it be avoiding reinventing the wheel or is it sub-optimizing on being clear about what you are looking for in external providers?

For those seeking to regulate the activity, a core question is: do you go it alone or to seek wider co-ordination across a number of bodies? (The latter path is more difficult but potentially has more rewards for participants and users alike.)

Another question is: do you focus upon regulating out by keeping those less fit to practice at a disadvantage in the market?

Or do you attempt to improve standards with a focus upon increasing the average effectiveness of practitioners?

PART IV

TOWARDS A THEORY OF COACHING AND MENTORING

A UNITED STATES PERSPECTIVE ON COACHING AND MENTORING

by
Dawn Chandler

CHAPTER OVERVIEW

This chapter discusses coaching and mentoring as United States practices and research foci. The discussion begins with an overview of coaching and mentoring as practices, starting with a brief review of their historical roots in the United States. The chapter then delves into the topics as subjects of research with a particular emphasis on their distinctiveness from each other. Next, the chapter turns to the American cultural bias that permeates much of the mentoring and coaching literature. Finally, areas for future research on both topics are offered.

INTRODUCTION

As practices, coaching and mentoring are flourishing in the United States. Among the trends, sole practitioners offer their services as executive, sports and life coaches, organizations implement formal mentoring programmes designed to enhance their human capital, and youth and educational mentoring continue to gain momentum (MENTOR, 2006a). As scholarly topics, mentoring has been a popular phenomenon since roughly the late 1970s (for example, Speizer, 1981; Chandler and Kram, 2007), while only more recently has coaching as a distinct focus of research begun to gain a foothold (Kampa-Kokesch and Anderson, 2001; Feldman and Lankau, 2005; Joo, 2005).

UNITED STATES COACHING AND MENTORING PRACTICES

United States' organizations have used coaching and mentoring as vehicles for employee and player learning, personal and team development and, in the case of non-sports organizations, career advancement. In addition, coaching and mentoring are considered to be strategies for employee retention, succession planning and career satisfaction.

The Gaining Popularity of Coaching

While sport coaching has been a mainstay in the United States since the inception of organized athletics, other types of coaching – with titles such as executive, life, business, reading, literary and counselling – have become more pervasive in recent decades. It is difficult to know with certainty when coaching (other than sports coaching) first began as a practice (Kampa-Kokesch and Anderson, 2001). Early influences on coaching date back to the early 1900s; William James, Carl Jung and Alfred Adler have been asserted as influences of modern-day coaching) (see Williams, 2003). Researchers have varyingly posited the emergence of coaching as a distinct, modern topic in the 1980s (Tobias, 1996; Natale and Diamonte, 2005) and 1990s (Feldman and Lankau, 2005).

For example, Natale and Diamante (2005) posit that executive coaching to the 1980s, when Thomas J., a financial planner in Seattle, Washington (USA) began offering life-planning consultations in 1992 and then formed Coach University, which was aimed at aiding professional development. Initially, executive coaching was formed to save talented individuals whose career was in jeopardy due to a particular flaw (McCauley and Hezlett, 2001). Over time, however, the other key recipients of coaching were high potential candidates who could climb the corporate ladder with appropriate development (McCauley and Hezlett, 2001).

Because of the array of coaching services an individual might provide (meaning that someone might identify as a life and/or personal coach), it is impossible to distinguish the growth of the life, personal and executive coaching segments of the industry from each other. As a general indicator of US involvement in coaching relative to the rest of the world, among the nearly 12,000 International Coaching Federation members – the largest global body of practitioners identifying as coaches – 53 per cent are United States based (ICF, 2007). As another indicator of coaching's popularity, a Society of Human Resource Management survey (2005) of 248 United States human-resource managers showed that 55 per cent of their organizations employed coaching as a means to aid employee development.

Finally, myriad organizations, public and private, such as 'Alcoa, American Red Cross, AT&T, Ford, Northwestern Mutual Life, 3M, and United Parcel Service' (Natale and Diamonte, 2005: 362), have begun implementing executive coaching programmes as a means to foster leadership talent and learning and bolster succession planning efforts. Organizations like the Center for Creative Leadership – a non-profit organization headquartered in North Carolina – and Right Management Consultants – a global consultancy firm owned by Manpower – offer leadership programmes and coaching services, respectively, to thousands of individuals who aspire to be or reside in managerial positions (Auerbach, 2005).

Arguably, the sport-coaching industry is the most advanced in terms of regulation and licensing standards. Programmes like the National Federation of State High School Associations' Coach Education Program, and organizations like the National Association for Sport and Physical Education (NASPE), ensure that an adequately qualified pool of various coaches oversee youth sports. For example, 'In 2006, NASPE called on experts from national governing bodies of sport, the United States Olympic Committee, National Federation of State High School Associations, and NASPE leadership to review and revise the popular 1995 standards for athletic coaches to be more consistent with current sport research and best practice' (NASPE web site).

In contrast, the United States 'business' coaching industry (which can generally be considered to encapsulate executive, life and personal coaching) is unregulated, leading to a proliferation of varying backgrounds, educational levels and overall qualifications among practitioners who identify as 'coaches' (Brotman et al., 1998; Harris, 1999). Therefore, coaching 'best practices' and required competencies have yet to be identified and standardized. However, United States and European organizations have begun to offer educational and credentialling programmes to enhance a coach's ability to meet clients' needs. For example, to become certified as an Associate Certified Coach (ACC), the first level of credentialling (there are two other levels not discussed here) with the International Coaching Federation, individuals must pass an oral exam and complete a minimum of 60 hours of coach-specific training and 100 hours of coaching experience. While the ICF's credential is not American per se, credentialling programmes are held in the United States and thousands of American practitioners gain ICF licensure for the purposes of educational enhancement and legitimacy in the field.

The 'Mentoring Movement'

While mentoring as a practice has arguably occurred throughout history across national settings, an explicit awareness of mentoring in a contemporary setting can largely be traced to the United States (see Speizer, 1981; Monaghan, 1992). Speizer (1981) asserted that the recent popularity of mentoring at the close of the 1970s was based on the research of Daniel Levinson, a Yale University professor, whose work captured researcher and public attention. Levinson et al.'s work (1978), which tracked a cohort of men throughout their lives, showed a mentor as a pivotal figure in assisting men through early adulthood as they seek to realize their dreams.

Consistent with Speizer's assertion of a United States' early influence on mentoring, Monaghan and Lunt (1992), wrote that 'In nursing the rise of mentoring (also called preceptorship) developed in the United States from the 1970s and 1980s' (p. 250) and 'In mentoring in business organizations there is again a strong American influence' (p. 251).

Since the 1980s, the United States' popular press and media have used the term 'mentoring movement' to convey the spread of mentoring practices and formalized programmes throughout the country (see Mecca, 2007; Youth Mentoring Connection, 2007). The growth of formal mentoring programmes was in part the result of the concurrent rise of the Human Resource Development Movement of the 1970s (Eng, 1986). Feldman (2001), in asserting the importance of mentoring for young scientists, wrote that mentoring relationships are 'common in nearly all professions' (p. 61).

Historically, formal programmes were initially developed on a 'work basis' with the aim of assisting a select group of individuals, in particular high-potential candidates and minorities (Kanter, 1977; Monaghan and Lunt, 1992). The recognition that US women and minorities were plateauing earlier and leaving organizations at higher rates than their male counterparts led to organizational mentoring efforts to redress the dual issues (Morrison et al., 1994). Likewise, the civil-rights movement and affirmative-action laws heightened the pervasiveness of formal mentoring programs (see Chandler and Kram, 2005).

Over time, formal programmes expanded to include a broader employee base, the goals being to enhance employee learning and development and knowledge transfer (Chao et al., 1992; Douglas and McCauley, 1997). Mentoring programmes span organizations of various sizes, including large, Fortune 500 organizations and small- and medium-size for-profit and non-profit organizations. With respect to the latter, for example, non-profit organizations such as Mentor.net, which aims to foster one-on-one e-mentoring relationships between protégés in universities and colleges and mentors from the engineering, mathematics and science industries, and MENTOR, which strives to connect adult mentors and youths, are proliferating.

Numerous programmes in the United States are designed specifically to foster American youths' full potential and minimize the likelihood of youth drug and alcohol use. To these ends, the Harvard Mentoring Project, MENTOR/National Mentoring Partnership and the Corporation for National Community Service created the National Mentoring Month (NMM), whose goal is to identify volunteers to help youth meet their full potential (MENTOR, 2006b). According to MENTOR, 30 per cent of all mentoring programmes are 'school-based' (MENTOR, 2006c). To ensure that youths' safety is not compromised in the pairing process, SafetyNet is an organization that conducted FBI-based background checks on all mentor volunteers (MENTOR, 2006d).

Other mentoring vehicles include faith and community-based mentoring programmes such as the Center for Urban Ministerial Education (CUME) in Boston and the YMCA, respectively. A more recent mentoring trend involves organization-to-organization mentoring. For example, in 1991, the Department of Defense established a 'Mentor-Protégé Program' that partners small, disadvantaged businesses (protégés) with more established businesses (mentors) as a means to help the protégé businesses compete for prime contract and subcontract awards http://www.acq.osd.mil/osbp/mentor_protege/). Likewise, organizations are forming mentoring partnerships to facilitate the spread of environmental best practices (Idaho Department of Environmental Quality, 2002).

In spite of the prevalence of formal mentoring programmes in the United States, noticeably absent are countrywide standards that could assist effective programme design and implementation. United States organizations can benefit from benchmarking proposed programs against the International Standards for Mentoring Programmes in Employment that were spearheaded by European Mentoring and Coaching Council (www.ismpe.com).

Researchers have asserted that the United States mentoring model in practice is one that favours protégé sponsorship, while Europe's model favours a 'developmental model' (see Clutterbuck, 2001, 2007b). A sponsorship model is one in which the primary aim of the mentoring relationship is to sponsor the protégé for career advancement through the provision of challenging opportunities and oversight of the protégé's careers; by comparison, the developmental model aims at personal growth, mutual learning and 'mentee' accountability for outcomes. Clutterbuck (2007b), in implicitly comparing the two models, commented that with the developmental model, 'Career outcomes are seen as outcomes of personal growth, rather than as the primary purpose of the relationship' (p. 14).

United States Research on Coaching and Mentoring

As noted earlier, the United States coaching literature is in a 'fledgling' stage of maturity relative to the mentoring literature, which has amassed an abundance of empirical studies over the past two-and-a-half decades. Here, both topics are reviewed, drawing comparisons between the literatures along relevant criteria, including the maturity of the field, the way each addresses practitioners, and key concepts and areas of interest to researchers. Table 14.1 compares the two topics along various criteria.

Maturity of Field

As noted earlier, the field of mentoring has developed over the past 25-plus years, while the field of coaching has begun to blossom in the past decade. As an indicator of the US's relative contribution to the mentoring literature, in the early 1990s, the mentoring literature body included over 900 articles, most of which were conducted in American settings and associated with management development (Segerman-Peck, 1991). Since Kram's work was published, mentoring research has flourished, building a US body of research around a nomological network of relationships, including mentoring antecedents, outcomes, processes and moderators.

By comparison, as noted in earlier chapters in this book, a body of studies on executive coaching emerged in the 1990s. The sports-coaching literature is relatively well established (a search of SPORTDiscus with Full Text yields

Table 14.1 Characteristics of the US mentoring and coaching literatures

	Mentoring literature	Coaching literature
Degree of definitional distinctiveness between mentoring and coaching	Undifferentiated	Differentiated
Methods	Positivistic	Case studies, qualitative
Practical implications	Derived from study findings	Considered at study's onset
Maturity of field	Mature	Nascent
Conceptual foci	Antecedents	Antecedents
	Outcomes (mentor, protégé, organizational)	Coaching interventions types, activities and process
	Developmental network	Proposed outcomes
	Formal mentoring programmes	Creation of a research agenda
	Types of relationships	Demarcation of coaching as a topic
Cohesiveness of literature	Fragmented (education, counselling, adult/youth)	Fragmented, yet less so (executive, sports, life, counselling) represent growing strands

articles dating back to 1974), yet is distinct in its focus on athletic relationships such as that between a coach and player rather than on work-related coaching relationships. Joo (2005), in his literature review on executive coaching, identified only 78 articles from select academic and practice articles. Joo's and other literature reviews (see Kampa-Kokesch and Anderson, 2001; Feldman and Lankau, 2005) do not differentiate between United States-based and other countries' research; however, one can assume a smaller number of studies.

Degree of Definitional Distinctiveness between Mentoring and Coaching

An influential factor in creating a distinct body of US knowledge is the topic's degree of definitional clarity. More specifically, it is important to define the topic of study as one that is distinct from other related concepts. While researchers have posited varying definitions of a 'mentor', there is relative clarity around its general notion (Wanberg et al., 2003) as a concept. The demarcation of mentoring from other concepts in essence creates 'definitional distinctiveness' that has enabled a topical literature to flourish.

A unique literature on coaching might have emerged earlier than roughly a decade ago, had a definition of coaching, as distinct from mentoring, emerged. This definitional vagueness led to the terms 'coach' and 'mentor' being used interchangeably.

Therefore, historical empirical research on mentoring encapsulates findings that probably include the relationships individuals had with their coaches.

Likewise, empirical studies on mentoring and developmental networks often operationalize the concept in such a way that a study participant could identify a coach as a mentor, thus further conflating the two phenomena. As an example of the ambiguity of the operationalization of the term 'mentor', the recently published Tharenou article (2005) noted in Chapter 2 'Researching Coaching and Mentoring' employed the mentor definition 'a higher-ranking person with advanced experience and knowledge who has played a committed role in the development of their careers' (p. 85). This definition has been advanced in a number of studies (see Kram, 1985; Scandura and Williams, 2001). A study participant presented with this definition might identify an external executive coach who is at a higher rank than the focal individual as a mentor. Similarly, research on developmental networks (Higgins and Kram, 2001) uses the definition 'a group of individuals who take an active interest in and action to advance a focal person's career' (p. 268). Again, an individual presented with this definition might identify an external coach as among his or her developers.

Degree of Cohesiveness of Literatures

Over the past few decades, various United States discipline researchers, for example business, educational, youth, sports, nursing and counselling, have examined mentoring. While discipline researchers occasionally cite studies from various literatures, it is common for a journal article or book chapter to focus almost solely on citing studies from a particular discipline. Therefore, the mentoring body is fragmented and 'silo-ed'.

As a testament to this fragmentation, Eby and Allen (2006: 1) wrote, 'Researchers from a wide range of disciplines (e.g., education, counselling, social work, psychology, management) have a mutual interest in mentoring relationships, yet researchers within disciplines rarely integrate theories or perspectives from other areas of mentoring scholarship to their own work'. As one means to create a more interdisciplinary body of mentoring research, the *Journal of Vocational Behavior* intends to publish a special edition called 'Bridging Disciplinary Divides in Mentoring Research' in 2008.

The coaching literature is fragmented, yet is much less so than the mentoring literature. For example, Kampa-Kokesh and Anderson (2001) noted that three distinct executive coaching bodies of literature, psychological, training and development, and management, have emerged. In addition, the authors noted that some studies highlight that managers and executives can act as coaches (Kampa-Kokesh and Anderson, 2001). Due to the relatively low numbers of published studies that mark the coaching field, it is arguably less fragmented than the mentoring literature. The degree of fragmentation that exists over time will be determined by the extent to which disciplines' researchers cross-cite studies from other disciplines.

Methods

Chapter 2 in this book described methodological distinctions between the mentoring and coaching literatures. A United States mentoring research study largely exemplifies the 'archetypal mentoring article' identified in Chapter 2. The typical article is well placed within established theory (e.g., noting mentoring functions, using current theory such as leader-member exchange), has a set of hypotheses, uses statistical analyses with large sample sizes, examines the relationship between two or three variables/concepts, and outlines limitations and practical contributions.

As shown earlier in Chapter 2, the coaching literature tends to be based on case studies and interviews with a relatively small number of respondents. It seems likely that as a US-based literature on coaching forms over time, a positivistic trend will develop.

Practical Implications

Another difference between United States and other countries' research (in this case, European research) lies in their approach to practice (aside from such noteworthy exceptions as those identified in the prior section). A typical United States mentoring research project begins with the aim of examining phenomena and then deriving practical implications on the basis of the study's findings. By way of comparison, European studies tend to place 'the emphasis [...] on identifying good practice (what works and doesn't work) and initiating subsequent quantitative or qualitative empirical investigation to elucidate underlying theory' (Clutterbuck, 2007b: 1).

The coaching literature's focus on business relevance and the stated aim of 'pragmatic enhancement of practice' (see Chapter 2) stand in contrast to US-based studies' tendency with consideration of practical implications. It seems likely that as a US-based executive coaching literature takes shape, studies will typically derive practical considerations from positivistic findings.

Topics of Focus in US Coaching and Mentoring

Table 14.1 shows topical foci for mentoring and coaching. Given coaching's newness as a field, researchers are working to carve out a *unique space for the topic* (by demarcating it from other helping relationships such as therapists and mentors) and to *create a robust agenda* to guide future efforts. Case studies and qualitative studies have served as a foundation for proposing *successful intervention processes and steps* (see Hall et al., 1999; Parsloe and Rolph, 2004; Feldman and Lankau, 2005; Natale and Diamonte, 2005). For example, Feldman and Lankau (2005: 837) outlined four major activities that occur in coaching relationships:

- Data gathering.
- Feedback.
- Implementation of the coaching intervention.
- Evaluation.

Numerous studies suggest positive *outcomes* associated with executive coaching, such as increased self-confidence, self-awareness and sensitivity to others, better time management, improved performance, organizational productivity, customer service and increased commitment (see Gegner, 1997; Olivero et al., 1997; Hall et al., 1999; Joo, 2005).

More recently, Joo (2005) proposed *antecedents* to coaching processes and outcomes that include coach characteristics such as his/her confidence, academic background and experience, and coachee characteristics such as his/her level of proactivity and goal orientation. To date, however, to the author's knowledge, these antecedents have yet to be empirically tested.

One of the driving forces behind the rise of executive coaching practices and research is purportedly the downsizing and delayering of United States organizations in the 1990s, which has led to isolated executives who need to develop skills after having been promoted yet receive too little support from others in the hierarchy (Carter, 2001).

The US mentoring literature foci include *antecedents, outcomes, formal mentoring programmes and developmental networks*. With respect to antecedents, researchers have examined mentor and protégé characteristics, e.g. education, job/career history, willingness to mentor, that influence relational processes and outcomes. Acknowledging that women and minorities have faced career challenges unlike their male, Caucasian counterparts in the United States, race and gender have been examined as antecedents. Myriad empirical studies have confirmed positive outcomes, for example career and job satisfaction, career advancement, personal learning, of mentoring for mentors, protégé and organizations, as well as negative outcomes such as sabotage that undermine mentoring (see Scandura, 1998; Eby et al., 2004).

Given the prevalence of formal mentoring programmes in the United States, researchers have been keen to understand the benefits of formal relationships in comparison to those offered by informal relationships as well as the value of having a mentor versus lacking one (Chao et al., 1992; Fagensen-Eland et al., 1997; Ragins and Cotton, 1999; Seibert, 1999). Very little research has examined what formal programme characteristics should be in place to lead to maximum programme effectiveness. Recently, however, Allen et al. (2006) found that mentor commitment and programme understanding mediated perceived programme effectiveness.

Shifts in the career environment including globalization, diversity, technology and downsizing act as a confluence of factors that have led to the unlikelihood that an individual (protégé) is able to gain all of his or her developmental needs with the assistance of a single mentor. People transition with greater frequency between and within organizations such that a long-term mentoring relationship between a mentor and protégé is unlikely. Furthermore, given the pace of organizational life today, people must learn quickly and potential mentors have less time to dedicate to their protégés (Kram and Hall, 1996; Higgins and Kram, 2001).

As raised in Chapter 8, today's employees are likely to have a developmental network, or portfolio of advisors (Higgins, 2000), who provide developmental assistance. 'Developers', members of the portfolio, can reside within or outside a focal individual's employing organization and stem from various social spheres, including within one's family and network of friends, and community-affiliated organizations (Higgins and Kram, 2001). The developmental network concept draws upon the social-network literature, which considers the strength and diversity of ties (relationships) as the basis of a network's structure. Since its introduction in the literature in 2001, it has been the basis of a growing number of empirical studies and discussion (see Higgins and Dobrow, 2005; Cummings and Higgins, 2006).

A UNITED STATES/WESTERN CULTURAL BIAS IN MENTORING AND COACHING RESEARCH AND PRACTICE

Neither the mentoring nor coaching literatures can be considered 'global' bodies of knowledge; both suffer from a lack of cross-cultural studies and have yet to transcend the United States assumptions that are embedded in most studies. For example, mentoring and coaching practices and research are arguably dually founded on Western cultural values. In support of this assertion, in a recent article comparing Saudi Arabian and US managerial coaching practices, Noer et al. (2007) commented that 'the foundations of coaching seem to be rooted in the modern Western (primarily US) managerial values of participation, accountability, and free choice' (p. 291; also see Hargrove, 1995; Whitworth et al., 1998). Later, they continued, 'From a global perspective, there has been no research that has examined the link between coaching behaviors and culturally defined values and norms outside the US or Western Europe' (p. 272).

One key reason that a United States/Western mentoring research bias exists lies in the use of United States study *participants*. In a more recent review of the mentoring literature, Chandler and Kram wrote, 'we want to point out to the reader that this chapter necessarily adopts an American focus, this perspective is taken because the mentoring research to date is overwhelmingly empirically based on American participant experiences' (2007: 242). Indeed, while there is a large body of literature relating to UK citizens, much of the extant literature is 'United States-bound' in that the findings relate to how Americans experience mentoring and cannot be generalized to other countries' citizens.

As an example of how a United States bias conceals how individuals from other countries experience mentoring, Bright (2005) asserted that Western mentoring, which includes American and European contexts, has taken on a more strategic emphasis than in Japan's context, which focusses more on the mentoring relationship in and unto itself. Human-resource departments have emphasized formal mentoring programmes in the West as a means to enhance employee retention and recruitment (Bright, 2005). By comparison, formal mentoring programmes are neither typically implemented nor part of a human-resource strategy (as would be the case if organizations 'strategized' how to further the informal formation of relationships) in Japan.

Given that mentoring and coaching practices are based on Western values and many, if not most, mentoring studies involve United States participants, it is critical to consider what American cultural assumptions are embedded in the topics' body of knowledge. Knowledge of these assumptions can aid the creation of a research agenda aimed at identifying mentoring and coaching practices and experiences in other national contexts.

Hofstede's (1980, 2001) national culture framework is useful to consider how Western/American assumptions cloak cross-cultural differences in mentoring and coaching. Hofstede's framework includes five key dimensions along which nations' culture differ: individualism/collectivism; power distance; masculine/feminine; uncertainty avoidance; and short-/long-term orientation. This section focusses on the first three dimensions.

Individualism/Collectivism

The United States culture is marked by a high level of individualism (Hofstede, 1980, 2001), which means that relationships between people are not tightly knit; individuals are expected to care for immediate family and themselves. Collectivism, the opposing cultural orientation, which characterizes countries such as China, Indonesia, West Africa and a number of Latin American countries, involves very close relationships between people that extend beyond immediate families (Hofstede, 1980, 2001). While the focus in individualistic societies is on respect for an individual's rights and personal responsibilities, collectivistic societies value respect for and loyalty to the group (Hofstede, 1980, 2001).

It may be that in a highly individualistic society like the United States, the looseness of ties between non-familial people are less likely to lead to strong affective, reciprocal bonds. While future research is needed to understand whether emotional closeness is a prerequisite for effective coaching relationships, studies have shown that it is a necessary condition for successful mentoring relationships (see Chapter 1).

Individualistic societies are less prone than their collectivistic counterparts to emphasize long-term employee contractual agreements. When the psychological contract (Rousseau, 1995) between an employee and organization is relatively short term, as is the case in the United States (Pfeffer, 1997), mentoring relationships that are formed may be shorter lived than in the case of long-term psychological contracts. Potential mentors and protégés may perceive fewer benefits of initiating a relationship if they perceive their tenure with the organization as short term. The duration of a relationship is likely to influence the amount of functional support provided to a protégé. The foregoing discussion suggests that, relative to collectivistic societies, mentoring in the United States may involve relatively fewer relationships that are of mentoring quality and shorter-term mentoring durations that may result in lesser amounts of mentoring support provided.

Another potential implication of US individualism involves the focus of the mentor and protégé's and coach and coachee's developmental efforts and aims. To the extent that the parties involved strive for protégé or coachee autonomy and independence, both of which are consistent with individualism, the development of a mutually rewarding relationship may become secondary to achieving the former aims.

As a comparison to US mentoring and coaching, Japan, a collectivistic nation, is prone to foster strong-tie, 'kinship' relationships between individuals who are not related due to cultural factors and organizational landscape (Bright, 2005). Japan has a culture of 'groupism', likely correlated with collectivism, which predisposes more experienced people to help those who are less experienced (Nakane, 1972; Bright, 2005). Heightening this tendency to form strong emotional ties that are necessary conditions for the occurrence of mentoring relationships, Japanese employees typically work for the same organizations throughout their entire careers; this context enables long-term relational bonds to flourish (Whitehill, 1991). Japan's career context stands in stark contrast to the United States' career context, in which individuals transition between jobs frequently as the result of flexible labour markets and a short-term psychological contract between employees and organizations (Rousseau, 1995).

Another example of the need to conduct more research on various national contexts is the case of China's guanxi relationships. Guanxi, a special type of relationship that bonds the exchange partners through reciprocal exchange of favours and mutual obligations (Alston, 1989; Luo, 1997), seems to similarly heighten the likelihood of naturally occurring mentoring relationships. The above cultural differences seem likely to account for the lack of formal mentoring programmes in either Japan or China. Thus, both Asian countries seem to naturally enjoy what the United States and other countries often 'manufacture'. To the extent that groupism and guanxi represent forms of collectivism, it seems likely that formal mentoring programmes may be more necessary in an individualistic society, in which most relationships are not characterized by strong enough ties to constitute mentoring or developmental relationships.

Power Distance

The United States is among those countries, others being Israel, New Zealand, Denmark and a number of Western European countries, characterized by low power distance. The degree of power distance refers to the extent to which a society's members accept a power inequality between people. In countries such as the United States, people are more likely to consider each other as equals; subordinates would desire and expect to have participation in decision-making. As contrasts, in countries such as Malaysia, Guatemala and the Philippines, which are high power countries, people expect those in higher positions of power to make important decisions and consider less equality given status differences.

Power distance has a number of potential implications for coaching and mentoring relationships. In lower-power-distance countries like the United States, protégés/coaches are likely to desire greater input into establishing goals and conveying their expectations for the relationship. Protégés in low-distance countries, because they perceive less of a power disparity between themselves and seniors, may feel more comfortable initiating mentoring relationships due to the perception that they can aid their mentors' careers as well. Mentors/coaches in low-power-distance countries may be more inclined to view their protégés as a potential threat given the lack of perceived power between the two individuals.

Masculine/Feminine

Noer et al.'s (2007) research showed that Saudi managers tended to use more supportive, nurturing behaviours than did United States managers. Included in these 'supporting' behaviours are 'attending', which involves the use of body language and other non-verbal communication aimed at creating a trusting, open environment, and 'affirming,' which aims at conveying that faith the coach has in the ability of the person being coached to develop. The authors posit that cultural differences can explain the coaching behavioural differences. Specifically, they posit that the Saudi culture is more 'feminine' (Hofstede, 1980, 2001) than the United States, which, by comparison, is more 'masculine'; a feminine culture places import on fostering and preserving relationships, while a masculine culture favours assertiveness and competitiveness (Hofstede, 1980, 2001). Another implication of masculinity is as a means to help the protégé 'beat' other employees perceived to be 'competitors', United States mentors and protégés may place an emphasis on sponsorship (behaviours aimed at advancing the protégé's careers).

US COACHING AND MENTORING RESEARCH AGENDAS

This section suggests several avenues for future inquiry for coaching and mentoring. As the prior section suggests, for a global perspective on mentoring and coaching to emerge in their respective literatures, much more research is needed that transcends United States' sample populations and studies based on Western assumptions and values. The agenda includes avenues for redressing the US/Western cultural bias and exploring topics that reflect practices and demographic trends in the United States.

The prior section's discussion suggests several questions related to cross-cultural research:

1. Are people in collectivistic nations more willing to mentor/coach than people in individualistic nations?
2. Do individuals from collectivistic nations have mentoring and/or coaching relationships that are longer in duration and stronger in affect and emotional closeness than individuals from individualistic nations?
3. Does the amount of mentoring and coaching protégés and coachees receive vary across national contexts?
4. Are potential protégés in low-power-distance countries more likely than potential protégés in high-distance countries to initiate mentoring relationships?
5. Are protégés in low-distance countries, due to their tendency to desire participation in the relationship, less likely to experience unmet expectations in mentoring and coaching relationships?
6. Is sponsorship as an outcome more likely to be emphasized by mentors and coaches in masculine countries than by mentors in feminine countries?
7. How do individuals in other countries define mentoring?
8. How do coaching behaviours and practices vary across national contexts?

Next, numerous more general avenues for coaching and mentoring research are offered.

A Coaching Agenda

The executive coaching literature would benefit from qualitative studies that mirror Kram's (1983, 1985) early research on mentoring phases and functions. Currently, executive coaching studies are prescriptive, supported by anecdotal and case study evidence to suggest what a successful intervention should look like. Given life and personal coaching seem conceptually distinct from executive coaching (although empirical investigation is needed), separate studies examining these relationships will be helpful to building the coaching literature. Ideally, the qualitative studies will ensure that internal coaches are considered as distinct from those that are external.

Until coaching relationships are more clearly delineated from mentoring relationships, it is likely that US mentoring studies will continue to empirically conflate the two and thus obscure findings relevant solely to executive or other coaching relationships. On the part of US mentoring researchers, measures that include questions designed to elicit responses around the type of relationship cited by the participant (e.g., external executive coach, organizational peer) would help disentangle coaching from other developmental relationships. Coaching studies should continue to illuminate areas of difference between the traditional mentoring relationship and an executive coach.

If coaching is to emerge as a distinct body of literature in the United States, it will likely mirror the mentoring literature in its positivistic focus. Researchers should explore the antecedents proposed in Joo's (2005) literature review and conduct rigorous, generalizable studies on coaching outcomes. Studies are needed that compare executive coaching in the United States to coaching in other countries.

To gain a better understanding of how to prepare global managers for cross-cultural coaching, more studies such as Noer et al.'s, which assess how coaching practices vary across national contexts, are needed.

A Mentoring Agenda

The United States literature is rich with studies that examine how women and minority groups experience mentoring. Most of the research focussed on African-American participants and, to a much lesser extent, on age. As the US baby-boomer generation heads toward retirement, age will become an influential factor in organizational life, given it is likely that a significant number of baby boomers will continue to work well into years at which retirement benefits begin. Two demographics that are under-researched are the Latino (the US will add 67 million people of Latin origin between 2000 and 2050 (US Census Bureau, 2005; see Blake-Beard et al., 2007)) and Asian-American/Pacific Islander populations. Research should also be dedicated to sources of 'hidden' US diversity (differences that are not physically manifest) such as sexual orientation, religion and disabilities.

Two practices that are gaining in popularity and in need of attention by researchers are reverse mentoring and organizational mentoring. Reverse mentoring involves a reversal of roles in the mentoring relationship, the junior employee acting as the mentor and senior employee as the protégé. In practice, reverse mentoring gained popularity when Jack Welch, Chairman of GE, ordered 600 senior employees to reach out to junior employees who were more knowledgeable about the internet.

To return to the earlier comment that the US enacts a sponsorship model on mentoring, which focusses on 'overseeing the career' of a protégé, Clutterbuck (2007b) asserted this model would not work in most Northern European countries, which have a very low power distance (Hofstede, 1980). Northern European employees encourage more personal responsibility for career management (Clutterbuck, 2007b). Early US research studies on mentoring supports this notion in that studies tended to examine career advancement and compensation. Since early mentoring programmes were aimed at women, diversity and high-potential candidates with the goal of aiding their advancement through the 'glass ceiling' and into senior positions overall, attentiveness to signs of advancement as outcomes seems appropriate. In practice, formal mentoring programmes in the United States may indeed still favour a sponsorship model. However, it can be argued that the United States research model is moving towards 'relational mentoring' processes and outcomes. A few trends support this assertion. First, as the mentoring literature has introduced more types of developmental relationships, researchers have recognized that mentoring benefits can be bi-directional (Kram and Hall, 1996). Second, more recently, positive organizational scholarship researchers have asserted the need to conceptualize mentoring relationships as 'high-quality connections' that lead to relational outcomes such as personal resilience (Dutton and Ragins, 2007; Higgins and Dobrow, working paper). Future research should examine the degree to which the American model is shifting in practice. Studies that consider outcomes such as relationship resilience move beyond traditional sponsorship measures.

The earlier discussion on how culture influences coaching and mentoring relationships highlights the need to conduct cross-cultural research. Given the paucity of studies using non-United States participants, it is important to consider how the underlying cultural values espoused by American participants (and by American researchers) influence research findings and how research projects are framed. Future studies should examine how mentoring and coaching varies based on cultural differences such as collectivism/individualism, power distance and masculinity/femininity. An application of Trompenaar and Hampden-Turner's (1993) cultural framework would also illuminate some potentially meaningful differences in how people across national contexts experience coaching and mentoring.

TOWARDS A THEORY OF COACHING AND MENTORING

CHAPTER OVERVIEW

This chapter pulls the themes raised throughout the book together in the form of a summary. We present a theoretical framework for coaching and mentoring which is comprised of antecedents, mediating concepts and practical applications. We then start to draw some conclusions from the themes and go on to project forwards into the future based on the trends and indicators that we see now. We place this into the public domain, not as a finished and tested theory but as a framework for debate and discussion. As we stated in the introduction of the book, we want this to be both a challenge and a basis for support. We value critical thinking and as such offer our thoughts up to criticism in the spirit of learning and the generation of new thinking.

SUMMARY OF THEMES

Theme 1 – The Context of the Knowledge Economy

We draw the themes for this book from an eclectic mix of social-science disciplines. For example, we draw on developmental and educational psychology, sociology, organizational theory, therapeutic psychology and sports psychology.

The debate in the book is located in the broader concept of learning and development as a contributor to social and economic development within a capitalist philosophy. From this is derived the concept of the 'knowledge economy'. This is a theme explicitly raised in Chapter 8 but it is present as an underlying assumption in other chapters. The argument is relatively simple and well rehearsed in a range of texts, for example Nonaka, 1991; Nonaka and Horotaka, 1995; Kessels, 1996b; Scarbrough et al., 1999; Barnett, 2000; Garvey and Williamson, 2002, and raises the question: how can knowledge be developed and used to add value to goods and services? We extend this view to the public and voluntary sectors.

There are associated links here to ideas on learning and development, education, creativity and innovation for example and the link to modern coaching and mentoring practice is clear. These are social and conversational approaches to developing, creating and sharing knowledge and understanding. It is here where a possible explanation for their exponential growth in recent years rests. Coaching and mentoring are an alternative and effective way to contribute to the knowledge economy.

Theme 2 – Mindset

Another theme raised throughout the book is that of mindset. We raise this in many of the chapters and it is a central theme to the book. We refer to and link 'mindset' to ideas such as dominant narrative, dominant discourse, gaze, dominant logic, mental models or ways of thinking. This can be a key factor in the ways different business sectors apply and understand coaching and mentoring activity. The concept also links to ideas presented throughout the book on power, goals, culture and diversity. Garvey and Williamson (2002: 183) suggest that 'mindset is 'a key determinant to the creation of a knowledge productive environment' and that it is linked to assumptions about the way people within social systems behave.

The idea that human systems are rational and that behaviour can be explained deterministically dominates the business world. The sense of 'rightness', 'provability' or 'one best way' associated with determinism discussed in this book is an important theme but, according to Von Krogh et al. (1994: 54), 'there is no longer a "right knowledge," but many coexisting conflicting pieces of knowledge'. The assumption of 'predictability' or 'determinism' is now increasingly challenged and giving way to the idea that human behaviour is based on a highly complex series of dependencies and variables that cannot be predicted. Garvey and Williamson (2002: 184) go on to say that 'this very dominant mode of thinking has been the driver of the modern industrialized world with the resultant knowledge being "characterized by a form of rationality that disengages the mind from the body and from the world" (Apffel-Marglin and Marglin, 1996: 3). Whilst it may be argued that the dominant deterministic logic (particularly prevalent in Western thinking) has been responsible for much progress in terms of industrial development, it could also be said that it is also responsible for 'social fragmentation' and 'environmental destruction' (Apeffel-Marglin and Marglin, 1996: 2)'.

Coaching and mentoring conversations offer the potential at least to create new mindsets and therefore the opportunity for people to think new thoughts, create new organizational structures and develop different, more tolerant, behaviours. This is a challenge as coaching and mentoring could easily become absorbed or even fade away as those who take a more deterministic view seek to annex them. This, in our view, is the threat of commodification raised and evidenced in several chapters throughout the book. Coaching and mentoring could be at risk of being reduced to 'tools' of management; indeed they are often extensively referred to as such (see, for example, Nankivell and Shoolbred, 1997; Broadbridge, 1999; King and Eaton, 1999; Chidiac, 2006; Henochowicz and Hetherington, 2006). The notion of 'tool' dehumanizes coaching and mentoring and aligns it to the idea that management is about the dominance of one group over another. It is a mechanical metaphor associated with discourses of control or perhaps manipulation. This is another sign of the worrying trend towards commodification – coaching and mentoring equate to tools and a tool can be 'sold' by the 'right' craftsperson – which is evidenced by the move to professionalization, qualifications, standards and the establishment of professional power bases.

The motivational theorist Abraham Maslow reminds of the risks of seeing human complexities as a tool when he once commented, 'if the only tool you have is a hammer, every problem looks like a nail.' (This saying is often attributed to him although we cannot find any direct written reference.) If all we can think of when we talk of coaching or mentoring is of 'banging in a nail', we destroy the sense of individualism, autonomy, creativity and the human spirit and contradict the very values that are embedded from coaching and mentoring's historical roots (see Chapter 1) – a confusing paradox indeed.

Theme 3 – Definitional Issues

As discussed in several chapters, coaching and mentoring activity, in our view, is fundamentally a learning and development activity.

Some, from a psychological background or, as we term it, psychologically minded (Lee, 2003), add performance, leadership and the development of expertise (Ericsson et al., 2007; Noer et al., 2007; Fleenor and Joyce, 2007; Lazovsky and Shimoni, 2007). Others, who are psychologically minded may view coaching and mentoring activity as an adjunct to therapy (see Sparrow, 2007) whereas some link the activities to the development of self-image and health-related concerns (Berglas, 2006).

Another body of work concerns itself with career progression and sponsorship with some considering mentoring and coaching as contributors to socialization processes (Kram, 1983; Colley, 2003; Rollag, 2007). Yet another body of literature links coaching and mentoring to education and educational attainment (see, for example, Miller, 2002; Garvey and Langridge, 2006).

Arguably, all these variations place coaching and mentoring in different social context and link them to different disciplines. As presented in Chapter 1, both coaching and mentoring have similar roots and the modern meanings are drawn from common discourses of the past. In Chapter 14, these differing views are explored from a US perspective with interestingly similar conclusions. The clarity of definition around mentoring in the US has enabled much good research. However, in the last ten years or so the term coaching has appeared in the literature and this has created greater variations of meaning and, in some cases, like the UK, the terms mentoring and coaching have become interchangeable. For the US style of positivistic research, this has created some difficulties as the terms coaching and mentoring have become conflated in research. What is clear is that some mindsets require differentiation through definition whereas others are content with ambiguity.

One area of commonality across the Atlantic is the view that mentoring is more of a 'movement' than coaching, and coaching is more associated with executive development.

In the UK, there are still attempts at differentiating of coaching and mentoring but the European Mentoring and Coaching Council has moved towards an integrated view. Within our Coaching and Mentoring Research Unit in Sheffield, we now refer to coaching and mentoring as one-to-one developmental dialogue. Despite a recent indication that this term may have some support (see Sparrow, 2007: 18), we do not believe that this term will necessarily 'catch on' but it does offer a clear description of the activity.

TOWARDS A THEORY

Coaching and mentoring activities are in need of a theory. As previously discussed, the challenges are considerable. Coaching and mentoring practice draw on at least five main bodies of knowledge and research:

- Sport.
- Developmental Psychology.
- Psychotherapy.
- Sociology.
- Philosophy.

Found within each discipline are sets of mediating concepts. These contribute to the multiple understandings, viewpoints and mindsets found within the specific discipline. These mediating concepts, in their turn, create practical applications.

The academic develops critical insights into theories and comments on practical applications. Many academics adopt positions and create brands. It is not surprising then that the pragmatic, positivistic manager is often dismayed and disappointed with academics who present so many choices. The manager is seeking practical solutions to management issues, in search of the magic bullet that will make his or her business bigger, better, cheaper, fast and more competitive. They would prefer a 'right' answer that is simple.

However, the positioning or branding mindset is also a victim of its own rhetoric in that it creates practice from the multiple understandings and mindsets found in each specific discipline; hence, the sheer variety of practice.

Table 15.1 Towards a theoritical description of coaching and mentoring

Antecedents	Mediating concepts	Some examples of practical applications
Sport	• Goals and targets • Measurement • Competitiveness • Performance	• GROW model • Mental rehearsal • Visioning • Goal focus • The inner game
Developmental psychology	• Education theory • Conversational learning theory • Motivations • Sense making • Theories of knowledge • Mindset • The role of language • Narrative theory • Situated learning • Adult development theories • Age transitions	• Levels of dialogue • Holistic learning • Knowledge productivity • Johari's window
Psychotherapy	• Emotional disturbance • Stress and well-being • Blindspots and resistance to change • Transference • Generativity • Narrative theory • Age transitions	• 7-eyed model of supervision • CBT techniques • Psychometrics • Challenge • Devil's advocacy • Visioning • Solution focus • The dream • The inner game • Johari's window
Sociology	• Organizational theory • Relationships • Change, power and emancipation • Language, culture and context • Dominant discourse • Strategy • Mindset • Narrative theory	• 360° Feedback • SWOT and PESTS • Performance management • Human resource management Practice • ROI • Discourse analysis
Philosophy	• Power, morality and mindset • Dominant discourses and meaning • The notion of expert	• Evidence-based coaching • Existential coaching • Ethical frameworks and standards

Clearly, there is a tension between theory and practice and this is particularly the case within the coaching and mentoring world.

Managers claim to want certainty, controllability and measurement. Some coaches and mentors are tempted to serve managers with the promise of the magic bullet and construct frameworks, inevitably drawn from research and scholarship, to serve this purpose. There is then disappointment if things do not work out and faddism when they do. Eventually, however, the fad grows beyond its capability, the market becomes flooded with a variety of approaches or brands all positioning for a place and the quality diminishes with new entrants, variations of practice grow and then professional bodies are formed to try and protect, inform, control and regulate.

Rather than promoting one theoretical position over another or one giving preference to one practice over another, we present here a heuristic which describes what we have come to know about coaching and mentoring. We offer it as a framework for discussion and in the knowledge that, as an heuristic, it will inevitably grow and change. In spirit, we agree with the sentiment expressed in the following quote by Phillips (2007: 38): 'One thing one learns from Freud's writing, and indeed from the practice of psychoanalysis, is the value of weak theory: theories that are obviously wrong invite conversation; strong theories create a fight-or-flight situation.' In other words, whilst we have tried to be robust in our thinking and in making our arguments, our aspiration is to invite conversation, rather than induce fight or flight. In this sense, we put the framework below in the category of weak theory.

As can be seen from looking at Table 15.1, there are some areas which occur more than once; for example, age transitions is a mediating concept that is rooted in both psychology and sociology. Furthermore, there is not always a perfect symmetry between mediating concepts and practical applications; returning to the sociology antecedent, we can see that organization theory and strategy come with more tools and practical applications than some of the other mediating concepts. Also, we acknowledge that we could have included other practical applications here.

Nevertheless, our purpose in developing the table is to make the point that coaching and mentoring theory and practice draws from a range of discourses. Any attempt to make sense of coaching and mentoring theory and practice must carry with it an understanding and appreciation of where the field has come from. Table 15.1 represents a reasonably complete overview of the main areas of contribution from theory within coaching and mentoring.

THE FUTURE

In this book, we have attempted to make sense of coaching and mentoring. This has required us to question and challenge some of the dominant discourses that are currently visible in the field but what of the future?

Research

A major point raised throughout the book is about the paucity of research in coaching. With the growth of interest in coaching and the development of academic courses in universities, this is likely to change. Our prediction is that there will be an explosion of published research on coaching in existing journals, as well as an expansion in the number of journals that publish such articles. We believe that these outputs will continue to be ROI and evaluative work but that larger-scale mixed method studies will also start to emerge.

There will also be books (like this one) that will also discuss and critically examine coaching and mentoring. The challenge will always be assessing the quality of the research. Within the mentoring literature, positivistic studies currently dominate. This is likely to change as social groups move away from demanding evidence related to proof of effectiveness towards understanding subtlety and complexity in specific cases.

The Implications for the HR Profession

For both coaching and mentoring there is a movement towards professionalism in practice and more informed controlling policies within the HR profession. This is a double-edged sword. While professionalization offers the promise of maintaining and improving standards, it also offers regulation and control (see Chapter 13). Regulation and control put at risk the voluntary nature and social movement philosophy, particularly found in mentoring, and threaten the strong intrinsic value of having a conversation with a purpose with a trusted person.

At the time of writing, we have just hosted a research event at Sheffield Hallam University. In an audience comprising academics, consultants, coaches and mentors, we debated the role that HRM departments play in relation to coaching, mentoring and people development more generally. There was a strong feeling that practices such as 360-degree feedback and other attempts to make people visible and knowable as subjects (see Townley, 1994 for an excellent discussion of this) are symptomatic of a profession in crisis. With development activities increasingly being ceded to line managers or, indeed, outsourced to consultants and executive coaches, instruments such as 360-degree feedback were seen by some as representing the 'death rattle' of conventional HRM practice.

As we have argued in Chapter 10, the use of competency models has proven useful to HR managers as they provide them with a language for managing the various apparatus of HRM practice – recruitment and selection; succession planning; talent management; appraisal; performance management; discipline; rewards and redundancy. Furthermore, the dominance of the GROW model (see Chapter 5) has been useful in creating *alignment* – a key word in HRM discourse – between individual and organizational goals. However, the recent Learning and Development survey conducted in the UK by the Chartered Institute of Personnel and Development (CIPD, 2007a) makes interesting reading for both coaches and HR professionals. According to the 2007 survey, 63 per cent of respondents claim to be engaging in coaching activities, compared with 79 per cent in the previous year. Although this might suggest that the popularity of coaching may be declining, it is also worth noting that 73 per cent of respondents expect coaching by line managers to increase in the next few years.

We see two main implications of these figures for the HR profession. First, it lends weight to the view that HR practitioners are struggling to redefine their roles within organizations (CIPD, 2007b), particularly as 74 per cent of respondents identify line managers as having primary responsibility for all learning and development activity, as opposed to HR professionals. Second, however, it also suggests that the use of external coaches and consultants may fall as manager practitioners become increasingly sophisticated and confident in their use of coaching and mentoring approaches.

Set against these trends are the linked issues of power within developmental relationships, raised in Chapter 7 and the social movement arguments made above. If line managers increasingly take on the role of coach and mentor to their direct reports, then, in addition to the 'magic bullet' arguments made earlier, it is likely that they will come up against the tension between managing performance and honouring the individual's development agenda (which may be different). This can present the coach-manager with an ethical and moral dilemma which returns us to a key question raised in Chapters 1, 4, 6 and 10 – 'Whose agenda is being followed here?'

Whilst this is not a new debate, we argue that this is likely to become more acute if the trends suggested above continue. Of course, it also re-ignites the debate around whether coaching and mentoring within organizations are simply aspects of good management practice. If this is the case, a strong focus on developing coaching and mentoring skills and processes with managers will become part of any management development programme.

It is our view, as we argue in Chapter 6, that there will always be a need for learning conversations which then lead to changing attitudes, behaviours and performance in the workplace. These deep-learning conversations may indeed, as Clutterbuck suggested in the 1980s, be best between people who do not have a direct line-management relationship, as this can avoid the distortions that legitimate power can bring. However, there is still a strong argument for the use of coaching and mentoring skills and qualities within line management relationships. This is because they have core values and principles embedded in them. These values are congruent with effective organizational membership within a capitalist economy and encourage people to take responsibility for their own decisions, develop individual autonomy, help people to develop, improve and progress and develop increased capacity for performance. This is what Lyotard (see Pedler et al., 2005 for a discussion of Lyotard's work) refers to as performative knowledge. Therefore, our prediction is that, whilst the balances of activities, will shift, there will be a need for both on-line and off-line coaching and mentoring relationships within organizations in the foreseeable future.

Drawing further on the arguments we make in Chapter 6, these two sorts of conversations are more likely to give sufficient space for all seven layers of dialogue, all of which have a part to play in organizational life. However, the form that these dialogues take may be quite different as we shall explore next.

New Modes and Formats

In Chapters 5, 8 and 9, in particular, we have examined the different modes and formats of coaching and mentoring. In Chapter 8, we examined the concept of communities of discovery by drawing on ideas taken from social-network theory. These ideas raise some serious challenges and questions about contemporary coaching and mentoring practice.

First, the idea of a network raises questions about the coaching or mentoring dyad. Coaching and mentoring, as we argued in Chapter 1, are mainly thought of as a one-to-one developmental dialogue between two people. In addition, there are some key drivers that we believe will move to change this as the dominant discourse around coaching and mentoring. These ideas – which we have raised in this book – are:

- Mutuality – the idea that the coach or mentor learns and gets value from the relationship.
- Changes in unit of analysis – the idea that the network, team or group can be the focus of attention for coaching and mentoring.
- Technology – the idea (examined in Chapter 9) that the changing nature of communicative technology impacts upon what is possible within coaching and mentoring.

Mutuality

Carden (1990) in relation to mentoring and Bagshaw (1998) in relation to coaching suggest that the learning is mutual and reciprocal, so, therefore, we ask: who should pay if both parties benefit from the learning conversation?

In an organizational scheme, the idea that internal coaches may benefit from the coaching as much as the coachee can be a positive and desirable outcome. The organization as the paying client is *for* both parties, so this may not present a challenge. However, where do external coaches and individual coaching relationships sit? If there is a genuine and equal mutual benefit, why does one party have to pay when both are getting value from it?

One argument in support of mutual learning is that the primary beneficiary is the coachee or mentee and that the coach's or mentor's learning is linked to their development as a coach or mentor or perhaps as an access to new networks. Nevertheless, this debate does connect with some of the challenges to conventional evaluation processes raised in Chapter 4, so what criteria are being used to make judgements about return on investment and added value?

Unit of Analysis

This also connects with the second point about unit of analysis. In our experience there is an increase in the use of the group as the mode to deliver coaching and mentoring where the form is one-to-several. As Pedler et al., 2005, argue, group mentoring and coaching is already taking place, although we might prefer to call it action learning.

Those who conceive of coaching and mentoring as essentially one-to-one dialogue may be challenged by the suggestion that they could also be group activities. Despite this, we predict that, as team coaching (discussed in Chapter 5) becomes more prevalent, so there will be an increased blurring of boundaries around helping activities such as coaching, mentoring, facilitation, consulting and action learning. This blurring of boundaries leads neatly on to the final point about technology.

Technology

As we argued in Chapter 9, the innovations in information technology have served to further break down conventional boundaries around effective communication and conversations. They have reduced (although not eliminated) the obstacles posed by time and distance. These innovations enable larger numbers of people to be involved in learning experiences, facilitated by open-access information technologies, for example Web 2.0 communications toolkits. As argued in Chapter 9, it is not yet clear how the protocols of such different modes of coaching and mentoring will influence relationships and conversations – more research is needed. However, other forms of social technology – for example, 'Open Space Technology' (Owen, 1997), 'Future Search' (Weisbord and Janoff, 1995) and 'World Café' (Brown, 2001) offer different ways to facilitate and empower people. Interestingly, there are now IT-enabled equivalents of Open Space events known as BarCamps (http://en.wikipedia.org/wiki/BarCamp) as well as other social-networking tools such as MySpace and Facebook, and even virtual worlds such as Second Life and There or Active Worlds. We predict that coaching and mentoring will increasingly integrate and engage with these environments and that coaches and mentors, as well as coachees and mentees, will need to become adept at working across a wider range of modes. In our view it is the core values and approach to facilitating others within coaching and mentoring that matters and this translates across different formats.

The Impact of Diversity

The term diversity has strong connections with mentoring scheme design (see Megginson et al., 2006), but, as we have argued in Chapter 12, diversity is strongly connected with the concept of mindsets and dominant discourses.

As argued in Chapter 7, dominant discourses can also have the impact of minimizing or playing down differences or silencing other discourses and, as asserted in Chapter 12, diversity presents one of the biggest challenges for humankind. As pointed out in Chapter 5, coaching and mentoring discourse is a 'broad church' which contains a range of competing assumptions and frameworks. Furthermore, as we argue in Chapter 13, these differences are replicated in a bewildering array of standards and the competencies. These have their advocates as well as their critiques in terms of the diverse philosophies that they represent. There is also the issue of societal culture and its influence. In Chapter 14 Chandler makes some interesting observations about the US perspective on coaching and mentoring which connects with our observations about research agendas in Chapter 2. However, she also makes some useful comparisons with other country philosophies, using Hofstede's framework.

We predict that, as organizations such as the EMCC and the ICF continue to expand, they will encounter some resistance from societal cultures where mentoring and coaching relationships may occur more naturally. Our Western bias may invite us to assume that countries that do not have branches of EMCC, ICF etc. may not be aware of, or be interested in, embracing coaching and mentoring but perhaps the opposite is true – they do not need to be adopted because they are already embedded. However, as we move towards 'a global village' perhaps the demands of operating within the global economy will require active engagement with more formal coaching and mentoring programmes.

Of course, being aware of diverse perspectives and mindsets does not simply refer to professional or societal constructs. As we argue in Chapter 10, we need to be aware of the diversity of agendas, goals and purposes of coaching and mentoring. Given that the organizational context is predominantly one of capitalism, we see no reason to assume that this will change significantly. In such organizations, there are competing tensions, goals, purposes and agendas and these are an inevitable part of organizational life. Perhaps the age of the unitarist organization is passing and the residue philosophies of 'alignment' and 'one best way' are taking time to diminish. Perhaps reductionism and simplification are giving way to an acceptance of complexity and diversity.

Our discussion in Chapter 3 includes an extended dimensions framework for positioning some of these differences. Interventions such as supervision, whether that be via action learning or one-to-one reflexive practice, can serve to help the individual coach or mentor to recognize the diverse influences and discourses that are influencing them.

In Chapter 11, we discussed how supervision itself is a borrowed term which has some tensions and challenges in it. Our view is that, as research on coaching and mentoring increases, we will see a more distinctive set of approaches to supervision emerge which will have less in common with psychotherapy and will be situated in coaching and mentoring praxis.

CONCLUDING REMARKS

In writing this book, we have tried to be critical yet constructive, non-partisan but passionate, offer ways forward but raise challenges and more questions. We have tried to represent our own philosophy of adult learning via coaching and mentoring whilst doing justice to the main debates and issues that are in the field. In essence, we have tried to be balanced but, in a sense, that aim was always unrealistic. As with any written account, this is a partial view of a fascinating and complex field. We offer any insights contained in the book to the reader in the hope that they may provide a starting point for them to make their own sense of coaching and mentoring theory and practice.

REFERENCES

Abraham, A., Collins, D. and Martindale, R. (2006) 'The coaching schematic: validation through expert coach consensus', *Journal of Sports Sciences*, 24(6): 549–64.

Allen, T.D. and Eby, L.T. (2003) 'Relationship effectiveness for mentors: factors associated with learning and quality', *Journal of Management*, 29(4): 469–86.

Allen, T.D. and O'Brien, K.E. (2006) 'Formal mentoring programs and organizational attraction', *Human Resource Development Quarterly*, 17(1), Spring: 43–58.

Allen, T.D., Eby, L.T. and Lentz, E. (2006) 'The relationship between formal mentoring program characteristics and perceived program effectiveness', *Personnel Psychology*, 59: 125–53.

Alred, G. and Garvey, B. (2000) 'Learning to produce knowledge: the contribution of mentoring', *Mentoring and Tutoring*, 8(3), December: 261–72.

Alred, G., Garvey, B. and Smith, R. (1997) *The Mentoring Pocket Book*. Alresford, Hants: Management Pocket Books.

Alred, G., Garvey, B. and Smith, R.D. (1998) 'Pas de deux – learning in conversations', *Career Development International*, 3(7): 308–14.

Alred, G., Garvey, B. and Smith, R. (2006) *The Mentoring Pocket Book*, 2nd edn. Alresford, Hants: Management Pocket Books.

Alston, J.P. (1989) 'Wa Guanxi, and Inhwa: managerial principles in Japan, China, and Korea', *Business Horizons*, 32(3): 2–88.

Appelbaum, S.H., Ritchie, S. and Shapiro, B. (1994) 'Mentoring revisited: an organizational behaviour construct', *International Journal of Career Management*, 6(3): 3–10.

Argyris, C. (1977) 'Double loop learning', *Harvard Business Review*, September–October. pp. 115–25 in J. Bowerman and G. Collins (1999) 'The coaching network: a program for individual and organizational development', *Journal of Workplace Learning: Employee Counselling Today*, 11(8): 291–7.

Argyris, C. (1986) 'Skilled incompetence', *Harvard Business Review*, September–October. pp. 74–9 in J. Bowerman and G. Collins (1999) 'The coaching network: a program for individual and organizational development', *Journal of Workplace Learning: Employee Counselling Today*, 11(8): 291–7.

Argyris, C. and Schön, D. (1996) *Organizational Learning II*. London: Addison Wesley.

Atkinson, P. (2005) 'One stop coaching: seven influencing strategies for personal change'. http://scholar.google.com/scholar?hl=en&lr=&q=cache:tX9rKfs47nkJ:www.transformations–uk.co.uk/pdf37.pdf (accessed 17/09/06).

Auerbach, J.E. (2005) 'Seeing the light: what organizations need to know about executive coaching'. 2005 State of the Coaching Industry. Sponsored by the College of Executive Coaching. http://www.executivecoachcollege.com/state_of_coaching_industry.htm

Back, L. (2004) 'Ivory towers? The academy and racism', in L. Law, D. Phillips and L. Turney (eds), *Institutional Racism in Higher Education*. Stoke on Trent: Trentham Books.

Bagshaw, M. (1998) 'Coaching, mentoring and the sibling organization', *Industrial and Commercial Training*, 30(3): 87–9.

Barnett, B. (1995) 'Developing reflection and expertise: can mentors make the difference?', *Journal of Educational Administration*, 33(5): 45–59.

Barnett, R. (1994) *The Limits of Competence*. Buckinghamshire, UK: Open University Press & SRHE.

Barnett, R. (2000) 'Working knowledge', in J. Garrick and C. Rhodes (eds), *Research and Knowledge at Work*. London: Routledge. pp. 15–32.

Barrett, I.C., Cervero, R.M. and Johnson–Bailey, J. (2004) 'The career development of black human resource developers in the United States', *Human Resource Development International*, 7(1): 85–100.

Barrett, R. (2002) 'Mentor supervision and development – exploration of lived experience', *Career Development International*, 7(5): 279–83.

Beard, C. and Wilson, J. (2006) *Experiential Learning: A Best Practice Handbook for Educators and Trainers*. London: Kogan Page.

Beck, U. (1992) *Risk Society: Towards a New Modernity*. London: Sage.

Beech, N. and Brockbank, A. (1999) 'Power/knowledge and psychological dynamics in mentoring', *Management Learning*, 30(1): 7–25.

Bennett, A. (2006) 'What can be done when the coaching goes "off–track?"', *International Journal of Mentoring and Coaching*, IV(1): 46–9.

Bennetts, C. (1995) 'Interpersonal aspects of informal mentor/learner relationships: a research perspective'. Paper in proceedings at the European Mentoring Centre Conference, London, 10 November.

Bennetts, C. (1996) 'Mentor/learner relationships – a research perspective', Making it Happen, South West Conference, The Grand Hotel, Torquay, 19 and 20 January.

Berg, I.K. and Szabó, P. (2005) *Brief Coaching for Lasting Solutions*. New York: W.W. Norton.

Berglas, S. (2002) 'The very real dangers of executive coaching', *Harvard Business Review*, 80(6): 86–92.

Berglas, S. (2006) 'How to keep a players productive', *Harvard Business Review*, 84(9): 104–12.

Berne, E. (1964) *Games People Play: The Psychology of Human Relationships*. Harmondsworth: Penguin.

Bernstein, B. (1971) 'On the classification and framing of educational knowledge', in M.F.D. Young, *Knowledge and Control: New Directions for the Sociology of Education*. London: Open University, Collier–MacMillan.

Bettis, R.A. and Prahalad, C.K. (1995) 'The dominant logic: retrospective and extension', *Strategic Management Journal*, 16: 5–14.

Bhavnani, R., Mirza, H.S. and Meetoo, V. (2005) *Tackling the Roots of Racism: Lessons for Success*. Bristol: Policy Press.

Blake-Beard, S., Murrell, A. and Thomas, D.A. (2007) 'Unfinished business: the impact of race on understanding mentoring relationships', in B.R. Ragins and K.E. Kram (eds), *The Handbook of Mentoring at Work: Theory, Research and Practice*. London: Sage.

Blattner, J. (2005) 'Coaching: the successful adventure of a downwardly mobile executive', *Consulting Psychology Journal: Practice and Research*, 57(1): 3–13.

Blitvich, J.D., McElroy, G.K. and Blanksby, B.A. (2000) 'Risk reduction in diving spinal cord injury: teaching safe diving skills', *Journal of Science and Medicine and Sport*, 3(2), June: 120–31.

Bloisi, W., Cook, C.W. and Hunsaker, P.L. (2007) *Management and Organizational Behaviour*. Maidenhead: McGraw–Hill.

Bluckert, P. (2005) 'Critical factors in executive coaching – the coaching relationship', *Industrial and Commercial Training*, 37(7): 336–40.

Bluckert, P. (2006) *Psychological Dimensions of Executive Coaching*. Maidenhead: Open University Press.

Borredon, L. and Ingham, M. (2005) 'Mentoring and organisational learning in research and development', *Research and Development Management*, 35(5): 493–500.

Boyer, N.R. (2003) 'Leaders mentoring leaders: unveiling role identity in an international online environment', *Mentoring and Tutoring*, 11(1): 25–41.

Bowerman, J. and Collins, G. (1999) 'The coaching network: a program for individual and organizational development', *Journal of Workplace Learning: Employee Counselling Today*, 11(8): 291–7.

Bright, M.I. (2005) 'Can Japanese mentoring enhance understanding of Western mentoring?', *Employee Relations*, 27(4/5): 325–39.

Broadbridge, A. (1999) 'Mentoring in retailing: a tool for success?', *Personnel Review*, 28(4): 336–55.

Brockbank, A. and McGill, I. (2006) *Facilitating Reflective Learning Through Mentoring and Coaching*. London: Kogan Page.

Brotman, L.E., Liberi, W.P. and Wasylyshyn, K.M. (1998) 'Executive coaching: the need for standards of competence', *Consulting Psychology Journal: Practice and Research*, 50: 40–6.

Brown, J. (2002) *The World Café: Living Knowledge Through Conversations That Matter*. Unpublished dissertation. Sheffield: Sheffield Hallam University.

Bruner, J. (1985) 'Vygotsky: a historical and conceptual perspective', in J.V. Wertsch (ed.), *Culture, Communication and Cognition: Vygotskian perspectives*. Cambridge: Cambridge University Press.

Bruner, J. (1990) *Acts of Meaning*. Cambridge, MA: Harvard University Press.

Brunner, R. (1998) 'Psychoanalysis and coaching', *Journal of Management Psychology*, 13(7): 515–17.

Burke, R.J., Bristor, J.M. and Rothstein, M.G. (1995) 'The role of interpersonal networks in women's and men's career development', *International Journal of Career Management*, 7(3): 25–32.

Burrell, G. and Morgan, G. (1979) *Sociological Paradigms and Organizational Analysis*. London: Heinemann.

Bush, T. and Coleman, M. (1995) 'Professional development for heads: the role of mentoring', *Journal of Educational Administration*, 33(5): 60–73.

Byrne, C. (2005) 'Getting to know me! Not getting results? Carmen Byrne explains how a lack of self–awareness can hold you back', *MW Coach*, April: 21, Profile New Zealand Publishing.

Caplan, J. (2003) *Coaching for the Future: How Smart Companies use Coaching and Mentoring*. London: CIPD.

Caraccioli, L.A. (1760) 'The true mentor, or, an essay on the education of young people in fashion', J. Coote at the Kings Arms in Paternoster Row, London.

Carden, A.D. (1990) 'Mentoring and adult career development; the evolution of a theory', *The Counselling Psychologist*, 18(2): 275–99.

Carr, W. and Kemmis, S. (1986) *Becoming Critical: Education, Knowledge and Action Research*. London: Falmer Press.

Carter, A. (2001) *Executive Coaching: Inspiring Performance at Work*. IES Report 379.

Caruso, R.E. (1996) 'Who does mentoring?' Paper presented at the 3rd European Mentoring Conference, London, 7–8 November.

Caulkin, S. (2006a) 'Friedman's unethical rot made wrongs into a right', *Observer*, Business & Media, 2 December.

Caulkin, S. (2006b) 'Why things fell apart for joined up thinking', *Observer*, 26 February.

Chandler, D.E. and Kram, K.E. (2005) 'Applying an adult development perspective to developmental networks', *Career Developmental International, Special Edition on Mentoring*, 10(6/7): 548–66.

Chandler, D.E. and Kram, K.E. (2007) 'Mentoring in the new career context', in H. Gunz and M. Peiperl (eds), *Handbook of Career Studies*. London: Sage. pp. 241–67.

Chao, G.T., Walz, P.M. and Gardner, P.D. (1992) 'Formal and informal mentorships: a comparison on mentoring functions and contrast with nonmentored counterparts', *Personnel Psychology*, 45(3): 619.

Chidiac, A.M. (2006) 'Getting the best out of executive coaching: a guide to setting up a coaching process', *Development and Learning in Organizations*, 20(3): 13–15.

CIPD (2007a) *Annual Survey Report: Learning and Development*. April, www.cipd.co.uk/surveys

CIPD (2007b) *Survey Report: The Changing HR Function*. September, www.cipd.co.uk/surveys

CIPD (2007) *Managing Change: The Role of the Psychological Contract*. www.cipd.co.uk (accessed 17/07/07).

Clawson, J.G. (1996) 'Mentoring in information age', *Leadership and Organization Development Journal*, 17(3): 6–15.

Clutterbuck, D. (1992) *Everyone Needs a Mentor*. London: IPM.

Clutterbuck, D. (1998) *Learning Alliances: Tapping into Talent*. London: CIPD.

Clutterbuck, D. (2002) 'Building and sustaining the diversity–mentoring relationship', in D. Clutterbuck and B.R. Ragins (eds), *Mentoring and Diversity: An International Perspective*. Oxford: Butterworth-Heinemann.

Clutterbuck, D. (2007a) *Coaching the Team at Work*. London: Nicholas Brealey International.

Clutterbuck, D. (2007b) 'An international perspective on mentoring', in B.R. Ragins and K.E. Kram (eds), *Handbook on Mentoring at Work: Theory, Research and Practice*. London: Sage. Chapter 26.

Clutterbuck, D. and Lane, G. (2004) *The Situational Mentor*. Aldershot: Gower Publishing Company.

Clutterbuck, D. and Megginson, D. (1995) *Mentoring in Action*. London: Kogan Page.

Clutterbuck, D. and Megginson, D. (1999) *Mentoring Executives and Directors*. Oxford: Butterworth Heinemann.

Clutterbuck, D. and Megginson, D. (2005) *Making Coaching Work, Creating a Coaching Culture*. London: CIPD.

Colley, H. (2003) *Mentoring for Social Inclusion: A Critical Approach to Nurturing Mentoring Relationships*. London: Routledge Falmer.

Colone, C. (2005) 'Calculating the return on investment in executive coaching for a corporate staff function in a large global financial services company', in J. Jarvis, D. Lane and A. Fillery–Travis (eds) (2006) *The Case for Coaching: Making Evidence-Based Decisions on Coaching*. London: CIPD. pp. 219–26.

Connor, M. (1994) *Counsellor Training: An Integrated Approach*. London: Kogan Page.

Cooperrider, D. (1995) *Appreciative Enquiry: An Emerging Direction for Organization Development*. Champaign, IL: Stipes.

Cottingham, J. (2007) *Western Philosophies: An Anthology*. Oxford: Blackwell.

Cox, E. (2000) 'The call to mentor', *Career Development International*, 5(4/5): 202–10.

Cramm, S. and May, T. (1998) 'Accelerating executive development; hey coach…', *Information Management and Computer Security*, 6(5): 196–8.

Cranwell-Ward, J., Bossons, P. and Gover, S. (2004) *Mentoring: A Henley Review of Best Practice*. Basingstoke: Palgrave Macmillan.

Cross, R. and Parker, A. (2004) *The Hidden Power of Social Networks*. Boston, MA: Harvard Business School Press.

Crossland, C. and O'Brien, M. (2004) 'Informal mentoring: a source of indirect entry into informal male networks?', *International Journal of Mentoring and Coaching*, III(1): 77–86.

Csikszentmihalyi, M. (2002) *Flow: The Classic Work on How to Achieve Happiness*. London: Rider.

Cummings, J. and Higgins, M. (2006) 'Relational instability at the network core: support dynamics in career developmental networks', *Social Networks*, 28(1): 38–55.

Daloz, L.A. (1986) *Effective Teaching and Mentoring*. San Francisco: Jossey Bass.

Dass, P. and Parker, B. (1996) 'Diversity: a strategic issue', in E.E. Kossek and S.A. Lobel (eds) (1996) *Managing Diversity: Human Resource Strategies for Transforming the Workplace*. Oxford: Blackwell.

De Bono, E. (1992) *I'm Right and You're Wrong: From This to the New Renaissance: From Rock Logic to Water Logic*. London: Penguin Books.

De Haan, E. (2008) *Relational Coaching: Journeys Towards Mastering One-to-One Learning*. Chichester, UK: John Wiley.

De Haan, E. and Burger, Y. (2005) *Coaching with Colleagues: An Action Guide for One-to-One Learning*. Basingstoke: Palgrave Macmillan.

De Janasz, S.C., Sullivan, S.E. and Whiting, V. (2003) 'Mentor networks and career success: lessons for turbulent times', *Academy of Management Executive*, 17(4): 78–91.

De Vries, K. and Miller, B. (1984) *The Neurotic Organization*. New York: Jossey Bass.

Department of Defense, Office of Small Business Programs (2007) *Mentor Protégé Program*, http://www.acq.osd.mil/osbp/mentor_protege/

Devins, D. and Gold, J. (2000) 'Cracking the tough nuts: mentoring and coaching the managers of small firms', *Career Development International*, 5(4): 250–5.

Dirsmith, M., Helan, J. and Covaleski, M. (1997) 'Structure and agency in an institutionalised setting: the application and social transformation of control in the Big Six', *Accounting, Organizations and Society*, 22(1): 1–27.

Dobrow, S.R. and Higgins, M.C. (2005) 'Developmental networks and professional identity: a longitudinal study', Special Issue on Mentoring, *Career Development International*, 10(6/7): 567–87.

Dobrow, S.R. and Higgins, M.C. (2005) 'Developmental networks and professional identity: a longitudinal study', *Career Development International*, 10(5): 567–83.

Douglas, C.A. and McCauley, C.D. (1997) 'A survey on the use of formal developmental relationships in organizations', *Issues & Observations*, 17: 6–9.

Downey, M. (2001) *Effective Coaching*. London: Orion.

Downey, M. (2003) *Effective Coaching: Lessons from the Coach's Coach*, (2nd edn). Mason, OH: Texere.

Drucker, P.F. (1955/1989) *The Practice of Management*. Oxford: Heinemann.

Dryden, W. (1991) *A Dialogue with Arnold Lazarus: It Depends*. Buckingham: Open University Press.

Du Toit, A. (2006) 'The management of change in local government using a coaching approach', *International Journal of Mentoring and Coaching*, IV(2): 45–57.

Dutton, J. and Ragins, B.R. (2007) 'Moving forward: positive relationships at work as a research frontier', in J. Dutton and B.R. Ragins (eds), *Exploring Positive Relationships at Work: Building a Theoretical and Research Foundation*. Mahwah, NJ: Lawrence Erlbaum and Associates. pp. 387–400.

Eby, L.T. and Allen, T.D. (eds) (2006) 'Call for papers', Special Issue on Bridging Disciplinary Divides in Mentoring Research, *Journal of Vocational Behavior*.

Eby, L.T., Butts, M., Lockwood, A. and Simon, S.A. (2004) 'Protégés' negative mentoring experiences: construct development and nomological validation', *Personnel Psychology*, 57: 411–47.

Eddy, E.R., Tannenbaum, S.I., Lorenzet, S.J. and Smith-Jentsch, K.A. (2005) 'The influence of a continuous learning environment on peer mentoring behaviours', *Journal of Managerial Issues*, XVII(3): 383–95.

Egan, G. (1993) 'The shadow side', *Management Today*, September: 33–8.

Ellinger, A.E., Ellinger, A.D. and Keller, S. (2005) 'Supervisory coaching in a logistics context', *International Journal of Physical Distribution & Logistics Management*, 35(9): 620–36.

Ellinger, A.D. and Bostrom, R. (1999) 'Managerial coaching behaviours in learning organizations', *Journal of Management Development*, 18(9): 752–71.

Eng, S.P. (1986) 'Mentoring in principalship education', in W.A. Gray and M.M. Gray (eds), *Mentoring: Aid to Excellence in Education, the Family and the Community*. British Columbia: Xerox Reproduction Centre.

Engstrom, T.E.J. (2005) *Individual Determinants of Mentoring Success*. Doctoral Dissertation. Newcastle: Northumbria University.

Ensher, E.A., Heun, C. and Blanchard, A. (2003) 'Online mentoring and computer-mediated communication: new directions in research', *Journal of Vocational Behaviour*, 63(2): 264–88.

Ericsson, K., Prietula, M. and Cokely, E. (2007) 'The making of an expert', *Harvard Business Review*, July–August: 114–21.

Erikson, E. (1950) *Childhood and Society*. Harmondsworth, Middlesex: Penguin Books Ltd.

Erikson, E. (1995) *Childhood and Society*. London: Vintage.

Eseryl, D. (2002) 'Approaches to the evaluation of training: theory and practice', *Educational Technology & Society*, 5(2): 93–8.

European Mentoring and Coaching Council (undated) *EMCC Coach Mentoring Standards*. Watford: EMCC.

Evers, W.J.G., Brouwers, A. and Tomic, W. (2006) 'A quasi-experimental study on management effectiveness', *Consulting Psychology Journal: Practice and Research*, 58(3): 174–82.

Fagenson-Eland, E.A., Marks, M.A. and Amendola, K.L. (1977) 'Perceptions of mentoring relationships', *Journal of Vocational Behavior*, 51: 29–42.

Fairbairns, J. (1991) 'Plugging the gap in training needs analysis', *People Management*, February: 43–5.

Feasey, D. (2002) *Good Practice in Supervision With Psychotherapists and Counsellors: The Relational Approach*. London: Whurr Publishers Ltd.

Feldman, D.C. and Lankau, M.J. (2005) 'Executive coaching: a review and agenda for future research', *Journal of Management*, 31(6): 829–48.

Feldman, G.C. (2001) 'Encouraging mentorship in young scientists', *New Directions for Child and Adolescent Development*, 93, Fall: 61–71.

Feltham, C. (1995) *What is Counselling?* London: Sage.

Fénélon, F.S. de la M. (1808) *The Adventures of Telemachus*, Vols 1 and 2, trans. Hawkesworth, J., Union Printing Office, St. John's Square, London.

Fénélon, F.S. de la M. (1835) *Oeuvres de Fénélon*, Vol. III, in P. Riley (1994) *Fénélon – Telemachus*. Cambridge: Cambridge University Press.

Fine, L. and Pullins, E.B. (1998) 'Peer mentoring in the industrial sales force: an exploratory investigation of men and women in developmental relationships', *Journal of Personal Selling and Sales Management*, XVIII(4): 89–103.

Finklestein, L.M., Allen, T.D. and Rhoton, L.A. (2003) 'An examination of the role of age in mentoring relationships', *Group and Organization Management*, 28(2): 249–81.

Flaherty, J. (1999) *Coaching: Evoking Excellence in Others*. Boston: Butterworth-Heinemann.

Fleenor, J. and Joyce, L.W. (2007) 'Coaching for leadership', (2nd edn), *Personnel Psychology*, Summer, 60(2): 528–30.

Flores, F. (1999) 'The world according to Flores', *Fast Company*, January: 144–51.

Foucault, M. (1979) *Discipline and Punish: The Birth of the Prison*. London: Penguin.

Fox, A. and Stevenson, L. (2006) 'Exploring the effectiveness of per mentoring of accounting and finance students in higher education', *Accounting Education: An International Journal*, 15(2): 189–202.

Fracaro, K. (2006) 'Mentoring for career guidance', *Supervision*, 67(6): 13–16.

Friday, E., Shawnta, S., Friday, A. and Green, L. (2004) 'A reconceptualization of mentoring and sponsoring', *Management Decision*, 42(5): 628–44.

French, Jr, J.R.P. and Raven, B. (1962) 'The bases of social power', in C. Dorwin (ed.), *Group Dynamics: Research and Theory*. Evanston, IL: Peterson. pp. 607–23.

Friedman, A.A., Zibit, M. and Coote, M. (2004) 'Telementoring as a collaborative agent for change', *Journal of Technology, Learning and Assessment*, 3(1): 2–41.

Gallwey, T. (1997) *The Inner Game of Tennis*, 2nd edn. New York: Random House.

Garrett, R. (2006) *NHS Expert Patient Programme Mentoring Pilot, Evaluation Report*. The Coaching and Mentoring Research Unit. Sheffield: Sheffield Hallam University.

Garvey, B. (1994a) 'A dose of mentoring', *Education and Training*, 36(4): 18–26.

Garvey, B. (1994b) 'Ancient Greece, MBAs, the Health Service and Georg', *Education and Training*, 36(2): 18–26.

Garvey, B. (1994c) 'Mentoring: erraringen in een groot bedrijf', in Opleiders in organisaties, Capita Selecta, *Mentoring en coaching*. Amstelveen, Netherlands: Kluwer Bedrijfswetenschapen.

Garvey, B. (1995a) 'Healthy signs for mentoring', *Education and Training*, 37(5): 12–19.

Garvey, B. (1995b) 'Let the actions match the words', in D. Clutterbuck and D. Megginson (eds), *Mentoring in Action*. London: Kogan Page.

Garvey, B. (1998) *Mentoring in the Market Place. Studies of Learning at Work*. PhD Thesis. Durham: University of Durham.

Garvey, B. (2004a) 'Call a rose by any other name and perhaps its a bramble?', *Development and Learning in Organizations*, 18(2): 6–8.

Garvey, B. (2006) 'Let me tell you a story', *International Journal of Mentoring and Coaching*, 4(1): 26–37.

Garvey, B. and Alred, G. (2000) 'Educating mentors, mentoring and tutoring', 8(2), September: 113–26.

Garvey, B. and Alred, G. (2001) 'Mentoring and the tolerance of complexity', *Futures*, 33(6), August: 519–30.

Garvey, B. and Galloway, K. (2002) 'Mentoring in the Halifax, a small beginning in a large organization', *Career Development International*, 7(5): 271–9.

Garvey, B. and Garrett–Harris, R. (2005) *The Benefits of Mentoring: A Literature Review*. Report for East Mentors Forum, Mentoring and Coaching Research Unit, Sheffield: Sheffield Hallam University.

Garvey, B. and Langridge, K. (2006) *The Pupil Mentoring Pocketbook*. Alresford, Hants: Teachers' Pocketbooks.

Garvey, B. and Megginson, D. (2004) 'Odysseus, Telemachus and Mentor: stumbling into, searching for and signposting the road to desire', *International Journal of Mentoring and Coaching*, 2(1): 16–40.

Garvey, B. and Williamson, B. (2002) *Beyond Knowledge Management: Dialogue, Creativity and the Corporate Curriculum*. Harlow, UK: Pearson Education.

Garvey, B., Alred, G. and Smith, R. (1996) 'First Person Mentoring', *Career Development International*, 5(1): 10–14.

Geertz, C. (1974) *Myth, Symbol and Culture*. New York: Norton.

Gegner, C. (1997) *Coaching: Theory and Practice*. Unpublished Master's thesis. San Francisco: University of California.

Gibb, S. (1994) 'Inside corporate mentoring schemes: the development of a conceptual framework', *Personnel Review*, 23(3): 47–60.

Gibb, S. and Hill, P. (2006) 'From trail-blazing individualism to a social construction community; modelling knowledge construction in coaching', *International Journal of Mentoring and Coaching*, 4(2): 58–77.

Gibb, S. and Megginson, D. (1993) 'Inside corporate mentoring schemes: a new agenda of concerns', *Personnel Review*, 22(1): 40–54.

Giglio, L., Diamante, T. and Urban, J. (1998) 'Coaching a leader: leveraging change at the top', *Journal of Management Development*, 17(2): 93–105.

Gill, J. and Johnson, P. (1997) *Research Methods for Managers*. London: Paul Chapman.

Gladstone, M.S. (1988) *Mentoring: A Strategy for Learning in a Rapidly Changing Society*. Research Document CEGEP. Quebec: John Abbott College.

Gladwell, M. (2002) *The Tipping Point: How Little Things can Make a Big Difference*. London: Abacus.

Godshalk, V.M. and Sosik, J.J. (2003) 'Aiming for career success: the role of learning goal orientation in mentoring relationships', *Journal of Vocational Behavior*, 63(3): 417–37.

Goldsmith, M. (2005) in H. Morgan, P. Hawkins and M. Goldsmith (eds), *The Art and Practice of Leadership Coaching*. Hoboken, NJ: Wiley. Chapter 9.

Goldsmith, M. (2006) 'Where the work of executive coaching lies', *Consulting to Management*, 17(2), June: 15–17.

Goodge, P. and Coomber, J. (2007) 'How to...get 360-degree coaching right', *People Management*, 3 May: 44–5.

Grant, A.M. (2003) 'The impact of life coaching on goal attainment, metacognition and mental health', *Sports Behaviour and Personality*, 31(3): 253–64.

Grant, A.M. (2006a) 'An integrative goal-focused approach to executive coaching', in D. Stober and A.M. Grant (eds), *Evidence Based Coaching Handbook*. New York: Wiley.

Grant, A.M. (2006b) 'Solution focused coaching', in J. Passmore (ed.), *Excellence in Coaching*. London: Kogan Page. pp. 73–90.

Grant, A.M. (2007) 'Enhancing coaching skills and emotional intelligence through training', *Industrial and Commercial Training*, 39(5): 257–66.

Grant, A.M. and Greene, J. (2001) *Coach Yourself: Make Real Changes in Your Life*. London: Pearson Momentum.

Grant, A.M., Franklin, J. and Langford, P. (2002) 'The self-reflection and insight scale: a new measure of private self-consciousness', *Social Behaviour and Personality*, 30(8): 821–36.

Grodski, L. and Allen, W. (2005) *The Business and Practice of Coaching: Finding Your Niche, Making Money and Attracting Ideal Clients*. London: Norton.

Gutting, G. (2005) *Foucault: A Very Short Introduction*. Oxford: Oxford University Press.

Habermas, J. (1974) *Theory and Practice*. London: Heinemann.

Hackman, R.J. and Wageman, R. (2005) 'A theory of team coaching', *Academy of Management Review*, 30(2): 269–87.

Hale, R. (2000) 'To match or mis-match? The dynamics of mentoring as a route to personal and organizational learning', *Career Development International*, 5(4/5).

Hall, D.T., Otazo, K.L. and Hollenbeck, G.P. (1999) 'Behind closed doors: what really happens in executive coaching', *Organizational Dynamics*, Winter: 39–53.

Hallett, C. (1997) 'Learning through reflection in the community: the relevance of Schön's theories of coaching to nursing education', *International Journal of Nursing Studies*, 34(2): 103–10.

Hamilton, B.A. and Scandura, T.A. (2003) 'Implications for organizational learning and development in a wired world', *Organizational Dynamics*, 31(4): 388–402.

Hansford, B. and Ehrich, L. (2006) 'The principleship: how significant is mentoring?', *Journal of Educational Administration*, 44(1): 36–52.

Hardingham, A. (2005) 'A job well done? The coach's dilemma', *People Management*, 11(8): 54.

Hardingham, A. (2006) 'The British eclectic model in practice', *International Journal of Mentoring and Coaching*, IV(1): 39–45.

Hardingham, A., Brearley, M., Moorhouse, A. and Venter, B. (2004) *The Coach's Coach, Personal Development for Personal Developers*. London: CIPD.

Hargrove, R. (1995) *Masterful Coaching: Extraordinary Results by Impacting People and the Way They Think and Act Together*. San Francisco, CA: Jossey-Bass/Pfeiffer.

Harquail, C.V. and Blake, S.D. (1993) 'UnMasc-ing mentor and reclaiming Athena: insights for mentoring in heterogeneous organizations'. Paper 8 in Standing Conference on Organizational Symbolism, Collbato, Barcelona, Spain.

Harris, M. (1999) 'Look, it's a 1–0 psychologist … no, it's a trainer… no, it's an executive coach', *TIP*, 36(3): 1–5.

Hasbrouck, J. and Denton, C.A. (2007) 'Student-focused coaching: a model for reading coaches', *The Reading Coach's Corner*, 60(7): 690–3.

Hawkins, P. and Schwenk, G. (2006) *Coaching Supervision*. Paper prepared for the CIPD Coaching Conference, September. London: CIPD.

Hawkins, P. and Shohet, R. (2006) *Supervision in the Helping Professions*, 3rd edn. Maidenhead: Open University Press.

Hawkins, P. and Smith, N. (2006) *Coaching, Mentoring and Organizational Consultancy: Supervision and Development*. Maidenhead: Open University Press.

Headlam-Wells, J., Gosland, J. and Craig, J. (2006) 'Beyond the organisation: the design and management of e-mentoring systems', *International Journal of Information Management*, 26: 272–85.

Henochowicz, S. and Hetherington, D. (2006) 'Leadership coaching in health care', *Leadership and Organization Development Journal*, 27(3): 183–9.

Higgins, M.C. (2000) 'The more, the merrier? Multiple developmental relationships and work satisfaction', *Journal of Management Development*, 19: 277–96.

Higgins, M.C., Dobrow, S.R. and Roloff, K.S. (2007) *Resilience and Relationships: The Role of Developmental Support Over Time*. Working Paper: Fordham University.

Higgins, M.C. and Kram, K.E. (2001) 'Reconceptualizing mentoring at work: a developmental network perspective', *Academy of Management Review*, 26(2): 264–88.

Hislop, D. (2005) *Knowledge Management in Organizations: A Critical Introduction*. Oxford: Oxford University Press.

Hjermstad, M. (2002) 'Bill Austin: The Industry's Popular, Demanding Teacher', *Bicycle Retailer & Industry News*, 10698493, 11(8).

Hoddinott, P., Lee, A.J. and Pill, R. (2006) 'Effectiveness of a breastfeeding peer coaching intervention in rural Scotland', *Birth*, 33(1): 27–36.

Hofstede, G. (1980) *Culture's Consequences: International Differences in Work-related Values*. Beverly Hills, CA: Sage.

Hofstede, G. (2001) *Culture's Consequences: International Differences in Work-related Values* (2nd edn). Thousand Oaks, CA: Sage.

Hollembeak, J. and Amorose, A.J. (2005) 'Perceived coaching behaviours and college athletes intrinsic motivation: a test of self determination theory', *Journal of Applied Sports Psychology*, 17(1): 20–36.

Honoria (1793) *The Female Mentor or Select Conversations*, Vols 1 & 2. London, The Strand: T. Cadell.

Honoria (1796) *The Female Mentor or Select Conversations*, Vol. 3. London, The Strand: T. Cadell.

Humble, J.W. (1971) *Management by Objectives*. London: Management Publications/BIM.

Hunt, J.M. and Weintraub, J.R. (2007) *The Coaching Organization: A Strategy for Developing Leaders*. Thousand Oaks, CA: Sage.

Hurley, A.E. and Fagenson-Eland, E.A. (1996) 'Challenges in cross-gender mentoring relationships: psychological intimacy, myths, rumours, innuendoes and sexual harassment', *Leadership & Organization Development Journal*, 17(3): 42–9.

Ibarra, H. and Lineback, K. (2005) 'What's your story?', *Harvard Business Review*, 83(1): 64–71.

Idaho Department of Environmental Quality, Pollution Prevention Program (2002) Environmental Mentoring, Business to Business, Peer to Peer, 20 June.

International Coach Federation (2007) http://www.coachfederation.org/ICF/

Irwin, G., Hanton, S. and Kerwin, D. (2004) 'Reflective practice and the origins of elite coaching knowledge', *Reflective Practice*, 5(3): 425–42.

Jackson, N. and Carter, P. (2000) *Rethinking Organizational Behaviour*. Harlow: Pearson Education.

Jackson, P.Z. and McKergow, M. (2002) *The Solutions Focus: The Simple Way to Positive Change*. London: Brealey.

Jacques, R. (1996) *Manufacturing the Employee: Management Knowledge From the 19th to 21st centuries*. London: Sage.

Jarvis, P. (1992) *Paradoxes of Learning – On Becoming an Individual in Society*. San Francisco: Jossey Bass Higher Education Series.

Jarvis, J., Lane, D. and Fillery-Travis, A. (2006) *The Case for Coaching: Making Evidence-Based Decisions on Coaching*. London: CIPD.

Jessup, G. (1991) *Outcomes: NVQs and the Emerging Model of Education and Training*. Oxford: Falmer.

Johnson, H.T. and Bröms, A. (2000) *Profit Beyond Measure*. New York: Free Press.

Johnson, S.K., Geroy, G.D. and Griego, O.V. (1999) 'The mentoring model theory: dimensions in mentoring protocols', *Career Development International*, 4(7): 384–91.

Jones, R.L. and Wallace, M. (2005) 'Another bad day at the training ground: coping with the ambiguity in the coaching context', *Sport, Education and Society*, 10(1): 119–34.

Jones, R., Rafferty, A. and Griffin, M. (2006) 'The executive coaching trend: towards more flexible executives', *Leadership and Organization Development Journal*, 27(7): 583–95.

Joo, B. (2005) 'Executive coaching: a conceptual framework from an integrative review of practice and research', *Human Resource Development Review*, 4(4): 462–88.

Jung, C. (1958) *Psyche and Symbol*. New York: Doubleday.

Kampa-Kokesch, S. and Anderson, M.Z. (2001) 'Executive coaching: a comprehensive review of the literature', *Consulting Psychology Journal: Practice & Research*, 53(4): 205–28.

Kanter, R. (1977) *Men and Women of the Corporation*. New York: Basic Books.

Kayes, D.C. (2006) *Destructive Goal Pursuit: The Mount Everest Disaster*. Basingstoke: Palgrave Macmillan.

Kellar, G.M., Jennings, B.E., Sink, H.L. and Mundy, R.A. (1995) 'Teaching transportation with an interactive method', *Journal of Business Logistics*, 16(1): 251–79.

Kennett, K. (2006) Unpublished Master's Thesis. Sheffield: Sheffield Hallam University.

Kessels, J. (1996a) *The Corporate Curriculum*. Inaugural Lecture. The Netherlands: University of Leiden.

Kessels, J. (1996b) *Knowledge Productivity and the Corporate Curriculum, in: Knowledge Management: Organization, Competence and Methodology*, Proceedings of the Fourth International ISMICK Symposium, 21–22 October, Rotterdam, The Netherlands.

Kessels, J. (2002) 'You cannot be smart against your will', in B. Garvey and B. Williamson (eds), *Beyond Knowledge Management: Dialogue, Creativity and the Corporate Curriculum*. Harlow: Pearson Education.

Kilburg, R.R. (2000) *Executive Coaching: Developing Managerial Wisdom in a World of Chaos*. Washington, DC: American Psychological Association.

Kilburg, R.R. (2004) 'Trudging toward Dodoville: conceptual approaches and case studies in executive coaching', *Consulting Psychology Journal*, 56(4): 203–13.

King, P. and Eaton, J. (1999) 'Coaching for results', *Industrial and Commercial Training*, 31(4): 145–51.

Kirkpatrick, D.L. (1959) 'Techniques for evaluating training programmes', *Journal of the American Society of Training Directors*, 13: 3–26.

Kochan, F.K. and Trimble, S.B. (2000) 'From mentoring to co-mentoring: establishing collaborative relationships', *Theory Into Practice*, 39(1), Winter: 20–8.

Kolb, D.A. (1984) *Experiential Learning*. Englewood Cliffs, NJ: Prentice Hall.

Krackhardt, D. (1992) 'The strength of strong ties: the importance of philos in organizations', in N. Nohria and R.G. Eccles (eds), *Networks and Organizations: Structures, Form and Action*. Boston: Harvard University Business School Press. pp. 216–39.

Krackhardt, D. and Stern, R.N. (1988) 'Informal networks and organizational crises: an experimental simulation', *Social Psychology Quarterly*, 51: 123–40.

Kram, K.E. (1980) *Mentoring Processes at Work: Developing Relationships in Managerial Careers*. Unpublished Doctoral Dissertation. New Haven, CT: Yale University.

Kram, K.E. (1983) 'Phases of the mentor relationship', *Academy of Management Journal*, 26(4): 608–25.

Kram, K.E. (1985) *Mentoring at Work*. Glenville, IL: Scott Foresman.

Kram, K.E. and Hall, D.T. (1996) 'Mentoring in a context of diversity and turbulence', in E.E. Kossek and S.A. Lobel (eds) (1996) *Managing Diversity: Human Resource Strategies for Transforming the Workplace*. Cambridge, MA: Blackwell Business. pp. 108–36.

Kram, K.E. and Isabella, L.A. (1985) 'Mentoring alternatives: the role of peer relationships in career development', *Academy of Management Journal*, 28(1): 110–32.

Krazmien, M. and Berger, F. (1997) 'The coaching paradox', *International Journal of Hospitality Management*, 16(1): 3–10.

Krohn, D. (1998) 'Four indispensable features of socratic dialogue', in R. Saran and B. Neisser (eds) (2004) *Enquiring Minds: Socratic Dialogue in Education*. Stoke on Trent: Trentham Books.

Kuhn, T.S. (1970) *The Structure of Scientific Revolutions*. Chicago: University of Chicago Press.

Lantos, G. (1999) 'Motivating moral corporate behaviour', *Journal of Consumer Marketing*, 16(3): 222–33.

Lave, J. and Wenger, E. (1991) *Situated Learning: Legitimate Peripheral Participation*. Cambridge: Cambridge University Press.

Lazovsky, R. and Shimoni, A. (2007) 'The on-site mentor of counseling interns: perceptions of ideal role and actual role performance', *Journal of Counseling and Development*, 85(3), Summer: 303–16.

Lee, G. (2003) *Leadership Coaching: From Personal Insight to Organizational Performance*. London: CIPD.

Legge, K. (1995) *Human Resource Management: Rhetorics and Realities*. Basingstoke: Macmillan.

Levinson, D.J., Darrow, C.N., Klein, E.B., Levinson, M.H. and McKee, B. (1978) *The Seasons of a Man's Life*. New York: Knopf.

Lievegoed, B. (1993) *Phases: the Spiritual Rhythms of Adult Life*. Bristol: Rudolf Steiner Press.

Lines, D. and Robinson, G. (2006) 'Tough at the top', *International Journal of Mentoring and Coaching*, IV(1): 4–25.

Lloyd, B. and Rosinski, P. (2005) 'Coaching culture and leadership', *Team Performance Management*, 11(3/4): 133–8.

Longenecker, C.O. and Neubert, M.J. (2005) 'The practices of effective managerial coaches', *Business Horizons*, 48: 493–500.

Luo, Y. (1997) 'Guanxi: principles, philosophies, and implications', *Human Systems Management*, 16(1): 43.

McAuley, M.J. (2003) 'Transference, countertransference and mentoring: the ghost in the process', *British Journal of Guidance and Counselling*, 31: 11–24.

McAuley, J., Duberley, J. and Johnson, P. (2007) *Organizational Theory: Challenges and Perspectives*. Harlow: Pearson Education.

McCauley, C.D. and Hezlett, S.A. (2001) 'Individual development in the workplace', in N. Anderson, D. Ones, H.K. Sinangil and C. Viswesvaran (eds), *Handbook of Industrial, Work and Organizational Psychology*. London: Sage. pp. 313–35.

McCauley, C.D., Moxley, R.S. and Van Velsor, E. (eds) (1998) *What Leaders Read.* Centre for Creative Leadership Handbook of Leadership Development, Jossey-Bass.

McElrath, M., Godat, L., Musson, J., Libow, J. and Graves, J. (2005) 'Improving supervisors' effectiveness: Mayo clinic finds answers through research', *Journal of Organizational Excellence*, Winter: 47–56.

McGovern, J., Lindemann, M., Vergara, M., Murphy, S., Barker, L. and Warrenfeltz, R. (2001) 'Maximizing the impact of executive coaching: behavioral change, organizational outcomes, and return on investment', *The Manchester Review*, 6(1): 1–9.

McIntosh, S. (2003) 'Work–life balance: how life coaching can help', *Business Information Review*, 20(4): 181–9.

MacLennan, N. (1995) *Coaching and Mentoring.* Farnborough: Gower Publishing.

McLeod, A. (2003) *Performance Coaching: A Handbook for Managers, HR Professionals and Coaches.* Bancyfelin, Carmarthen: Crown House.

McMahan, G. (2006) 'Doors of perception', *Coaching at Work*, 1(6): 36–43.

Mecca, A.M. (2007) *Mentoring Works: California Programs Making a Difference.* California Mentoring Association, http://www.calmentor.org/mentoringmovement_scorecard.fsp

Megginson, D. (1994) 'Planned and emergent learning: a framework and a method', *Executive Development*, 7(6): 29–32.

Megginson, D. (1996) 'Planned and emergent learning: consequences for development', *Management Learning*, 27(4): 411–28. Reprinted in C. Grey and E. Antonacopoulou (eds) (2004) *Essential Readings in Management Learning.* London: Sage. pp. 91–106.

Megginson, D. and Boydell, T. (1979) *A Manager's Guide to Coaching.* London: BACIE.

Megginson, D. and Clutterbuck, D. (1995) *Mentoring in Action.* London: Kogan Page.

Megginson, D. and Clutterbuck, D. (2005a) *Techniques for Coaching and Mentoring.* Oxford: Butterworth-Heinemann.

Megginson, D. and Clutterbuck, D. (2005b) 'The meaning of success', *Training Magazine*, October: 19.

Megginson, D. and Stokes, P. (2004) 'Development and supervision for mentors', in D. Clutterbuck and G. Lane (eds), *The Situational Mentor: An International Review of Competences and Capabilities in Mentoring.* Gower, Aldershot. pp. 94–107.

Megginson, D., Stokes, P. and Garrett-Harris, R. (2003a) *MentorsByNet – an E-mentoring Programme for Small to Medium Enterprise (SME) Entrepreneurs.* Evaluation Report on behalf of Business Link Surrey.

Megginson, D., Garrett-Harris, R. and Stokes, P. (2003b) *Business Link for London E-mentoring scheme conducted by Prevista.biz – for Small to Medium Enterprise (SME) Entrepreneurs/Managers.* Evaluation Report for Business Link London.

Megginson, D., Clutterbuck, D., Garvey, B., Stokes, P. and Garrett-Harris, R. (2006) *Mentoring in Action*, 2nd edn. London: Kogan Page.

MENTOR (2006) *MENTOR's SafetyNET Program*, http://apps.mentoring.org/safetynet/index.adp

MENTOR (2006) *Mentoring in America 2005: A Snapshot of the Current State of Mentoring*, www.mentoring.net

MENTOR (2006) *National Mentoring Month: Share What You Know. Become a Mentor*, http://www.mentoring.org/mentoring_month/

MENTOR (2006) *School-Based Mentoring*, www.mentoring.org/program_staff/re-search_corner/school_based_mentoring

Merrick, L. and Stokes, P. (2003) 'Mentor development and supervision: a passionate joint enquiry', *International Journal of Coaching and Mentoring* (e-journal), 1, www.emccouncil.org

Miller, A. (2002) *Mentoring Students and Young People: A Handbook of Effective Practice*. London: RoutledgeFalmer.

Monaghan, J. and Lunt, N. (1992) 'Mentoring: person, process, practice and problems', *British Journal of Educational Studies*, 40(3): 248–63.

Morgan, G. (1986) *Images of Organization*. Beverly Hills: Sage.

Morgan, G. (1993) *Imaginization: The Art of Creative Management*. Newbury Park, CA: Sage.

Morgan, G. (2006) *Images of Organization*, 3rd edn. London: Sage.

Morgan, H., Hawkins, P. and Goldsmith, M. (eds) (2005) *The Art and Practice of Leadership Coaching*. Hoboken, NJ: Wiley.

Morrison, A., White, R., Velsor, E. and the Center for Creative Leadership. (1994) *Breaking the Glass Ceiling: Can Women Reach the Top of America's Largest Corporations?* Reading, MA: Addison-Wesley.

Mulec, K. and Roth, J. (2005) 'Action, reflection, and learning – coaching in order to enhance the performance of drug development project management teams', *R&D Management*, 35(5): 483–91.

Mullen, C.A. (2007) 'Naturally occurring student-faculty mentoring relationships', in T.D. Allen and L.T. Eby (eds), *The Blackwell Handbook of Mentoring: A Multiple Perspectives Approach*. Oxford: Blackwell.

Murray, E. (2004) 'Intuitive coaching – summary', *Industrial and Commercial Training*, 36(5): 203–6.

Nakane, C. (1972) *Japanese Society*. Berkeley: University of California Press.

Nankivell, C. and Shoolbred, M. (1997) 'Mentoring: a valuable tool for career development', *Librarian Career Development*, 5(3): 98–104.

NASPE (2007) http://www.aahperd.org/naspe/template.cfm

Natale, S.M. and Diamante, T. (2005) 'The five stages of executive coaching: better process makes better practice', *Journal of Business Ethics*, 59: 361–74.

Neenan, M. (2006) 'Cognitive behavioural coaching', in Jonathan Passmore (ed.), *Excellence in Coaching*. London: Kogan Page. pp. 91–105.

Neff, T. and Citrin, J. (2005) *You're in Charge – Now What?* Bancyfelin, Carmarthen: Crown Business.

Nehamas, A. and Woodruff, P. (1989) *Plato. The Symposium, HPC Classics Series*. Indianapolis: Hackett Publishing.

Nelson, D.L. and Quick, J.C. (1985) 'Professional women: are distress and disease inevitable?', *Academy of Management Review*, 10(2): 206–18.

Neilson, T. and Eisenbach, R. (2003) 'Not all relationships are created equal: critical actors of high-quality mentoring relationships', in *International Journal of Mentoring and Coaching*, 1(1) EMCC, www.emccouncil.org

Niehoff, B.P. (2006) 'Personality predictors of participation as a mentor', *Career Development International*, 11(4): 321–33.

Noer, D.M., Leupold, C.R. and Valle, M. (2007) 'An analysis of Saudi Arabian and US coaching behaviours', *Journal of Managerial Issues*, 19(2), Summer: 271–87.

Nonaka, I. (1991) 'The knowledge creating company', *Harvard Business Review*, Nov./Dec.: 96–104.

Nonaka, I. (1996) 'The knowledge-creating company', in K. Starkey (ed.), *How Organisations Learn*. London: International Thompson Business Press.

Nonaka, I. and Horotaka, T. (1995) *The Knowledge-creating Company: How Japanese Companies Create the Dynamics of Innovation*. Oxford: Oxford University Press.

Oliver, Richard (2006) *Purposive Drift*. http://www.changethis.com/31.06.PurposiveDrift

Olivero, G., Bane, K.D. and Kopelman, R.E. (1997) 'Executive coaching as a transfer of training tool: effects on productivity in a public agency', *Public Personnel Management*, 26(4): 461–9.

O'Neill, D.K. and Harris, J.B. (2004) 'Bridging the perspectives and developmental needs of all participants in curriculum-based telementoring programmes', *Journal of Research on Technology in Education*, 37(2): 111–28.

O'Neill, R.M. (2005) 'An examination of organizational predictors of mentoring functions', *Journal of Managerial Issues*, XVII(4), Winter: 439–60.

Orenstein, R. (2002) 'Executive Coaching – it's not just about the executive', *Journal of Applied Behavioural Science*, 38(3): 355–74.

Otago, L., Swan, J. and Ramage, S. (2005) 'The risk management knowledge of basketball coaches and their influence on the injury prevention strategies of their players', *Journal of Science and Medicine in Sport*, 8(4).

Owen, H. (1997) *Open Space Technology: A User's Guide*, 2nd edn. San Francisco: Berrett-Koehler.

Oxford Reference Online (2006) Oxford University Press, Sheffield Hallam University, http://www.oxfordreference.com.lcproxy.shu.ac.uk/views/ENTRY.html?subview=Main&entry=t54.e314 (accessed 23 February 2006).

Parker-Wilkins, V. (2006) 'Business impact of executive coaching: demonstrating monetary value', *Industrial and Commercial Training*, 38(3): 122–7.

Parsloe, E. (1992) *Coaching, Mentoring and Assessing*. London: Kogan Page.

Parsloe, E. and Rolph, J. (2004) 'Coaching: survey respondents have their say', *Training Journal*, June: 36–9.

Parsloe, E. and Wray, M. (2000) *Coaching and Mentoring: Practical Methods to Improve Learning*. London: Kogan Page.

Passmore, J. (ed.) (2006) *Excellence In Coaching*. London: Kogan Page.

Pearson, M. and Kayrooz, C. (2004) 'Enabling critical reflection on research supervisory practice', *International Journal for Academic Development*, 9(1): 99–116.

Peat, D.F. (1995) *Blackfoot Physics: A Journey into the Native American Universe*. London: Fourth Estate.

Pedler, M., Burgoyne, J. and Brook, C. (2005) 'What has action learning learned to become?', *Action Learning: Research and Practice*, 2(1): 49–68.

Pegg, M. (1999) 'The art of mentoring', *Industrial and Commercial Training*, 31(4): 136–41.

Pemberton, C. (2006) *Coaching to Solutions: A Manager's Toolkit for Performance Delivery*. Oxford: Butterworth-Heinemann.

Pfeffer, J. (1995) 'Producing sustainable competitive advantage through the effective management of people', *Academy of Management Executive*, 9(1): 55–69.

Pfeffer, J. (1997) *New Directions for Organization Theory: Problems and Prospects*. New York: Oxford University Press.

Phillips, A. (1995) *Terrors and Experts*. London: Faber.

Phillips, A. (2007) 'After Strachey', *London Review of Books*, 4 October: 36–8.

Pickstone, J.V. (2000) *Ways of Knowing: A New History of Science Technology and Medicine*. Manchester: Manchester University Press.

Plato (1997) *The Republic*. Translated by J. Davies and D. Vaughan. London: Wordsworth Classics.

Plato (2004) *The Trial and Death of Socrates*. Translated by Benjamin Jowett, introduction by David Taffel. New York: Barnes and Noble.

Plato (1989) *The Symposium*. Translated by Alexander Nehamas and Paul Woodruff, HPC Classics Series. Indianapolis, IN: Hackett Publishing Company, Incorporated.

Platt, G. (2001) 'NLP – no longer plausible', *Training Journal*, May: 10–15.

Porter, M., Lorsh, J. and Nohria, N. (2004) 'Seven surprises for new CEOs', *Harvard Business Review*, 82(10): 62–72.

Post, D. (2006) 'Important flight parameters in the shot put', *Track Coach*, 175: 5601–2.

Potrac, P., Jones, R. and Armour, K. (2002) 'It's all about getting respect: the coaching behaviours of an expert English soccer coach', *Sport, Education and Society*, 7(2): 183–202.

Ragins, B.R. and Cotton, J.L. (1999) 'Mentor functions and outcomes: a comparison of men and women in formal and informal mentoring relationships', *Journal of Applied Psychology*, 84: 529–50.

Revans, R.W. (1978, 1983, 1998) *ABC of Action Learning*. London: Lemos and Crane.

Rhodes, J.E., Reddy, R. and Grossman, J.B. (2005) 'The protective influence of mentoring on adolescents' substance use: direct and indirect pathways', *Applied Developmental Science*, 9(1): 31–47.

Rigsby, J.T., Siegal, P.H. and Spiceland, J.D. (1998) 'Mentoring among management advisory services professionals: an adaptive mechanism to cope with rapid corporate change', *Managerial Auditing Journal*, 13(2): 107–16.

Riley, P. (1994) *Fénélon – Telemachus*. Cambridge: Cambridge University Press.

Roberts, A. (1999) *Homer's Mentor: Duties Fulfilled or Misconstrued?* http://home.att.net/~nickols/homers_mentor.htm

Robertson, L. (2005) 'The cost of missed opportunities', *Strategic Communication Management*, 9(3), April/May: 5.

Robinson, J. (2005) 'GROWing service improvement within the NHS', *International Journal of Mentoring and Coaching*, III(1): 87–91.

Rogers, C.R. (1969) *Freedom to Learn*. Columbus, Ohio: Merrill.

Rollag, K. (2007) 'Defining the term "new" in new employee research', *Journal of Occupational and Organizational Psychology*, March, 80(1): 63–75.

Rorty, R. (1989) *Contingency, Irony and Solidarity*. Cambridge: Cambridge University Press.

Rosinski, P. (2003) *Coaching Across Cultures*. London: Nicholas Brealey.

Ruona, W.E.A. and Lynham, S.A. (2004) 'A philosophical framework for thought and practice in human resource development', *Human Resource Development International*, 7(2): 151–64.

Rousseau, D.M. (1995) *Psychological Contracts in Organizations: Understanding Written and Unwritten Agreements*. Newbury Park, CA: Sage.

Salimbene, F., Buono, A.F., Van Steenberg Lafarge, V. and Nurick, A.J. (2005) 'Service-learning and management education: the Bentley experience', *Academy of Management Learning & Education*, 4(3): 336–44.

Samier, E. (2000) 'Public administration mentorship: conceptual and pragmatic considerations', *Journal of Educational Administration*, 38(1): 83–101.

Scandura, T.A. (1998) 'Dysfunctional mentoring relationships and outcomes', *Journal of Management*, 24: 449–67.

Scandura, T.A. and Williams, E.A. (2001) 'An investigation of the moderating effects of gender on the relationships between mentor initiation and protégé perceptions of mentoring functions', *Journal of Vocational Behavior*, 59: 342–63.

Scandura, T., Tejeda, M., Werther, B. and Lankau, M. (1996) 'Perspectives on mentoring', *Leadership & Organization Development Journal*, 17(3): 50–6.

Scarbrough, H., Swan, J. and Preston, J. (1999) *Knowledge Management: A Literature Review*. London: IPD.

Schön, D.A. (1987) *Educating the Reflective Practitioner: Towards a New Design for Teaching and Learning in the Profession*. San Francisco, CA: Jossey-Bass.

Schön, D. (1991) *The Reflective Practitioner: How Professionals Think in Action*. Aldershot: Ashgate Arena.

Schostak, J.F. (2002) *Understanding, Designing and Conducting Qualitative Research in Education*. Buckingham: Open University Press.

Schwartz, J.P., Thigpen, S.E. and Montgomery, J.K. (2006) 'Examination of parenting styles of processing emotions and differentiation of self', *Family Journal: Counselling and Therapy for Couples and Families*, 14(1): 41–8.

Segerman-Peck, L. (1991) *Networking and Mentoring: A Woman's Guide*. London: Piatkus.

Seibert, S. (1999) 'The effectiveness of facilitated mentoring: a longitudinal quasi-experiment', *Journal of Vocational Behavior*, 54: 483–502.

Senge, P.M. (1992) *The Fifth Discipline*. Chatham, Kent: Century Business.

Shanklin, N. (2007) 'How can you gain the most from working with a literacy coach', *Voices from the Middle*, 14(4): 44–7.

Sheehy, G. (1974) *Passages: Predictable Crises of Adult Life*. New York: E.P. Dutton.

Sheehy, G. (1996) *New Passages: Mapping Your Life Across Time*. London: Harper Collins.

Sheehy, G. (2006) *Passages: Predictable Crises of Adult Life*, 2nd edn. Columbia: Ballantine Books.

Sherman, S. and Freas, A. (2004) 'The Wild West of executive coaching', *Harvard Business Review*, 82(11), November: 82–90.

Sieler, A. (2003) *Coaching to the Human Soul: Ontological Coaching and Deep Change*. Melborne, Australia: Newfield.

Simmel, G. (1950) *The Sociology of Georg Simmel*, ed. K.H. Wolff, New York: Free Press.

Smither, J.W., London, M., Flautt, R., Vargas, Y. and Kucrie, I. (2003) 'Can working with an executive coach improve multisource feedback ratings over time? A quasi-experimental field study', *Personnel Psychology*, 56(1): 23–44.

Sparrow, S. (2007) 'Model behaviour', *Training and Coaching Today*, April: 24–5.

Speizer, J.J. (1981) 'Role models, mentors and sponsors: the elusive concepts', *Journal of Women in Culture*, 6(4): 692–712.

Spreier, S.W., Fontaine, M.M. and Mallery, R.L. (2006) 'Leadership run amok', *Harvard Business Review*, 84(6): 72–82.

Stake, R.E. (2004) 'Case studies', in N.K. Denzin and Y.S. Lincoln (eds), *Strategies of Qualitative Inquiry*. London: Sage. pp. 88–109.

Stokes, P. (2007) *The Skilled Coachee*. Paper presented at the European Mentoring and Coaching Conference, Stockholm, October.

Tabbron, A., Macaulay, S. and Cook, S. (1997) 'Making mentoring work', *Training for Quality*, 5(1): 6–9.

Tharenou, P. (2005) 'Does mentor support increase women's career advancement more than men's? The differential effects of career and psychosocial support', *Australian Journal of Management*, 30(1), June: 77–109.

Thomas, D.A. and Gabarro, J.J. (1999) *Breaking Through: The Making of Minority Executives in Corporate America*. Boston, Havard Business School Press.

Tobias, L.L. (1996) 'Coaching executives', *Consulting Psychology Journal: Practice & Research*, 48(2): 87–95.

Toffler, A. (1970) *Future Shock*. Oxford: The Bodley Head.

Torrance, E.P. (1984) *Mentor Relationships; How they Aid Creative Achievement, Endure, Change and Die*. Buffalo, New York: Bearly.

Townley, B. (1994) *Reframing Human Resource Management: Power, Ethics and the Subject at Work*. London: Sage.

Trevitt, C. (2005) 'Universities learning to learn? Inventing flexible (e)learning through first- and second-order action research', *Educational Action Research*, 13(1): 57–83.

Trompenaars, F. and Hampden–Turner, C. (1993) *Riding the Waves of Culture*. London: Brealey.

Tucker, R. (2005) 'Is coaching worth the money? Assessing the ROI of executive coaching', in H. Morgan, P. Hawkins and M. Goldsmith (eds), *The Art And Practice of Leadership Coaching.* Hoboken, NJ: Wiley. pp. 245–54.

Turban, D. and Dougherty, T. (1994) 'Role of protégé personality in receipt of mentoring and career success', *Academy of Management Journal*, 37(3): 688–702.

Turner, B. and Chelladurai, P. (2005) 'Organizational and occupational commitment, intention to leave and perceived performance of intercollegiate coaches', *Journal of Sports Management*, 19: 193–211.

US Census Bureau (2005) Fact sheet for race, ethnic, ancestry group, http://factfinder.census.gov

Van Emmerik, H., Baugh, S.G. and Euwema, M.C. (2005) 'Who wants to be a mentor? An examination of attitudinal, instrumental, and social motivational components', *Career Development International*, 10(4): 310–24.

Von Krogh, G., Roos, J. and Slocum, K. (1994) 'An essay on corporate epistemology', *Strategic Management Journal*, 15: 53–71.

Vermaak, H. and Weggeman, M. (1999) 'Conspiring fruitfully with professionals: new management roles for professional organizations', *Management Decision*, 37(1): 29–44.

Vidmar, D.J. (2005) 'Reflective peer coaching: crafting collaborative self-assessment in teaching', *Research Strategies*, 20(3): 135–48.

Vygotsky, L.S. (1978) *Mind in Society: The Development of Higher Psychological Processes.* Cambridge, MA: Harvard University Press.

Wanberg, C.R., Welsh, L. and Hezlett, S. (2003) 'Mentoring: a review and directions for future research', in J. Martocchio and J. Ferris (eds), *Research in Personnel and Human Resources Management.* Vol. 22, Oxford: Elsevier Science Ltd. pp. 39–124.

Warr, P., Bird, M. and Rackham, N. (1978) *Evaluation of Management Training.* London: Gower.

Watts, R.E. and Pietrzak, D. (2000) 'Alderian encouragement and the therapeutic process of solution-focused brief therapy', *Journal of Counselling and Development*, Fall: 442–7.

Wasylyshyn, K.M. (2003) 'Executive coaching: an outcome study', *Consulting Psychology Journal: Practice and Research*, 55(2): 94–106.

Watkins, M. (2005) *The First 90 Days.* Boston: Harvard Business School Press.

Weick, K. (1995) *Sensemaking in Organizations.* London: Sage.

Weisbord, M. and Janoff, S. (1995) *Future Search: An Action Guide to Finding Common Ground in Organizations & Communities.* San Francisco: Berrett-Koehler Publishers.

Whitmore, J. (2002) *Coaching for Performance: GROWing People, Performance and Purpose*, 3rd edn. London: Nicholas Brealey.

Whitworth, L., Kimsey-House, H. and Sandhal, P. (1998) *Co-active Coaching: New Skills for Coaching People Toward Success in Work and Life.* New York: Davies-Black.

Wild, A. (2001) 'Coaching the coaches, to develop teams, to accelerate the pace of change', *Industrial and Commercial Training*, 33(5): 161–6.

Willis, P. (2005) 'European Mentoring and Coaching Council', *Competency Research Project: Phase 2*, June. Watford: EMCC. www.emccouncil.org

Wilson, J.A. and Elman, N.S. (1990) 'Organisational benefits of mentoring', *Academy of Management Executive*, 4: 88–94.

Whitehill, Arthur, M. (1991) *Japanese Management: Tradition and Transition.* London: Routledge.

Wilson, C. (2004) 'Coaching and coach training in the workplace', *Industrial and Commercial Training*, 36(3): 96–8.

Young, A.M. and Perrewé, P.L. (2004) 'The role of expectations in the Mentoring Exchange: an analysis of mentor and protégé expectations in relation to perceived support', *Journal of Managerial Issues*, XVI(1), Spring: 103–26.

Youth Mentoring Connection (2007) www.youthmentoring.org

Zeus, P. and Skiffington, S. (2000) *The Complete Guide to Coaching at Work*. Sydney: McGraw-Hill.

Žižek, S. (2008) *Violence*. London: Profile.

Zuboff, S. (1988) *In the Age of the Smart Machine: The Future of Work and Power*. New York: Basic Books.

INDEX

coactive coaching 81
co-creation of power 123
coercive power 112, 114, 116
cognitive behavioural coaching 82
coherence 195
collaborative learning 99
collectivism 215–16
Colley, H. 72, 76, 90
Collins, G. 126, 128–9
co-mentoring 92–3, 186
commodification 24, 25, 82
community of discovery 135–8, 229
community of practice 135
competence-based learning 97–8
competencies 188–201
competency models 157, 227
complexity 131–3, 135
compliance mindset 128
concrete experience 17
confidentiality 19, 184
consensus 17
context *see* social context
contractual arrangements 126
conversation, as dance 102–5
conversational learning 96–107, 153, 228
Coomber, J. 195–6
Cooperrider, D. 61
Copenhagen Process 199
Corporation for National Community
    Service 208
countertransference 115, 116–17,
    120–1, 123
Cox, Mary 172
Cranwell-Ward, J. 77
credibility 73–4
creep-in approach 59, 63
critical science 29
Cross, R. 132, 133
Csikszentmihalyi, M. 61
culture 53–66
    intolerance 180–1
    language 180
    western bias 214–17, 231
customer-led concept 118

dance, conversation as 102–5
Dass, P. 177, 178, 179
De Bono, E. 186–7
deficiency model 191
deficit or appreciative inquiry 59, 60–1
de Haan, E. 17, 18, 58, 176
delegation 65
design 67–79
Developing Mentor 168, 170–1
development 75, 112, 116–17, 166
developmental coaching 57–8
developmental model 209

developmental networks 132, 133, 135, 211,
    213, 214
developmental psychology 225
developmental relationships
    128–9, 228
Diamante, T. 46, 85–6, 206
difference 76
dimensions 25–6
Dirsmith, M. 117–18, 119
discourses 121, 122, 174
distance from participants 39–40
diversity 127, 177–87, 230–1
diversity mentoring 90
dominant culture 54
dominant discourse 121, 123, 230–1
dominant logic 24
Dougherty, T. 55
Downey, M. 63, 84, 118
Drucker, P.F. 153
Du Toit, A. 166
dyadic mentoring 90–1
dyadic relationships 19–21, 25, 229

Eby, L.T. 211
eclecticism 30
economy, knowledge 125, 128, 135,
    159, 221–2
e-development 140–50
education 223
    faith schools 179–80
    mentoring 90, 92
Egan, G. 152
Eisenbach, R. 20, 125
eligibility 73
Ellis, Albert 82
embedded level 56
EMCC *see* European Mentoring and
    Coaching Council
e-mentoring 93–4, 140–50
emergent and episodic approach 178–9
emotional intelligence 165
emotional self 23
employment trends 126
the ending 19–20
engagement mentoring 72, 76
Engstrom, T.E.J. 13
Ensher, E.A. 147
entrepreneurial mentoring 130
environment 100
    best practice 209
    folk wisdoms 10–11
Erikson, E. 99
Eseryl, D. 70
ethics 197
European Mentoring and Coaching
    Council (EMCC) 23, 30–1, 47,
    195, 200, 224, 231

Monaghan, J. 207
monoculture 191
moral relativism 181
Morgan, G. 24, 29, 77
motivation 74
Mulec, K. 46, 87–8
Mullen, C.A. 132
multiculturalism 177
  strategic 178, 179–80
multiple relationships 55, 125–39
mutuality 22, 92–3, 229

Nakane, C. 216
nascent level 56
Natale, S.M. 46, 85–6, 206
National Association for Sport and Physical
    Education (NASPE) 207
National Federation of State High School
    Associations 207
National Health Service (NHS) 113–17
  Expert Patient Mentoring Programme 72–3
needs model 61
Neilson, T. 20, 125
networks 128–31, 132–5, 229, 230
  analysis 133
  developmental 132, 133, 135, 211,
      213, 214
Neubert, M.J. 46
new initiative approach 76–7
Newton, Sir Isaac 136
Noer, D.M. 214, 217
Nonaka, I. 55
non-linear conversations 101–2, 105, 158
non-linear learning 102, 105
Novice Mentor 168, 169–70

objectivism 24, 25, 29, 97, 181
Odysseus 14
Oliver, Richard 191–2
O'Neill, D.K. 94, 142
ontological coaching 82
open/closed dimension 25, 26
open curriculum 75
Open Space Technology 230
opportunistic mentoring 130
orchestration 83
organic approach 77
organizational mentoring 219
organizations
  design and evaluation 67–79
  goal assumption 151–60
  impact 53–66
  mindset 24
  performance 71
  structure changes 127
  structure chart 133
outcomes 98, 213

Parker, A. 132, 133
Parker, B. 177, 178, 179
Parker-Wilkins, Vernita 33–4
Parsloe, E. 192–3
passivity 32, 39, 118, 174
Pedler, M. 230
peer mentoring 91–2, 93
Pemberton, C. 58
performance
  organizational 71
  or whole life 59, 63
performance coaching 128
performative knowledge 228
personal coaching 206, 218
Pfeffer, J. 125, 216
phenomenology 29, 69, 71–2
Phillips, A. 115, 226
philosophy 225
Pietzak, D. 88
Plato 11, 18
Platt, G. 58–9
polarization 186–7
police, mentoring 182–6
political agendas 177–8
Porter, M. 64
Positive Action Mentoring Scheme (PAMS)
    74, 182–6
positivism 29, 30, 38–40, 41, 45, 50–2
  evaluation 69, 78
  purpose 71
Potrac, P. 83
power 49, 111–24, 228
  distance 217, 219
  goals 55, 152
  organizations 55
  social 133
practitioner studies 38–9, 40
Prahalad, C.K. 24
Pratchett, Terry 189
primary e-development 147
problem
  identification 61
  or solution 59, 61–2
  solving 65
professionalization 188–201, 227
programmatic approach 178, 179
protégés 32, 39, 91, 118, 219
psychoanalysis 164, 226
psychological mindedness 164, 165, 166, 223
psychological training 164, 165
psycho-social dysfunction 72
psychotherapy 225
public/private dimension 25, 26
Pullins, E.B. 92
pure e-development 147
purpose, design 71–2
purposive drift 191–2

technology 230
  alienation 148
  e-mentoring 93–4, 140–50
Telemachus 12, 13, 14, 132
telementoring 142
Thackeray, William Makepeace 18
Tharenou, Phyllis 31–3, 38, 211
thick description 25, 131
Thomas, D.A. 127
time
  evaluation 69
  management 105, 106
tolerance 180–2, 186–7
tools 223
traditional mentoring 90–1, 130
training gap 191
transactional analysis 114
transaction costs 193
transference 113, 115, 116–17, 120–1, 122, 123
Trimble, S.B. 92–3
triviality 20
Trompenaars, F. 220
trust 122
Turban, D. 55

understanding 17
unit of analysis 230
United States 57–8, 205–20, 223–4

voluntarism 22, 77, 90, 227
Von Krogh, G. 222
Vygotsky, L.S. 100, 101, 106

Wageman, R. 87
Wallace, M. 83
Wanberg, C.R. 86
Warr, P. 70
Wasylyshyn, K.M. 45, 46, 47
water logic 186–7
Watts, R.E. 88
Weick, Karl 142
Weintraub, J.R. 57–8
Welch, Jack 219
Wenger, E. 55, 75, 101, 135
Whitehill, Arthur M. 216
Whitmore, J. 63
Wild, A. 173
Williams, E.A. 211
Williamson, B. 53, 61, 75, 125, 127, 136,
    180, 222
Willis, P. 190
women
  female mentor 13, 16
  mentor support 31–3
  role models 14
work–life balance 85
World Café 230
Wray, M. 192–3

YMCA 208
Yorkshire Police PAMS 182–6

zone of proximal development 100
Zuboff, S. 148

Research Methods Books from SAGE

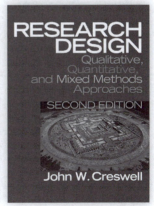

The Qualitative Research Kit

Edited by Uwe Flick

Read sample chapters online now!

Doing Ethnographic and Observational Research — Michael Angrosino

Using Visual Data in Qualitative Research — Marcus Banks

Doing Focus Groups — Rosaline Barbour

Designing Qualitative Research — Uwe Flick

Managing Quality in Qualitative Research — Uwe Flick

Analyzing Qualitative Data — Graham Gibbs

Doing Interviews — Steinar Kvale

Doing Conversation, Discourse and Document Analysis — Tim Rapley

The SAGE Qualitative Research Kit — Edited by Uwe Flick

www.sagepub.co.uk

SAGE